PENGUIN BOOKS

THE MEDIEVAL MACHINE

Jean Gimpel is a medieval scholar and social historian whose previous book, *The Cathedral Builders,* was highly praised both in the United States and in Europe. He has lectured at Yale and other universities in the United States and at present lives in London.

Jean Gimpel

The Medieval Machine

The Industrial Revolution of the Middle Ages

PENGUIN BOOKS

Penguin Books Ltd, Harmondsworth,
Middlesex, England
Penguin Books, 625 Madison Avenue,
New York, New York 10022, U.S.A.
Penguin Books Australia Ltd, Ringwood,
Victoria, Australia
Penguin Books Canada Limited, 2801 John Street,
Markham, Ontario, Canada L3R 1B4
Penguin Books (N.Z.) Ltd, 182–190 Wairau Road,
Auckland 10, New Zealand

First published in French under the title
La Révolution Industrielle du Moyen Age
First published in the United States of America by
Holt, Rinehart and Winston 1976
Published in Penguin Books by arrangement with
Holt, Rinehart and Winston 1977
Reprinted 1980, 1981

LIBRARY OF CONGRESS CATALOGING IN PUBLICATION DATA
Gimpel, Jean.
The medieval machine.
Reprint of the 1976 ed. published by Holt, Rinehart
and Winston, New York.
Includes bibliographical references and index.
1. Economic history—Medieval, 500–1500.
I. Title.
[HC41.G5   1977]   330.9′02   77-6676
ISBN 0 14 00.4514 7

Printed in the United States of America by
The Murray Printing Company, Westford, Massachusetts
Set in Linotype Caledonia

An article based on Chapter 4 was first published in
slightly different form in *Environment and Change*.

Map and plan of the Clairvaux monastery is reprinted from
The Maze of Ingenuity by Arnold Pacey.
Copyright © Arnold Pacey, 1974. Reprinted by
permission of Holmes & Meier Publishers, Inc.

Contents

A Note on Currency

Sums of money are referred to in this book by the abbreviations £, s., and d. These signify *livres*, *sous*, and *deniers*, which were the units of currency in both France and England during the medieval period, and which continued in use in England as symbols for the later pounds, shillings, and pence.

Preface

The recent international energy crisis, which precipitated the present economic and financial depression, has made many people deeply apprehensive that our Western technological society could be doomed to decline and perish like all the world's previous civilizations. It is hardly surprising that there is a revival of interest in the works of Oswald Spengler. In 1931, in an essay entitled "Man and Technics," Spengler suggested that perhaps the "machine-technics" of our civilization would one day "lie in fragments, *forgotten*—our railways and steamships as dead as the Roman roads and the Chinese wall, our giant cities and skyscrapers in ruins like old Memphis and Babylon. The history of this technics is fast drawing to its inevitable close. It will be eaten up from within, like the grand forms of any and every Culture."[1] He observed, too, that "where there is coal, or oil, or water-power, there a new weapon can be forged against the heart of the Faustian Civilization. The exploited world is beginning to take its revenge on its lords."[2]

Events have proved that Spengler's view was an oversimplification, but while one may disagree with his scholarship, his dogmatism, and his metaphysical theories, he nevertheless projected some astonishing insights into the future of Western civilization. Spengler's interest in technology led him to infer that the foundations of our present technologically oriented society were laid not in the Italian Renaissance or in the English Industrial Revolution, but in the Middle Ages. This is the main theme of my study.

The Middle Ages was one of the great inventive eras of mankind. It should be known as the first industrial revolution in Europe. The scientists and engineers of that time were searching for alternative sources of energy to hydraulic power, wind power, and tidal energy. Between the tenth and the thirteenth centuries, western Europe experienced a technological boom. Both that boom and the subsequent decline can now be seen to offer striking parallels to Western industrial society since 1750, and to the present situation in the United States in particular. Some of the features that accompanied this first industrial revolution seem strangely familiar.

There was a great increase in population, which led to massive movements of people. They emigrated; they opened up and colonized new lands; they founded and built new towns. Conditions favored free enterprise, and this led to the rise of self-made men. Capitalist companies were formed and their shares were bought and sold. Entrepreneurs were fully prepared to use ruthless business methods to stifle competition. They introduced extensive division of labor to increase efficiency, and their enterprises called into being a proletariat whom they could exploit. The workers retaliated with wage claims, absenteeism, and strikes.

Energy consumption increased considerably. Technological innovations brought about improvements in the efficiency of existing methods and also led to a successful search for new sources of energy. Many of the tasks formerly done by hand were now carried out by machines. Concurrently there was a revolution in agricultural methods, which enabled farmers to produce enough food for an expanding population and provide a more varied diet. There was a marked increase in the general standard of living. The growth of industry and the search for new sources of raw materials led to extensive industrial pollution of waterways and, on a wider scale, posed a severe threat to the environment, with grave long-term consequences.

The entrepreneurs, the landowners, and the financiers were able to extract large profits from this industrial expansion, and the growth of capitalism brought about modern methods of accountancy and banking, which in turn led to further expansion. The people with financial power also wielded political power, and economic sanctions could be employed very effectively for political ends. The period was characterized by a sense of optimism, a rationalist attitude, and a firm belief in progress.

At a certain point the dynamism of the Middle Ages began to fail and symptoms of decline became evident. The population ceased to grow, differences between the classes hardened, and there was less social mobility. Restrictive practices were introduced in many industries, and there was a growth of violent unrest in the big industrial centers. There were increasing indications that the level of efficiency was dropping and at the same time there was a resistance to change. Energy production and mechanization had reached a peak and the standard of living began to decline. Inflation began to get out of hand; currencies were devalued and banks crashed.

There was a decline in the old moral values. People became less public-spirited, and with this went a growth of permissiveness. There was a growing awareness of aesthetic values. Many people turned away from traditional religion to embrace new esoteric cults. Rationalism gave way to mysticism.

If this picture of the medieval world does not sound like the Dark Ages, or like the age of romance and chivalry, it is because the history of technology has been so universally neglected, thanks largely to the age-old attitude of academics and intellectuals toward manual work and engineering. Plato, in the *Gorgias*, gives evidence of the contempt in which engineers were held by philosophers in his time: "You despise him and his art, and sneeringly call him an engine-maker, and you will not allow your daughter to marry his son or marry your son to his daughter."[3]

The scorn of men of letters for engineers throughout history has kept them, all too often, oblivious to the technology created by those engineers who were of lower social status and worked to earn their living. They had no idea that in this other world there was an uninterrupted tradition of technological writing. Leonardo da Vinci is a case in point. As an engineer he was despised by the literati of his time, and they, like the majority of Western intellectuals today, were ignorant of the fact that Leonardo had borrowed a great many of his inventions from technological treatises by engineers of previous generations.

Our Western civilization has seen the development of two parallel systems of education—that of the mechanical arts for engineers and that of the liberal arts for men of letters. These are the two cultures of C. P. Snow. Historians steeped in the prejudices of the liberal arts have rarely thought it worthwhile to cross the gap in order to study or to write the history of the mechanical arts, the history of technology. Since the Renaissance, whenever Western man has tried to make historical comparisons, he has usually turned to the Roman Empire, not the Middle Ages, in spite of the fact that the medieval industrial revolution is remarkably comparable to the English Industrial Revolution and its subsequent development in America. The creative time span of each of these great technological eras lasted for some two and a half centuries before symptoms of decline became apparent. Our own last two decades demonstrate that today Western technological society is revealing much the same pattern of history as its medieval predecessor.

We are witnessing a sharp arrest in technological impetus. No more fundamental innovations are likely to be introduced to change the structure of our society. Only improvements in the field of preexisting innovations are to be expected. Like every previous civilization, we have reached a technological plateau.

The main purpose of this study is to examine closely, and with new perspectives, the industrial life and institutions of the Middle Ages, and the genius of their inventiveness. Comparisons with our own society will be apparent throughout, and a detailed study of parallels between the two great inventive eras, medieval and modern, will be found in the epilogue. While I hope that the reader of *The Medieval Machine* will want to pursue his own comparisons, I must point out one alarming contrast. The economic depression that struck Europe in the fourteenth century was followed ultimately by economic and technological recovery. But the depression we have moved into will have no end. We can anticipate centuries of decline and exhaustion. There will be no further industrial revolution in the cycles of our Western civilization.

JEAN GIMPEL
London
June 1975

The
Medieval
Machine

1

The Energy Resources of
Europe and Their Development

The Middle Ages introduced machinery into Europe on a scale
no civilization had previously known. This was to be one of the
main factors that led to the dominance of the Western hemisphere over the rest of the world. Machines were known in the
classical world, of course, but their use in industry was limited.
Cogs and gears were employed only for creating toys or automata. In medieval society, however, machinery was made to
do what previously had been done only by manual, and often
hard, labor.

It is an astonishing concept to the modern mind that medieval man was surrounded by machines. The fact is, machines
were not something foreign or remote to the townsman or to
the peasant in his fields. The most common was the mill, con-
verting the power of water or wind into work: grinding corn,
crushing olives, fulling cloth, tanning leather, making paper,

Commercial life on the Grand Pont, the main bridge of medieval Paris. In the bottom scene, a boat delivers grain to the bridge's gristmills. Courtesy Bibliothèque Nationale, Paris.

and so on. These were the factories of the Middle Ages. In the towns and villages the citizen could stand on a bridge over a river or canal and observe the different types of water mill: mills built along the banks, others floating midstream or moored to the banks, and, if he cared to look under the bridge, he might find the same machines built between the arches. If he walked upstream he would find the river dammed to provide a sufficient fall of water to drive the mills' machinery.

These groups of machines were more than mere factories; they were often local meeting places, in particular the corn mills, where townspeople or country folk lined up, waiting their turn to have their grain ground. At times there were such gatherings outside the buildings that prostitutes would come to tout for clients up and down the line. Saint Bernard, the leader of the Cistercian order in the twelfth century, was scandalized to hear of the prostitutes' activities and wanted to have the mills closed. If such a thing had occurred—if the mills had been closed down, not only those in the cities and in the countryside, but those powering the hundreds of Cistercian factories—the European economy would have grown at a far slower rate. The effect would have been in some way comparable to that produced by the decision in 1973 of the oil-producing countries in the Middle East to raise the price of oil and put an embargo on supplies to certain countries of the Western world. The economy of the West has been affected by these measures, and oil in the twentieth century plays much the same role as did waterpower in the Middle Ages.

A twelfth-century report on the use of waterpower in a Cistercian monastery (that of Clairvaux in France) shows how far mechanization had become a major factor in European economy. The importance of this report, this great hymn to technology, is that it could have been written 742 times over; for that was the number of Cistercian monasteries in the twelfth century, and the report would have held true for practically every one of them.

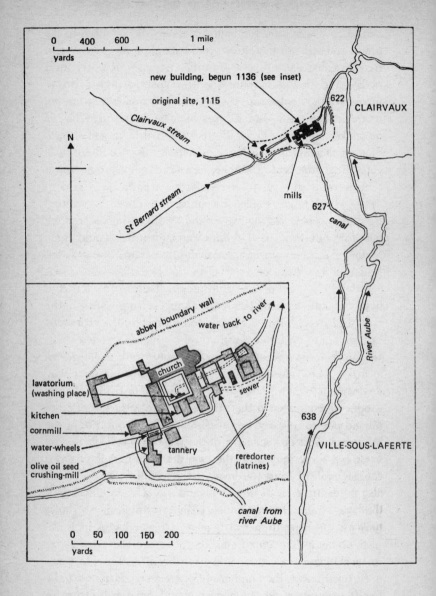

Map and plan of the Clairvaux monastery. Reprinted by permission of Holmes & Meier Publishers, Inc.

Monasteries built in countries separated by thousands of miles—Portugal, Sweden, Scotland, Hungary—all had very similar waterpowered systems within almost universally similar plans for the monasteries themselves. It has been said that a blind Cistercian monk moving into any of the monasteries would instantly have known where he was. In certain ways the discipline imposed by Saint Bernard on his monks—the rigid timetable, the impossibility of deviating from the Rule without facing punishment—brings to mind the work regulations that Henry Ford imposed on his assembly lines.

The capacities of a Cistercian factory could vary, in that the raw materials available in some regions of Europe were not available in others and the machinery had to be adapted to different processes. For example, olives were found in Provence and crushed to produce olive oil by specially built grinding stones, but olives were not to be found in the north of France. Where iron was available, hammer forges were built. If a wine crop failed, as described in the Clairvaux report, beer was produced in its place.

In the Clairvaux report, four distinct industrial operations are mentioned that required waterpower: crushing wheat, sieving flour, fulling cloth, and tanning. It is possible that waterpower also activated bellows for the flames that heated the vats in which beer for the monks was produced. Running water was used for domestic purposes, as well as for industrial ones. It was carried in lead or wooden pipes to the kitchen for cooking and washing and to the gardens for watering. It was also used to clean out the drains, presumably situated under the lavatories, or *necessaria*, and to carry away the waste so as to "leave everywhere spotless."

Entering the Abbey under the boundary wall, which like a janitor allows it to pass, the stream first hurls itself impetuously at the mill where in a welter of movement it strains itself, first to crush the wheat beneath the weight of the millstones, then to shake the fine sieve which separates flour from bran. Already it has reached the next building; it replenishes the vats and surrenders itself to the flames which heat it up to prepare beer for the monks, their liquor when the vines reward the wine-growers' toil with a barren crop. The stream does not yet consider itself discharged. The fullers established near the mill beckon to it. In the mill it had been occupied in preparing food for the brethren; it is therefore only right that it should now look to their clothing. It never shrinks back or refuses to do anything that is asked for. One by one it lifts and drops the heavy pestles, the fullers' great wooden hammers . . . and spares, thus, the monks' great fatigues. . . . How many horses would be worn out, how many men would have weary arms if this graceful river, to whom we owe our clothes and food, did not labour for us. . . .

When it has spun the shaft as fast as any wheel can move, it disappears in a foaming frenzy; one might say it had itself been ground in the mill. Leaving it here it enters the tannery, where in preparing the leather for the shoes of the monks it exercises as much exertion as diligence; then it dissolves in a host of streamlets and proceeds along its appointed course to the duties laid down for it, looking out all the time for affairs requiring its attention, whatever they might be, such as cooking, sieving, turning, grinding, watering, or washing, never refusing its assistance in any task. At last, in case it receives any reward for work which it has not done, it carries away the waste and leaves everywhere spotless.[1]

Over a millennium earlier, the poet Antipater of Thessalonica, living under the reigns of Augustus and Tiberius, had celebrated in terms no less enthusiastic the role of waterpower. Rejoicing that the water nymphs were liberating mankind from the hard labor of grinding corn, he wrote:

Hold back your hands from the mill, O maids of the grindstone;
*   slumber*
Longer, e'en though the crowing of cocks announces the morning.
Demeter's ordered her nymphs to perform your hands' former
*   labours.*
Down on the top of the wheel, the spirits of the water are leaping,
Turning the axle and with it the spokes of the wheel that is whirling
Therewith spinning the heavy and hollow Nisyrian millstones.[2]

Both writers express a similar admiration for waterpower, but the societies they lived in reacted differently toward its industrial use; medieval society gave itself wholeheartedly to mechanization, while the classical world adopted it to only a limited extent.

The availability of slaves and, in Mediterranean countries, the scarcity of streams flowing all year round restricted the use of water mills in antiquity. Water mills are of no economic interest if the flow of water is only seasonal, and although the Romans sometimes overcame this difficulty by building aqueducts to bring water to the mills, it was a costly undertaking.

The first water mills were built by engineers possibly toward the end of the second century B.C. The first mention of a water mill is found in the writings of the first-century B.C. Greek geographer Strabo, who records the existence of one at Cabira, in the palace of Mithridates, king of Pontus, where it aroused the wonder of Pompey's conquering troops in 63 B.C.

The earliest water mills had no gears. A waterwheel revolving horizontally drove the upper millstone by means of a vertical shaft. Its energy output of approximately 0.5 horsepower was equivalent to that of a donkey mill.

By the end of the first century B.C., the Roman engineers had increased the power of the water mills sixfold—to 3 horsepower—by building a vertical undershot waterwheel fitted with blades, which drove the upper millstone through 90-de-

7

Gearing details of a twelfth-century vertical undershot waterwheel

gree gearing. The gearing permitted a much higher speed of rotation in the stones than in the wheels. Vitruvius, a Roman architect and engineer who lived just before the turn of the millennium, was the first to describe this machinery, which was to play such a vital role in the industrialization of medieval Europe.

East of Monte Cassino, at Venafro on the Volturno, a Roman water mill has been unearthed with a wheel 7 feet in diameter. If the millstones made 46 revolutions per minute, they could grind 150 kilograms of corn per hour or 1,500 kilograms (roughly 1½ tons) in 10 hours. To see the extraordinary economy in manpower achieved by such a mill, it is only necessary to compare these figures with the quantity of corn ground by two slaves with a rotary hand-mill in one hour:

7 kilograms, or 70 kilograms in 10 hours. So over 40 slaves would have had to work 10 hours to grind the same 1,500 kilograms.

The ultimate in Roman waterpower was reached at Barbegal, near Arles in Provence, where engineers constructed the largest known industrial complex of the Roman Empire, a factory to produce flour sufficient for eighty thousand people. It was built on a hillside; the water, flowing from an aqueduct down the steep hill at an angle of 30 degrees, in a double millrace, fell 19 meters (62 feet). Sixteen waterwheels—eight on each millrace—were each driven by the tail flow from the wheel above and coupled to a pair of millstones with a grinding capacity of 150 to 200 kilograms, bringing the total hourly capacity of the factory to 2,400 to 3,200 kilograms, or approximately 28 tons in a 10-hour day.

While these figures show the enormous potential of waterpower and mechanization, they should not lead one to suppose that the Romans ever had a policy of mechanization like the Cistercians in the Middle Ages. For every mill that was powered by water, like the ones at Venafro or Barbegal, many others were still powered by human energy. Slave energy.

The Romans seem to have realized that a thoroughgoing policy of mechanization would have had drastic effect on the employment level of both free wage earners and slaves. Suetonius, for example, wrote that the Emperor Vespasian (A.D. 69–79) turned down a labor-saving device on these grounds: "To a mechanical engineer who promised to transport some heavy columns to the Capitol at small expense, he gave no mean reward for his invention, but refused to make use of it, saying 'you must let me feed my poor commons.'"[3] In this case, his commons were the free wage earners, not the slaves.

Roman mills and Roman slavery both survived the fall of the Roman Empire. Mills built in Rome on the Janiculum hill, powered by water carried from Lake Sabatinus by the old aqueduct of Trajan, were still in working order when the

Byzantine general Belisarius was besieged in the city in 537 by the Ostrogoths led by Totila. To deprive the city of these mills the besieging army cut off the water supply. But Belisarius's engineers were not to be outwitted. They moved the machinery of the mills into barges moored in the Tiber and fitted them with waterwheels to be driven by the current of the river, thus maintaining the supply of flour for the defenders of the city. Belisarius's floating mills were to be carried over into the Middle Ages, when mills were often moored under the arches of bridges. As for slavery, the practice continued after the fall of Rome, but gradually declined and reached a low point in the ninth century—at the time when medieval waterpower was beginning to become important.

In the ninth century—around the year 845—on the twenty-three domains belonging to the monastery of Montier-en-Der, in the arrondissement of Saint-Dizier in the Haute-Marne, there were eleven water mills on the river Voire, three of them separated by less than 6 kilometers. In the same century, on the land owned by the famous medieval monastery of Saint Germain-des-Près—now renowned for its literary cafés the Flore, the Lipp, and the Deux-Magots—there were no less than 59 water mills. The majority of these mills were built on quite small streams. Aqueducts were no longer needed to drive the waterwheels. The corn-grinding industry had been decentralized and there were to be no more Barbegals.

The rate of expansion of the water mills in the succeeding centuries was spectacular. There was nothing comparable in antiquity. For example, on the banks of the Robec, which joins the Seine at Rouen, there were 2 mills in the tenth century, 4 in the eleventh century, 10 in the thirteenth century, and 12 at the beginning of the fourteenth century. In the department of l'Aube, 14 water mills are mentioned in the eleventh century, 60 in the twelfth, and over 200 in the thirteenth century.

Thanks to the Domesday tax collectors' scrupulous attention to fiscal detail, we have an exceptionally clear picture

The Domesday water mills and river systems. Courtesy *Antiquity* magazine.

of English waterpower in the latter part of the eleventh century. The commissioners, whom William the Conqueror sent out in 1086 to make the survey, had a number of questions to be answered, and one concerned mills, which were regarded as an important source of revenue. The commissioners covered roughly thirty-four of the English counties and reported on 9,250 manors. They found that there were 287,045 tenants and occupiers of land, and if each of these is taken to have been the head of a family of 5, we reach a population figure for the area covered by the Domesday Book of approximately 1,400,000.

A grand total of 5,624 water mills was recorded. Of the 9,250 manors, more than one-third, 3,463, had one mill or more. Only about 2 percent of the mills have not been located. On many of the sites listed in the Domesday Book, mills were still in use at the time of the Industrial Revolution of the eighteenth century, and after modernization some survived into the nineteenth and even the twentieth centuries.

Thus, on a nationwide basis, each of the eleventh-century water mills may be presumed to have supplied an average of 50 households. Some counties were better equipped than others, particularly the corn-growing counties and those with especially good water systems. Wiltshire, for example, had 390 mills for 10,150 households, or a mill for every 26 households, whereas in Suffolk there were 93 households to each mill.

A map of England's river system with the 5,624 Domesday water mills is an amazing sight. It is literally covered with dots, especially the areas to the south of the Severn and the Trent. On rivers like the Wylye in Wiltshire the concentration of mills is remarkable: thirty mills along some 10 miles of water; three mills every mile.

One of the main reasons for this "mill-building craze" was financial. Once the initial investment had been made—and this was relatively high—mills could bring in substantial rents. These rents varied considerably: from a low of 3d. to a high of 60s. On the Wylye they ranged from a low of 5s. at Hanging Longford to a high of 20s. at Fisherton de la Mare and at South Newton (where two mills were worth 40s. together). The interesting thing about some of these mills is that they were owned by two, three, four, or even five parties, each with an equal share in the profits. The Hanging Longford mill was divided between the Count of Mortain and Wakeran the Huntsman, each of whom had a half share in the mill worth 30d. In the following century in France the citizens of

Toulouse set up a company, that of the Bazacle,[4] where the shares of the mills on the Garonne were subject to annual fluctuations in value. The mill shares were bought and sold freely like shares on a contemporary stock exchange. The Société du Bazacle may well be the oldest capitalistic company in the world. It survived into the middle of the twentieth century when it was nationalized by the Electricité de France.

So the site of a medieval mill was valuable financially, and for this reason was protected commercially. A millowner had the right to prevent the erection of any new mill that would be damaging to his own. Or else he could accept compensation, a custom that existed well into the nineteenth century. In 1840 the city of Leeds had to pay £40,000 compensation to millowners for the right to put up their own mills.

Domesday Book records that two mills in Somerset were paying rents with blooms of iron, which suggests that these water mills were being used not to grind corn, but to forge iron. If this is so, these mill mechanisms were substantially different from those of the corn mills. Instead of a rotary movement to drive the millstones around and around, a reciprocal motion was needed to reproduce mechanically the action of the smith. This was done by cams projecting from the axle of a waterwheel, which raised and then released the pivoting trip- or tilt-hammer.

The engineers of the classical world—men like Hero of Alexandria—knew the use that could be made of the cam, but applied it only to animate toys or gadgets. Although the Chinese operated trip-hammers for hulling rice as early as A.D. 290, the use of the cam evidently failed to spread to other industries in the following centuries. In fact, it is a feature of Chinese technology that its great inventions—printing, gunpowder, the compass—never played a major evolutionary role in Chinese history. The introduction of the cam into medieval industry, on the other hand, was to make an important contri-

13

bution to the industrialization of the Western hemisphere. Today practically every automobile coming off the assembly line has a camshaft.

In Europe, from the end of the tenth century the cam enabled millwrights to mechanize a whole series of industries which up to then had been operated by hand or by foot. In France, one of the first mills for making beer is mentioned in a document relating to the monastery of Saint-Sauveur at Montreuil-sur-Mer between 987 and 996; water-driven hammers seem to have been operating as early as 1010 at Schmidmühlen in Oberpfalz in Germany. Hemp seems to have been treated mechanically in the Graisivaudan in 1040. The earliest mentioned fulling mill operating in France was in a village in Normandy about 1086. A tanning mill is mentioned in an 1138 document belonging to the chapter of Notre-Dame de Paris. Paper, which was manufactured by hand and foot for a thousand years or so following its invention by the Chinese and adoption by the Arabs, was manufactured mechanically as soon as it reached medieval Europe in the thirteenth century. This is convincing evidence of how technologically minded the Europeans of that era were. Paper had traveled nearly halfway around the world, but no culture or civilization on its route had tried to mechanize its manufacture.

The first paper mills to be driven by waterpower were those of Xativa, near Valencia in Spain, mentioned in documents of 1238 and 1273. Seven water-driven paper mills were in active service in 1268 in Fabriano in Italy. The first known French paper mill is the Moulin Richard-de-Bas, on the river Dore, near Ambert, department of the Puy-de-Dôme. It was manufacturing paper in 1326, and to this day linen and cotton rags are still being pulped by a battery of long wooden hammers, the heads of which are lifted and dropped in turn by a horizontal camshaft. Many contemporary artists use Moulin Richard-de-Bas paper with the original watermark, with its date of 1326.

Of all the medieval industries that adopted machinery fitted with a camshaft, none underwent a greater transformation than the fulling industry. Fulling was an important operation in cloth making. After leaving the loom the cloth had to be scoured, cleansed, and thickened by beating it in water. Originally this was done by men trampling the cloth in a trough; eventually the feet of the men were replaced by two wooden hammers which were alternately raised and dropped upon the cloth on the tilt-hammer system by means of a revolving drum attached to the spindle of a waterwheel. A whole series of hammers could replace a large group of fullers and could be operated with only one overseer.

In England in the thirteenth century, fulling mills brought in substantial profits, to a point where many lords of the manor not only built new fulling mills but also transformed corn mills into fulling mills. They made it obligatory for their tenants to bring their cloth to be fulled at the manorial mill, just as they had always insisted that their peasants' grain be ground at the manorial corn mill. They were monopolists. But this was not to the liking of the tenants, who resented paying a due to the miller and sometimes having to trek many miles across country.

The hostility to the waterpowered mills is reflected in a milling epic enacted on the land owned by the monastery of Saint Albans (Hertfordshire). The Abbot John (1235–60) had spent over £100 repairing all the mills on his land, and his successors were anxious to have their tenants bring their cloth and corn to the manorial mills. The tenants refused to obey these injunctions and continued to full at home, free of charge. Things came to a head in 1274 when Abbot Roger, one of John's successors, had certain houses searched to confiscate the cloth. The tenants resisted physically, then opened a fighting fund, and when Queen Eleanor came to Saint Albans they had their womenfolk appeal to her, "since it is hard satisfactorily to calm the anger of women." But as the Queen came from Provence it is not certain she understood exactly what these women were complaining about in English. The townsmen contested the case in the King's Court, but in vain. They had to abandon fulling by foot and bring their cloth to the abbey mills to be fulled by the machines.

In the following century, in 1326, a more violent dispute arose between the inhabitants of Saint Albans and the monastery. It led to an insurrection during which the monastery was twice besieged. The quarrel this time was over the right of the tenants of Saint Albans to grind their corn at home with their hand mills. Five years later, in retaliation, Abbot Richard had all the houses searched and the millstones seized. The stones were brought to the monastery, where the Abbot had the courtyard paved with them, for the humiliation of the common people. Their bitterness remained and when fifty years later, in 1381, the Peasants' Revolt broke out led by Wat Tyler, the people of Saint Albans rushed eagerly to the monastery to break up the millstone courtyard, the symbol of their humiliation.

The introduction of the fulling mill has been described as an industrial revolution of the thirteenth century, "a revolution which brought poverty and discontent to certain old centres of the industry but wealth, opportunity and prosperity to the country as a whole and which was destined to alter the face of medieval England."[5] The mechanization of fulling was "as decisive an event as the mechanization of spinning and weaving in the eighteenth century."[6]

The example of Paris in the early fourteenth century shows how close to one another water mills were built in a medieval city. There were sixty-eight in the upstream section alone of the main branch of the Seine. This went from the rue des Barres on the right bank, on the level of the present church of Saint-Gervais, across the Grand Pont (which stood on the site of the present Pont-aux-Changes, which links the place du Châtelet with the boulevard du Palais) to the eastern tip of the Île Notre-Dame, a distance of under a mile (1450 meters). Such a concentration of mills formed a real industrial complex in the center of Paris

Under the Grand Pont were moored floating mills of the type created by Belisarius in Rome eight centuries earlier. By anchoring them under the arches instead of in the middle of the river, the medieval millwrights considerably increased the efficiency of the mills. The flow of the river rushing through the arches turned the wheels, and therefore the millstones, faster. Productivity was thus much higher. There were thirteen such mills under the Grand Pont in 1323.

The millwrights of Toulouse worked out another solution to the problem of the relatively low productivity of the floating mills on the Garonne. They built majestic dams, possibly the largest ever erected up to that time. In the second half of the twelfth century, before the dams were built, there were over 60 floating mills in three groups. In the first group, that of the Château-Narbonnais at the upstream entrance to the town, there were 24 floating mills; in the second group, that of La Daurade, there were at least 15; and by the downstream entrance to the city, in that of Le Bazacle, there were 24. These floating mills had certain disadvantages. They interfered with navigation, and in times of flood they often broke away from their moorings and either crashed into boats or finished up as wrecks on someone's section of the riverbank, resulting in innumerable lawsuits. Toward the end of the twelfth century the city engineers therefore did away with the floating mills, built three dams barring the fast-flowing Garonne, and erected 43 water mills on its right bank. The Château-Narbonnais dam drove 16 of the earthbound mills, the Daurade dam drove 15, and the Bazacle dam 12. The reduced number of earthbound mills suggests that they were more efficient.

The building of the dams was a remarkably intricate feat of engineering. In no way comparable to rivers like the

Seine or the Thames, the Garonne has an average flow of 350 cubic meters per second (approximately 12,360 cubic feet per second), with maximums of 9,000 cubic meters per second in times of flood, while the width of the river varies between 150 and 200 meters (500 and 650 feet).

The Bazacle dam, first mentioned in a document of 1177, was some 400 meters (1300 feet) long and was situated diagonally across the river to offer more efficient resistance to the onrushing waters. Like the other dams, it was built by ramming thousands of oak piles approximately 6 meters long into the riverbed by means of a ram or piledriver. The dam engineers thus formed a series of parallel palisades and filled the spaces between with earth, wood, gravel, and boulders to reinforce the dam and make it watertight. Breakwaters were built in front of the dams to protect them against floating debris.

The height of the dam was of paramount importance, as it determined the fall of the water, which drove the waterwheels. The higher the dam, the higher the waterfall, and the faster the grain would be ground. But the height of the waterfall was also determined by the height of the dams downstream. If the level of the water retained by the lower dam was too high, the upstream dam would not have a waterfall sufficiently high to drive the waterwheels. In Toulouse, the height of the waterfall of the Château-Narbonnais dam was dependent on the height of the Daurade dam, and the latter dependent on that of the Bazacle dam. The Bazacle dam was the only one of the three whose waterpower was not dependent on the height of another dam, there being no further downstream dam.

Time and again through the centuries there were complaints followed by lawsuits because the owners of the downstream dams illegally raised the height of their dams to increase their waterpower. In the second half of the thirteenth century the owners of the Château-Narbonnais mills sued the

Daurade owners for having taken advantage of repairwork to raise their dam. They won their case on June 8, 1278. Experts were appointed to bring the Daurade dam back to the height originally agreed on. But twice in the next century they again raised their dam and twice, in 1308 and 1329, they were successfully prosecuted by the Château-Narbonnais.

In 1316 La Daurade in their turn sued Le Bazacle for raising their dam. Just as the Château-Narbonnais had won their cases against La Daurade, La Daurade won their case against Le Bazacle, and on October 27, 1316, five dam experts met to determine officially the height of the dam and to confirm the shape and width of the *navière*—the passageway left for the boats moving up and down the river. The *navière* was always to be a problem. The water flowing through it was a volume of water lost to drive the mills. So the millowners were continually closing the *navière*, to the fury of those navigating the Garonne.

Forty years later, in 1356, a new lawsuit was brought against Le Bazacle by La Daurade. It was to last over half a century, ending only in 1408. It began, as usual, as a result of the dam being raised under cover of repairs. But this time it was more dramatic, because the Bazacle dam had been raised to such a height as to put the Daurade mills out of action. And this time the Bazacle owners refused to comply with an order, made in 1358, to lower the dam. Le Bazacle appealed against this decision to high-ranking persons and then to the Parliament in Paris. La Daurade fought on, claiming considerable damages for lost opportunities. In 1366 the Parliament confirmed the 1358 order and ordered Le Bazacle to pay damages. But Le Bazacle managed by devious means not to have the dam lowered. They asked for a postponement of the decision, then offered to do the destruction work themselves, but of course did nothing. By this time La Daurade was beginning to run out of money to pay for the court fees, with their mills having been idle for many years. The lawsuit was abandoned in 1368. By the time it was resumed ten years later, many of the Daurade owners had withdrawn in view of the hopelessness of the situation. Le Bazacle bought up the Daurade shares in the following year, and by 1408 only one shareholder was left. He decided to sell, and with that La Daurade ceased to exist. Le Bazacle had in hand a total victory, achieved by men who for over fifty years continuously used unscrupulous methods to reach their goal.

The millowners of the Château-Narbonnais, La Daurade, and Le Bazacle were all shareholders, men and women who had either inherited or bought their company shares. From the early thirteenth century we find no millers among the shareholders. We are faced here with a division between capital and labor. The millers were employees who had no say in the company's decisions, and the shareholders were wealthy Toulouse citizens who had no special knowledge of or interest in milling, except to receive profit from it. These citizens were small capitalists exploiting other men's labor.

The price of the shares fluctuated like any contemporary shares quoted on the Stock Exchange. The market price varied according to the economic situation and the good or bad working order of the mills. Shares rose, for example, to a very high level in the years following 1350, after the Black Death. They fell whenever the dam or the mills were battered by a Garonne flood. As in modern times, the price of shares anticipated results. On the average they brought in a return of 10 percent to 25 percent a year, a very high yield, which accounts for the great interest shown in the mills by the financially minded citizens of Toulouse.

The shares were called *uchaus*. One *uchau* was worth one-eighth of a mill. So for the twelve mills of Le Bazacle, there were ninety-six shares. Shares could be inherited, donated, exchanged, or purchased. The most common transactions were those involving the purchase of shares and were carried out in the presence of a solicitor (*notaire*) who drew up the official documents. There were sales of a quarter of an *uchau*, or a third or a half, and of one, two, or three *uchaus*. The solicitor drew up a document enumerating all the rights that the new owner was entitled to. While the annual dividends from the *uchaus* were paid in kind—grain from the corn mills—the sales of the *uchaus* were paid in hard cash.

When in the twelfth century the *uchau* owners of the floating mills all met to discuss the plans for building the dams and the earthbound mills, they had to make numerous and difficult decisions concerning their future association. They had to innovate, as there were no known examples of such associations in the past. They first had to agree on the common expenses. The building of the dams and their upkeep were to be the main ones, requiring from all concerned an important outlay of capital. It was decided that the mills would be built and paid for by those who owned the *uchaus* of the floating mills.

Among the other problems to be solved were those resulting from the income from fishing rights, which would be quite substantial. The dams were to be one long fishing net laid across the river, and to make sure that the salmon would not jump over the dams, the engineers laid latticework all along the tops. The revenues from the fishing rights were to be paid in cash to the shareholders in proportion to their shares.

Progressively the shareholders realized that it was in their interest to pool all their profits and losses. This they did, and by the 1370s the Château-Narbonnais and the Bazacle associations had practically formed themselves into what one would now call limited companies—the Daurade association having ceased its activity after its long-drawn-out lawsuit with Le Bazacle. The mills were valued, and from then on the shareholders no longer had a share in one mill but a share in the Societé du Bazacle or du Château-Narbonnais. Le Bazacle had a particularly difficult problem to resolve, because two of the original twelve corn mills of the late twelfth century had become fulling mills. The two fulling mills were finally bought out by the shareholders of the corn mills, but not before a lawsuit had been fought, which ended only in 1403.

There were annual general meetings of the shareholders, where the accounts of the previous year were rendered and where managers were elected who would act for the shareholders until the following year. These were entitled to buy real estate, houses, mills, building material; to sign contracts with the employees or tradesmen; and to lease the meadows owned by the companies to tenant-farmers. They had to defend the interests of the shareholders in the numerous lawsuits that arose. Perhaps for this reason, many of the managers were chosen from the legal profession.

A plan was made in 1374 for a merger between the sociétés du Bazacle and du Château-Narbonnais, but it was never realized. The ruling citizens of Toulouse may have intervened to protect the public interest, for such a monopoly could eventually have manipulated the price of grain in time of famine. In the following centuries—in the years 1507, 1574, 1666, and 1702—the two companies. nonetheless came to limited agreements on such issues as common purchases of raw materials and employees' working conditions.

The two medieval limited companies moved smoothly into modern times. In the eighteenth century the word *actionnaire* (shareholder) appears in the companies' archives, and in the nineteenth century the word *action*, which then tends to replace the old French word *uchau*. In 1840 the dividends were paid in cash and no longer in grain. The Société des Moulins du Bazacle became the Société Civile Anonyme du Moulin du Bazacle. In the nineteenth century the Bazacle dam was used to produce electricity—it had been rebuilt after the medieval dam had been destroyed in 1709 by an exceptionally powerful flood—and the company then took the name of Société Toulousaine d'Electricité du Bazacle. Then, after the 1939–45 war, the French government nationalized (along with all the other French companies producing electricity) what was certainly the oldest French company and probably also the oldest limited company in the world—nearly eight centuries old. It is a great tribute to medieval engineering that contemporary engineers built their dam on the exact site of the twelfth-century dam.

Medieval engineers harnessed not only fast-flowing rivers like the Garonne, but also the energy of the sea. So remarkable was their choice of sites for tidal mills that the first twentieth-century tidal-powered plant, built after World War II by the Electricité de France—L'usine marémotrice de la Rance—dammed a river along which lay a whole series of medieval tidal mills which were still in active use, on La Rance, near Saint-Malo in Brittany.

Tidal mills—unknown in classical times—are typical of the medieval urge to discover new sources of energy. In the twelfth century, tidal mills are mentioned on the Adour near Bayonne, and at Woodbridge on the Deben Estuary in Suffolk. In the thirteenth century the number of recorded tidal mills greatly increases. This trend continues through the centuries, although the growth of water mills slows down. We know of 3 tidal mills in Devon and Cornwall in the thirteenth century, 5 in the fourteenth, 9 in the sixteenth, 11 in the seventeenth, 14 in the eighteenth, and 25 in the nineteenth century.

Tidal mills were generally built in low-lying areas where the gradients of the rivers were too slight to provide a sufficiently powerful flow to drive water mills. Along shallow tidal creeks—often quite a distance inland—dams were built to create ponds as large as 13 acres. Swinging gates were built in the dam to allow the incoming tide to flow into the ponds. As the tide turned, the pressure of the water, now greater inside, automatically closed the gates. The miller waited until the level of water below the mill had dropped sufficiently and then allowed the dammed water to escape through the mill-race, to drive the waterwheels.

There were disadvantages to tidal mills. Since the time of high tide changes every day, the miller's working hours did as well; and, more important, the tidal mills could only be worked a limited number of hours per day. Tidal mills, which were only used to grind corn, were never to play as decisive a role as the water mills in the economy of medieval Europe.

In the twelfth century, medieval engineers turned their attention to harnessing wind power. They adapted the mechanism of the water mill for this purpose, and with remarkable success. The waterwheels driven by hydraulic power were replaced by sails driven by the power of the wind. But while water always flows in the same direction, the airstream is apt to flow from many directions. The windmill engineers solved this problem very ingeniously by mounting the framed wooden body, which contained the machinery and carried the sails, on a massive upright oak post free to turn with the wind.

This so-called "post-mill" seems to have been an independent Western invention and to owe no debt to the horizontal windmill (mounted on a vertical axle), which is known to have existed from the seventh century onward on the plateaus of Iran and Afghanistan (where the wind always blows from one direction). At the time of the Third Crusade (1189–92) post-mills were in fact exported to the Middle East, where they had been previously unknown. An eyewitness relates:

> *The German soldiers used their skill*
> *To build the very first windmill*
> *That Syria had ever known.*[7]

The industrial revolution of medieval Europe was sufficiently established to export its technological innovations.

Early drawing of a raised windmill. Courtesy Bodleian Library, Oxford.

From 1180 onward there are innumerable documents relating to windmills. There were so many windmills, bringing in such high profits, that Pope Celestine III (1191–98) imposed a tax on them. They mushroomed wherever there was a lack of fast-flowing streams, and since, unlike water mills, they could operate in freezing winter conditions, they were erected in large numbers on the great plains of northern Europe. There were as many as 120 windmills operating in the immediate vicinity of Ypres in the thirteenth century, and in the same century windmills were introduced into Holland.

The importance attached to windmills is proved (as with the water mills) by the desperate means with which some owners tried to protect their monopolies. Often, when someone built a windmill near one owned by someone else, the prior owner would try to bring the intruder before a tribunal or else resort to violence and have the offending mill destroyed.

A famous chronicler, Jocelin of Brakelond, chaplain to Samson, Abbot of Bury Saint Edmunds, relates in 1191 how angry the Abbot was when he heard that Herbert the Dean

25

had built a windmill for his own use. The story of this "industrial dispute" of the late twelfth century is told so vividly by Jocelin of Brakelond that I quote it in full:

Herbert the Dean set up a windmill on Habardun; and when the Abbot heard this, he grew so hot with anger that he would scarcely eat or speak a single word. On the morrow, after hearing mass, he ordered the Sacrist to send his carpenters thither without delay, pull everything down, and place the timber under safe custody. Hearing this, the Dean came and said that he had the right to do this on his free fief, and that free benefit of the wind ought not to be denied to any man; he said he also wished to grind his own corn there and not the corn of others, lest perchance he might be thought to do this to the detriment of neighbouring mills. To this the Abbot still angry, made answer: "I thank you as I should thank you if you had cut off both my feet. By God's face, I will never eat bread till that building be thrown down. You are an old man, and you ought to know that neither the King nor his Justiciar can change or set up anything within the liberties of this town without the assent of the Abbot and the Convent. Why have you then presumed to do such a thing? Nor is this thing done without detriment to my mills, as you assert. For the burgesses will throng to your mill and grind their corn to their hearts' content, nor should I have the lawful right to punish them, since they are free men. I would not even allow the Cellarer's mill which was built of late, to stand, had it not been built before I was Abbot. Go away," he said, "go away; before you reach your house, you shall hear what will be done with your mill." But the Dean, shrinking in fear from before the face of the Abbot, by the advice of his son Master Stephen, anticipated the servants of the Abbot and caused the mill which he had built to be pulled down by his own servants without delay, so that, when the servants of the Sacrist came, they found nothing left to demolish.[8]

In the following century the monks from the royal Cistercian monastery of Royaumont, near Chantilly, were outraged when a certain Pierre de Baclai built a windmill that was in direct competition with their own mill at Gonesse. Threats were of no avail and the monks went to court to force the issue, but after hearing both sides the judge decreed that Pierre de Baclai's windmill should not be destroyed.

The large income to be derived from leasing out windmills or water mills would account for the millowners' concern for their power-producing machines. When undertaking a series of capital improvements on their land in the fourteenth century, the estate administration of Glastonbury Abbey in Somerset voted to invest some of their capital in a new post-mill at Walton, with a view to renting it out to a miller, reckoning that this would be more profitable than exploiting it themselves. The building account for 1342–43 totaled £11 12s. 11d. (By comparison, a fulling mill built in 1208–1209 at Brightwell for the Bishop of Winchester cost £9 4s. 4d.) An attractive lease was drawn up and a yearly rental of £3 was asked with an entry fee of £1. William Pyntel, a farmer who had in the previous years accumulated some small capital, was attracted by this concession and signed a life tenancy. The Glastonbury estate had made an excellent investment; it gave them an annual return of 25.75 percent on their capital.

The burden of the high rentals demanded by the water-, wind-, and tidal-millowners often encouraged the millers to exceed the legal levy of meal or flour, which was normally one-sixteenth of the grain ground. This practice was immortalized by Chaucer in the Reeve's Tale:

> *At Trumpington, not far from Cambridge town*
> *A bridge goes over where the brook runs down*
> *And by that brook there stands a mill as well.*

. . .

There was a miller lived there many a day
As proud as any peacock and as gay

. . .

This miller levied toll beyond a doubt
On wheat and malt from all the land about
Particularly from a large-sized college
In Cambridge, Solar Hall. 'Twas common knowledge
They sent their wheat and malt to him to grind it.
Happened one day the man who ought to mind it,
The college manciple, lay sick in bed,
And some reported him as good as dead.
On hearing which the miller robbed him more
A hundred times than he had robbed before;
For up till then he'd only robbed politely,
But now he stole outrageously, forthrightly.
The Warden scolded hard and made a scene,
But there! The miller didn't give a bean
Blustered it out and swore it wasn't so.[9]

2

The Agricultural Revolution

The first impact of the new sources of energy was on agriculture. Throughout the Middle Ages probably more than 90 percent of the population of Europe still lived directly off the land. However, not only did cultivation become far more intensive, both to serve the growing population and to provide surpluses for commerce, but there was also a breakdown of the old manorial system, under which the peasants had cultivated both their own strips of land and the demesne lands of the manor. An important factor in these changes was the climate.

Scientific and historical research in the last few decades has shown that the climate of Europe was milder and drier around the year 1000 than in the twentieth century. Although the average temperature was perhaps no more than one or two degrees higher, this resulted in a quite different type of climate and goes a long way to explain the extent of the medieval agricultural revolution.

There are now a number of methods used to determine climatic changes, and their findings are generally in agreement. One of the most highly developed is dendroclimatology, based on the study of the rings of trees, which reflect meteorological conditions. This method is of great importance in countries like the United States, where thousand-year-old trees are to be found, but in Europe more valuable results have been obtained from the study of the advance and retreat of glaciers. In the Alps, the most remarkable glacier from this point of view is the Fernau glacier in the Tyrol.

The advance and retreat of the Fernau glacier, like others in the Alps, clearly shows the warm and cold periods during the last seven or eight thousand years. From the glacier's behavior in the past three millennia, we can conclude that the first millennium B.C. was on the whole a cold period, especially between 900 B.C. and 300 B.C. In Roman times, from 300 B.C. to A.D. 400, the glacier retreated and later advanced again. Then, from 750 onward Europe became warmer and drier. This very important historical period, in which the birth of Europe really took place, lasted until approximately 1215. Known as the "little climatic optimum," it was followed by a limited cold spell which ended around 1350. The next cold spell, which lasted from 1550 to 1850, with a very cold seventeenth century, is often called the "Little Ice Age." In the middle of the nineteenth century another warm era began, reaching a peak around the 1930s. Unfortunately, since 1940 the trend has reversed, and the climatologists are not prepared to predict how long the current cycle will continue.

It is difficult to measure precisely how the medieval climatic optimum influenced demographic and agricultural expansion in western Europe, although it is easy to see how favorable weather conditions must have helped the Norsemen in their voyages and migrations to the northern regions of the

Western hemisphere. They moved into Iceland in the ninth century, into Greenland at the end of the tenth century, and a short time later into Newfoundland. It seems that in this period the North Sea and the Atlantic were less stormy, and that icebergs rarely moved south of the 70th parallel.

Greenland itself was so named because of the luxuriant pastures of the southern fjords. While the difference in temperature in western Europe between the Middle Ages and our own time is approximately 1 to 2 degrees, in Greenland the difference is as great as 2 to 4 degrees. The settlements there were prosperous for the first two centuries or so, but the changing weather of the thirteenth century brought icebergs down the east coast and the Greenlanders became more and more cut off from supplies from Iceland and the mainland. Communities died out one after another, and by the beginning of the sixteenth century there were no Norsemen left in Greenland.

In western Europe the drier period certainly helped to slow down the natural expansion of the forests, which then covered vast areas of the continent, and in certain regions pollen analysis shows that forests actually retreated. This phenomenon must have made easier the task of clearing forest lands to make way for the plow.

Cereal growing in Europe must also have profited from the medieval climate of the "little optimum," just as it had flourished in the exceptionally sunny fourth millennium B.C., when cereals were grown in Europe for the first time (between 3200 and 3000 B.C., in the Magdeburg-Cologne-Liège area).

The influence of the climate on trees and crops can be measured with some accuracy in the mountainous areas. Between 1300 and 1500 the altitudinal limits of various species of trees in the Vosges and the Black Forest fell by 100 to 200 meters. After 1300 there was a reduction in the cultivation of fruit and grain crops in the mountain districts of central Europe, and in Baden, in southwestern Germany, the altitudinal limit of vineyards fell by 220 meters. On the hills of northern England, the plow reached its highest levels in the twelfth and thirteenth centuries—beyond the limits of the wartime emergency plowing campaign of 1940–44.

Progress in climatological studies in recent decades has led medieval historians to accept the fact that climate must have been one of the decisive factors in raising the level of agriculture. A critical contribution also came from the exploitation of another source of energy, the horse.

An example of medieval horsepower is given in the building accounts of Troyes. From quarries 50 kilometers away, carters on an average journey drove pairs of horses that pulled wagons weighing 2,500 kilograms and loaded with 2,500 kilograms of stone. When, infrequently, the wagons were loaded with 3,900 kilograms of stone, the horses were pulling 6,400 kilograms. This is a very heavy load in comparison with the maximum load, 500 kilograms, a pair of horses was authorized to pull on roads in Roman times.

The Theodosian Code of 438 decreed that anyone caught harnessing horses to a load in excess of 500 kilograms would be severely punished. So exceptionally low was Roman horsepower that horses were never used in agriculture. How then did the Middle Ages increase horsepower to pull such heavily laden wagons, and plow the heavy soil of northern Europe?

Until Lefebvre des Noëttes, a retired French cavalry officer, published his book on harnessing, *L'Attelage—le cheval à travers les ages* (subtitled *Contribution à l'histoire de l'esclavage*) in 1931, no academic had ever realized how inefficient the classical world had been in using animal power and how inventive medieval man was in this respect. Lefebvre des Noëttes's theory was that the Greeks and Romans had never found the correct way to harness horses but had simply adapted the yoke harness of the ox, with minor modifications, to the horse without ever realizing how inefficient this system was. As soon as the horses started to pull, the neck straps pressed on their jugular veins and windpipes, strangling them and making them throw back their heads like the horses of the Parthenon. Lovers of Greek art have always celebrated the rare genius of the Greek sculptor who gave such dignity to the horse, without realizing that the horse they celebrated had his head raised to avoid strangulation.

In 1910, Lefebvre des Noëttes conducted a series of experiments in Paris to verify his theories. He harnessed horses as they are depicted in Greek and Roman monuments and found that a pair of horses harnessed in this fashion had difficulty in pulling loads in excess of 500 kilograms, proving the merits of the regulations in the Theodosian Code.

The correct way of harnessing horses was to build rigid padded collars, which would rest on the shoulder blades of the animal and not interfere with its breathing. This "modern" harness seems to have been used for the first time somewhere in the steppes separating China from the Siberian forests, and was originally designed for camels. It was introduced into Europe sometime in the eighth century, and in 800 we find its first European application. By the end of the ninth century we hear of horses used for plowing on the northern coast of Norway, no doubt with the new harness. This is the very first mention of horses employed in agriculture. The earliest representations of horses working in the fields appear in the border of the Bayeux tapestry (eleventh century), where there is one pulling a harrow; and a tapestry of the Creation in the Cathedral of Gerona from around the same time shows a team of horses plowing the land with a revolutionary heavy-wheeled plow. From then onward an increasing number of works represent horses plowing with the modern harness. And the horses no longer raise their heads.

The horsepower achieved by the rigid collar was further increased in the Middle Ages by the nailing of iron shoes to the horses' hooves as protection against wear and tear, especially in moist climates. Previously, types of sandals made of cord or leather had been used, but these quickly wore out;

they were supplanted by iron sandals, to be attached to the hooves with thongs or wires, but these used to fall off as soon as the horse trotted or galloped. (Their inefficiency did not prevent them from becoming status symbols, for Nero had his mules provided with silver sandals while Poppaea had her mules wear sandals of gold.)

The nomadic riders of the Yenisei region in Siberia are perhaps the first to have actually nailed iron shoes to horses' hooves, judging from archaeological remains that have been uncovered at gravesites dating from the ninth to tenth centuries. Soon afterward, we hear of iron shoes in Byzantium and in the West. By the eleventh century they were common. Domesday Book reveals that in Hereford six smiths were each obliged to make 120 horseshoes yearly for the king. By the twelfth century, horseshoes were mass-produced, and the great iron-producing center of the Forest of Dean in southwest England carried out an order for fifty thousand for Richard I's Crusade. In the next century, in 1254, the iron center situated in the Weald of Sussex and Kent, now growing to rival the Forest of Dean, manufactured thirty thousand horseshoes and sixty thousand nails (though there must have been more than two nails to each horseshoe). Iron shoes had become one of the vital necessities of war, transport, and agriculture. And from the eleventh century onward, horseshoes appear in drawings with the nails very clearly shown. In his sketchbook, the thirteenth-century architect-engineer Villard de Honnecourt drew three horses with iron shoes and went to great lengths to indicate the high quality of shoeing in his time.

There was one more harnessing technique unknown to the Romans that was discovered by the Middle Ages and that allowed them to take full advantage of horsepower for transport and agriculture. This was to hitch horses one behind the other, and thus to distribute the weight to be pulled equally among as many as four horses.

Lefebvre des Noëttes, who had demonstrated how, technically, this had been achieved, curiously enough did not see that the horse thus harnessed and shod was to become a progressive element in the development of medieval agriculture.

The horse, like the tractor that superseded it, was certainly not adopted everywhere and at the same time. As with the tractor, there was a prejudice against the horse. It went against tradition; for centuries Europeans had used only the ox for plowing. A horse in the Middle Ages, like a tractor in the twentieth century, involved a substantial investment, and its upkeep cost considerably more than that of an ox. The farmer had to learn how to raise and feed horses and care for them. Horses had to have special food—oats—and this confronted the farmer with a fundamentally new problem, as oats had to be specially grown. For all these reasons horses—like tractors—were at first bought only by the richer and more progressive landowners.

Table 1 shows clearly the reason horses gradually took over from oxen.

The horse and the ox exert roughly the same pull, but as the horse moves 50 percent faster—3.6 feet per second to the 2.4 feet per second of the ox—it produces 50 percent more foot-

TABLE 1.   *Muscular Power of a Man and of Various Animals*[1]

	Pressure exerted (pounds)*	Velocity (feet per second)	Foot-pounds per second†	Ratio
Average draft horse	120	3.6	432	1.00
Ox	120	2.4	288	0.66
Mule	60	3.6	216	0.50
Donkey	30	3.6	108	0.25
Man, pumping	13.2	2.5	33	0.076
Man, turning winch	18	2.5	45	0.104

* The pressures exerted here are effective pressures as recorded by dynamometer, not the weights transported.

† 500 foot-pounds per second = 1 horsepower.

pounds per second, 432 as compared to 288. Horses also have greater endurance and can work two hours longer per day in the fields.

George Duby, the French medievalist, writes:

> the horse was speedier, much speedier than the ox, and its use accelerated considerably the work of the farm and made it possible to increase the number of ploughings and to drag the harrow, shown in the Bayeux tapestry being pulled by a horse in the eleventh century. Giving up the ox team in favour of the horse also meant the spread of oat growing, which in its turn was connected with a more regular practice of the three-year rotation. Countries where this took place witnessed an improvement in the preparation of the land and thus in its fertility, a reduction in the duration of the fallow, and a rise in return on seed sown. The whole process marked the advent of a much more productive agrarian system.[2]

The superiority of the horse is reflected in the fact that in the twelfth century in the Slavic lands, east of Germany, the unit of labor was what one horse or two oxen could plow in one day.

An increasing number of horses begin to appear in many account books. In 1125, at Elton (an estate of Ramsey Abbey), there were 40 oxen and only 2 horses, but sometime after 1160 the number of oxen had fallen to 24 and the number of horses had multiplied fourfold. By the thirteenth century there were regions like Normandy where horses had apparently taken over almost completely from oxen. The same is true of the region around Paris, where at Palaiseau by 1218 and at Gonesse by 1277 only horses were plowing.

Nevertheless, there were regions in Europe in the thirteenth century, such as southeastern France, where horses had not overtaken oxen. This may have been due in part to the difficulty of growing oats, which are better suited to cold and wet soils.

Strangely enough, it was in thirteenth-century England that there seems to have been a real setback in the increasing use of horses for plowing. Walter of Henley, the famous English agronomist of that time, strongly recommended the use of oxen to young estate administrators. As he wrote in his treatise on farming: "With an ox plough you shall till rather than with a horse plough if the land be not stony so that the ox cannot help himself with his feet. Wherefore, I will tell you; the horse is more costly than the ox."[3]

He dismissed the fact that the horse was so much faster than the ox by accusing the plowmen of what is probably the first known work slowdown in history: "And the ox plough shall till as much in the year as the horse plough shall because the malice of the ploughmen do not allow that the horse plough shall break pace more than the ox plough."[4]

Walter of Henley went on to prove in great detail how much more the upkeep of a horse cost. The horse, in winter, ate as much as 8s. 2d. worth of oats (½d. of oats a day for twenty-eight weeks), whereas the ox ate only 2s. 8d. worth for the same number of days. Thus, food for the horse cost three times as much as food for the ox. In summer Walter estimated that out in the fields the horse and ox would cost the same amount in grass: 12d. We can accept these figures but, unfortunately, in his eagerness to prove his point Walter went too far and quoted quite unrealistic costs for the shoeing of a horse, figures flatly contradicted by other treatises and accounts. He stated that shoes would cost the estate 4s. 4d. a year, when we know for a fact that shoeing actually cost only 6d. to 9d.

Walter then gave a final reason for disregarding the horse: "And when the horse is old and worn out then hath he nothing but his skin. But when the ox is old with 10d. of grass he will be made fat to kill or to sell for as much as he cost you."[5] Walter's arguments show at least that serious thought was given to economic considerations. The great value of the horse, particularly when used with the heavy plow and the three-field system, was that it led to a very great increase in productivity; but in areas where there was no great increase in the density of population—and this varied throughout Europe—there was no real need for greater productivity, and the innovations, particularly where they involved higher outlays, took hold only gradually.

Walter of Henley's treatise on estate management and farming is only one of several remarkable treatises written in thirteenth-century England that reveal a very modern approach to agricultural methods and economics. In general, they encouraged the adoption of experimental techniques and advised that a systematic effort be made to run the estates on a rational basis. They advocated efficient organization, accurate methods of accounting, and the setting up of a yearly control of the accounts by auditors. These treatises were extremely popular and were copied and recopied for the benefit of many landlords who worked to increase the productivity of their land. Of Walter of Henley's treatise alone, thirty-two copies have survived. The other best-known treatises are those of Robert Grosseteste (written 1240–42), the anonymous *Seneschaucy*, and the anonymous *Husbandry*.

The exceptional success of these treatises coincides with a decision of Parliament in 1285 made to combat the innumerable frauds committed by estate officers—stewards and bailiffs. The new laws authorized auditors to imprison any officers found defrauding an estate, which in turn provided a useful impetus for lords of manors to increase their demesne farming (on the parts of their lands not held by their tenants) by improving their organization.

As they became interested in farming themselves, the lords of the manors needed highly trained estate administrators, knowledgeable not only in farming but in accountancy and law. They found them in towns like Oxford, where there were "courses in business management, instruction in the art of letter writing, the formulation of writs, deeds and accounts."[6] Walter of Henley, who had perhaps acquired his farming experience as a bailiff on some large estate in the West Midlands, may have "read his treatise as a visiting lecturer," "taking the draft away with him after permitting that a copy was made for use in teaching."[7]

Walter of Henley is, quite rightly, often quoted in history books as one of the first men known to have applied experimental methods to agriculture. His writings reveal a very independent character bound by no tradition; he never hesitated to defend the unorthodox views resulting from his personal observations, and he sometimes invited his audience to verify these theories for themselves: "And will you see it? When the corn is come up above the ground, go to the one end of the furlong and behold the corn along towards the other head, or end, and you shall find it true which I tell you."[8]

To read Walter of Henley brings many medieval technological problems vividly to life. He discusses at length the relative merits of the "two-field" and "three-field" systems, supporting his views with detailed calculations. The question of the rotation of crops has always been considered of great importance in medieval agriculture, and the adoption of the three-field system was a major technological breakthrough. The Romans knew only the two-crop rotation. Under this system one of two fields would be left fallow—that is, unsown —every other year, to let the earth rest. Animals would be kept on the fallow land to enrich it with manure. The "three-field" system—which first appears in the eighth century—is more complex. A plot of land is divided equally into three fields. In the first year the first field is planted with a winter crop, such as wheat, the second field is planted in spring with a spring crop, like oats, and the third field is left fallow. The second year the field that was fallow is planted with a winter

		1st year		2nd year		3rd year
1st field	A U T U M N	- - - -	A U T U M N	· · · · ·	A U T U M N	
2nd field		· · · · ·				- - - -
3rd field				- - - -		· · · · ·

Winter planting = - - - - -   Spring planting = · · · · ·

FIGURE 1. *The Three-Field System*

crop, the first field instead of having another winter crop is sown with a spring crop, and the second field which was previously planted with a spring crop is left fallow. The third year, the first field is left fallow, the second field is planted with a winter crop, and the third field is sown with a spring crop. And the fourth year, the three-year cycle begins all over again.

The three-field system had many advantages. As only 30 percent of the land lay fallow in any year, as against 50 percent with the two-field system, there was a higher proportion of land under cultivation. Secondly, the fact that there were two crops harvested at different times of the year was a protection against a failing crop, and it spread the plowing more evenly through the year. And as a further advantage it allowed farmers who wanted to plow with horses to have a spring crop of oats, which would feed the horses.

But the most far-reaching changes in medieval agriculture were certainly due to the general adoption of the heavy-wheeled plow. It was of far greater importance than either horsepower—which in many areas had still not replaced ox power—or the three-field system—which was only adopted to a limited extent in Europe. Improvements in the plow had been made over the centuries, probably since late Roman times, so that by the end of the tenth century the heavy plow was a very formidable agricultural weapon, equipped with a colter cutting vertically into the sod, a flat plowshare cutting the grass horizontally at the roots, and a moldboard designed to turn the slice of turf. Its two wheels enabled the plowman to move from field to field and helped him regulate the depth of the furrows. In the eleventh century, which saw the development of the great capitalist estates and the opening up of new lands by colonists to accommodate the dramatic growth of population, this powerful plow could be used to help clear the forests and also to cultivate vast new areas, such as the rich alluvial lowlands, which had been avoided by earlier settlers.

Use of this plow resulted in many other changes, some of lasting importance. In the first place, the deep plowing of heavy soils made it necessary to team up a greater number of plow animals—eight oxen, or six oxen and two horses, or two horses, or four horses. As these long teams were difficult to turn when they reached the end of the field, the fields were extended to the maximum possible length, wherever the land permitted. All over Europe the deep plow tended to change the shape of the fields, from a squarish form to a longitudinal form. A second consequence of the heavy plow was the development of cooperative agricultural communities, as few small landowners could possibly own, alone, the expensive machine and all its animals. It also led to the invention of a new agricultural implement, the harrow, because the deep plow eliminated the need for cross-plowing. Drawn across the field at right angles to the furrows, the more easily handled harrow leveled the soil and helped mix the seeds with the earth.

Walter of Henley told his audience how to use the plow on fallow land, explaining that the first plowing of the fallow ought to be made with a deep, broad furrow—provided that there was a good depth of fertile soil which could thereby be brought to the surface—but that the plowman should be care-

A team of horses with rigid collars yoked to the revolutionary high-wheeled plow. Courtesy Vatican Library, Rome.

The deep plow. Courtesy British Museum, London.

ful that no subsoil be plowed up. For the second plowing of the fallow his advice was:

> Stir not your land too deep but so that you may destroy the thistles and the weeds utterly; for if the land be stirred very deep and be sopped in water when you should plow for sowing then the plough cannot get to any firm ground but will flounder in the mud. And if the plough can go two fingers' breadth deeper at seed time than when it was stirred at second fallow, it will find firm ground and thus it be cleansed and rid of the water the which maketh the tillage good.[9]

The new technique of medieval plowing brought about a substantial increase in grain yield. It has been calculated that between the eleventh and thirteenth centuries the average yield increased from approximately 2.5 to approximately 4. That is, for every measure of grain sown, the harvest yielded 4 measures. This meant that the portion of the harvest to be disposed of by the producer doubled—from 1.5 to 3. The anonymous author of the *Husbandry* may have been misleading his readers when he stated that the yield for barley was 8, 7 for rye, 5 for wheat, 4 for oats—as we know that the average yield on the estates of the Bishop of Winchester for the period 1200–1350 was only 3.8 for barley, 3.8 for wheat, and 2.4 for oats. It is nevertheless true that on some fertile lands, like those of Artois, yields from the large estate could be higher even than those quoted in the *Husbandry*. In the Artois, on the demesne of Thierry d'Hireçon at Roquetoire, the wheat in 1319 reached a yield of 7.5, in 1321 of 11.6, and at Gosnay in 1333 of 11 and in 1335 the record figure of 15. This last figure approaches the yields of 20 which are achieved today in the region of Neufbourg in Normandy, where in the early fifteenth century the yield of wheat was only 3.2.

It was not until the agricultural revolution of the eighteenth century that yields rose to a substantially higher level than those reached in the thirteenth and early fourteenth centuries. It took nearly half a millennium before medieval agricultural technology was overtaken. Medieval agronomists had given high priority to increasing the yield; more than 10 percent of Walter's treatise is devoted to this problem. He recommends sowing the winter crop with purchased corn:

> Change yearly your seed corn at Michaelmas for more increase shall you have of the seed that grew upon another man's land than by that which groweth upon your own land. And will you see it? Cause the two lands to be ered [plowed] in one day and sow the one with the bought seed and the other with the seed which grew of your own and at harvest you shall find that I say truth.[10]

Following this, Walter of Henley enumerates the different fertilizers in current use and methods of improving them, and explains when and how they should be spread on the arable land and plowed in. Dealing with the same subject, the anonymous author of the *Seneschaucy* writes: "No stubble should be sold from any manor and only as much as is needed for the thatching of houses ought to be reaped and gathered; the rest ought to be ploughed in."[11] The corn was cut high and the stubble allowed to ripen. If there is any surplus of "straw and fern it ought to be gathered and thrown on roads and lanes in order to make compost."[12]

Walter discusses the merits of marl, a rich soil containing a mixture of calcium carbonate and argillaceous matter. Marl was found in certain regions of England, in the Île-de-France, in Normandy, and in Anjou, and was used as a fertilizer. The practice of marling was known to the classical world, was lost and, it seems, rediscovered at the time of Charlemagne.

Manure was highly prized, for it was a rare and precious

product, none of which must be wasted. The most blessed of all the animals was the sheep. Sheep were led ceremoniously to fertilize the fallow land, and a sheep's hoof was known, justifiably, as the "golden hoof." All contemporary treatises made much of sheep. The author of the *Seneschaucy* considered that a shepherd should not be deterred from his duty even by a "wrestling match." Walter of Henley estimated that twenty ewes could produce as great a benefit as two cows and yield one stone of cheese and half a gallon of butter per week.

For the medieval farmer, sheep were more useful than any other animal. Their "golden hooves" were a great asset; the farmers could drink their milk, make butter and cheese, eat mutton, and with the skin they could make parchment. With the educational boom of the twelfth century, there was a substantial increase in the demand for books, and the premium for parchment was high. A comparative study of medieval parchment manuscripts over the Middle Ages shows parchments themselves increasing in size when one reaches the twelfth and thirteenth centuries, remarkable evidence of the successful selective breeding of sheep!

But the prime value of sheep was their wool. With selective breeding, long-haired sheep were developed. Selected rams such as those of Lindsey in Lincolnshire were exported to other parts of England for breeding purposes. In 1196 the sheriff of Sulby in Northamptonshire spent an additional 33s. 4d. to "replace sheep with coarse wool by 100 curly-fleeced sheep."[13] The investment was profitable and the annual revenue of the lands rose from £9 2s. 4d. to £10.

Profits on investments could be higher still: Thierry d'Hireçon in 1320 purchased 160 sheep at 8s. 6d. per head. The following year he resold them—only 2 had died in the interval —at 10s. 6d. per head. He had invested £68; it brought him £83. But that was not all; he sold the wool for £52 so that in one year he made a total profit on the operation of approximately 100 percent.

Wool was the chief raw material of Europe in the Middle Ages, and the great capitalistic cloth industries of Flanders and Florence used tens of millions of fleeces each year. Indeed, their survival depended on the regular delivery of these vast amounts of wool. And when a country like England, the major supplier, threatened to cut the supplies, the cloth industries were faced with a dramatic unemployment problem. This happened in 1297, the year of a great wool famine in Flanders. The lands of Flanders were said to be practically empty "because the people could not have the wools of England."

The demand for English wool—the most sought-after wool in Europe—encouraged small farmers and larger landowners in England, Wales, and Scotland to raise sheep for export. In 1273 some 8 million sheep were sheared and their fleeces, weighing over 7 million pounds, were packed in 32,743 sacks and shipped overseas to the industrial centers.

The foreign buyers from Flanders and Italy were always anxious to sign long-term contracts with the Cistercian monasteries, whose whole agricultural economy—at least in England—was geared to raising sheep for export. Fountains Abbey in Yorkshire had up to 18,000 sheep, Rievaulx 14,000, and Jervaulx 12,000; they could export respectively 76, 60, and 50 sacks annually. By signing contracts with the Cistercians, the buyers had the advantage of being able to purchase a uniform product and, due to careful breeding, a particularly high-quality wool. They also had the benefit—due to the highly centralized Cistercian organization—of having to deal with only one individual, the cellarer, who was responsible for the material and financial administration of the monastery.

Again we see evidence of the Cistercians as an important force in the medieval economy. The order was founded by Robert, Abbot of Molesmes, who in 1098 retired with a few companions to Cîteaux, in one of the forests of Burgundy, in an attempt to follow the original rule of Saint Benedict (c. 480–c. 547). The movement really only expanded with the arrival in 1112 of Saint Bernard, but soon found itself in a controversial position—not for its ideals, which were much admired, but for the economic consequences of these ideals. In their sincere desire to flee the worldly and commercial life of the cities the Cistercians went to live in areas "remote from habitation of man." But by attempting to become independent of the outside world, they created an economic empire based on a highly centralized administration and on up-to-date technological expertise.

They were running the most modern factories in Europe. The report on the use of hydraulic power in a Cistercian monastery, quoted at length in chapter 1, is evidence of the high degree of technological efficiency reached by this religious order. In a later chapter we will show what an important part they played in spreading metal technology throughout Europe, and in agriculture we have just seen how the English monasteries geared their economy to an export market. All over Europe the Cistercians set up around their monasteries a whole series of granges, or model farms, which played a major role in opening up for agriculture hundreds of thousands of acres of woodlands and wastelands by forest clearing, draining, or irrigation. For example, for the monastery of Les Dunes, the lay brothers converted some 25,000 acres of the sandy and marshy deserts of Flanders coastline into fertile soil, while for the monastery of Chiaravalle, near Milan, they built an irrigation canal, completed in 1138, to bring water to the crops.

While in England many lay brothers reared sheep and exported wool, in certain regions in France and Germany they planted vineyards and exported wine. The motherhouse of Cîteaux, situated in the great wine-growing region of Burgundy, set an example by planting what became one of the world's most famous vintages, that of the Clos-Vougeot, and is where the wine connoisseurs, the Chevaliers du Tastevin, meet each year. In Germany, the Cistercians of Eberbach, who seem to have been the first to discover the advantages of cultivating vines on terraced hillsides, transported in their own ships approximately 53,000 gallons of wine yearly down the Rhine, mostly to Cologne, where it was sold wholesale to local merchants.

The great demand for wine which these figures reflect is linked to the rise in the standard of living of western Europe in the twelfth and thirteenth centuries. It led to a considerable extension of the vineyards into land formerly plowed for grain. A large proportion of the present famous French and German vineyards are medieval. The techniques of grape growing and winemaking that were developed between the eleventh and thirteenth centuries remained practically unchanged until the disastrous phylloxera epidemic that struck the French vineyards in the second half of the nineteenth century.

An Italian Franciscan friar, Salimbene, passing through Auxerre, the center of a wine-growing region, about 1245, expressed his astonishment because "These people sow nothing, reap nothing and gather nothing into their barns. They only need to send their wine to Paris on the nearby river which goes straight there. The sale of wine in this city brings them in a good profit which pays entirely for their food and clothing."[14]

That the Cistercians, one of the most austere religious orders in the whole history of mankind, should have cultivated vineyards may at first seem rather surprising. The primary reason for their decision was that wine was indispensable for Holy Communion (until the thirteenth century Holy Communion was received in both kinds, bread and wine, by all the faithful, priest and lay). The second reason was that Saint Benedict had in his rules allowed the monks to drink, if "sparingly," and if they could abstain they would be rewarded. Saint Benedict did not specify the reward.

Yet, considering the infirmity of the weak, we think that one pint of wine a day is sufficient for each: but let those to whom God gives the power of abstinence know that they shall have their proper reward. If, however, the situation of the place, the work, or the heat of the summer require more, let it be in the power of the Superior to grant it; taking care at all times that surfeit or drunkenness creep not in. And although we read that wine ought by no means to be the drink of Monks, yet since in our times Monks cannot be persuaded of this, let us at least agree not to drink to satiety, but sparingly: because "wine maketh even the wise to fall away." But where the necessity of the place alloweth not even the aforesaid measure, but much less, or none at all, let those who dwell there bless God, and not murmur. This above all we admonish, that there be no murmuring among them.[15]

As in Saint Benedict's time, the Cistercian lay brothers often could not be restrained from "murmuring." From the end of the twelfth century their murmurings certainly became very loud, for the lay brothers had been told that wine or beer was prohibited on the farms. This decision was put to the vote and then partially repealed several times, until in 1237 "the general chapter forbade the use of wine and intoxicating drinks only during the period from the first Sunday of Advent until Easter Sunday."[16] In the following year, even this attempt to set some limit to what had become an "ancient custom" failed. Over a hundred serious disturbances are recorded, many of them related to the problem of drink. It may be that drinking was even a direct cause of the decline of the Cistercian order. It certainly provoked the lay brother proletariat to frequent rebellion, involving bloodshed and sometimes deaths.

The celebrated Benedictine Abbess of Bingen, writing in the period 1148–79 about the lay brothers of Eberbach, where the growing of wine was the principal industry, seems to detect in this "class of men" a certain revolutionary frame of mind. The Cistercians, she writes, "draw a certain other class of men to themselves, whom they call conversi, of whom very many do not convert themselves to God in their habits because they love perversity rather than uprightness and perform their duties with the noise of temerity saying thus of their prelates: 'Who and what are they? And what were we?' 'Or what are we?' "[17]

In 1206 at Margam the lay brothers were responsible for a violent and ludicrous outbreak. They threw the cellarer from his horse, armed themselves and chased the Abbot some fifteen miles, barricaded themselves in their dormitory, and denied food to the monks. At the monastery of Garendon in Leicestershire, one night in the infirmary a lay brother, who had evidently made his plans with his confrères, seriously wounded Abbot Reginald. At Eberbach, about 1261, a series of disturbances culminated in the murder of the Abbot by a lay brother.

Our Italian friar, Salimbene, who, like his French and English friends, enjoyed drunken parties and must have appreciated "good wines," wrote:

> So the French delight in good wine, nor need we wonder for wine "cheereth God and men," as it is written in the ninth chapter of Judges. . . . It may be said literally that the French and English make their business to drink full goblets. Wherefore the French have blood-shot eyes; for from their ever-free potations of wine their eyes become red-rimmed, and bleared and bloodshot. And in the early morning, after they have slept off their wine, they go with such eyes to the priest who had celebrated Mass, and pray him to drop into their eyes the water wherein he has washed his eyes. But Brother Bartolommeo Giuscola of Parma was wont to say at Provins (as I have often heard with mine own ears) "ale, ke malonta ve don Dé; metti de l'aighe in le vins, non in lis ocli"; which is to say, "Go; God give you evil speed. Put the water in your wine

when ye drink it, and not in your eyes!" The English indeed delight in drink, and make it their business to drain full goblets; for an Englishman will take a cup of wine and drain it, saying, "Ge bi: a vu" which is to say "It behoveth you to drink as much as I shall drink" and therein he thinketh to say and do great courtesy, and he taketh it exceeding ill if any do otherwise than he himself hath taught in word and shown by example. And yet he doth against the scripture which saith, ". . . Wine also in abundance and of the best was presented, as was worthy of a king's magnificence. Neither was there any one to compel them to drink that were not willing." (Esther 1:7) Yet we must forgive the English if they are glad to drink good wine when they can, for they have but little wine in their own country. In the French it is less excusable, for they have greater plenty; unless, indeed, we plead that it is hard to leave our daily wont. Note that it is written thus in verse: "Normandy for sea-fish, England for corn, Scotland (or Ireland?) for milk, France for wine."[18]

The higher standard of living was also reflected in the food eaten, and some historians are quite prepared to attribute the dynamism of the Middle Ages in large measure to the relatively well-balanced diets of the time.

It was not merely the new quantity of food produced by improved agricultural methods, but the new type of food supply which goes far towards explaining, for northern Europe at least, the startling expansion of population, the growth and multiplication of cities, the rise in industrial production, the outreach of commerce, and the new exuberance of spirits which enlivened that age. In the full sense of the vernacular, the Middle Ages from the tenth century onwards were "full of beans"[19]

Beans are important. So are field peas and all other vegetables, as they contain protein. The Romans using the two-crop rotation evidently did not plant vegetables in any sufficient quantity. But with the introduction in the Middle Ages of the triennial rotation, vegetables were regularly planted with the spring crop and became generally available to the population, although they were never very abundant. The medieval peasant found more of the proteins that his body required in the cereals he grew, and also in milk, whey, cheese, and eggs.

In 1289 on the manor of Ferring belonging to Battle Abbey, the carters expected cheese in the morning and meat or fish to go with their rye bread and beer at noon. And in the years 1300–1305, the workmen building the spire of the Church of Bonlieu-en-Forez were offered cheese, meat, and a large quantity of wine, as well as rye bread and bean soup.

In a leper colony in Champagne in the twelfth century, each leper received a daily ration of three loaves of bread, a cake, and a measure of peas. And in 1325 it was recommended that as well as bread, oil, salt, and onions, the lepers be served meat three days a week and eggs or herring on the other days.

Two remarkable detailed accounts of expenditure on food have been analyzed by the historian L. Stouff. The first document was the outcome of an inquiry in 1338 into the cost of food in four commanderies belonging to the Order of the Hospitalers in Provence. Table 2 shows the annual expenses for the different categories of religious and lay workers of the commanderies of Arles, Manosque, Roussillon, and Puimoisson.

Figure 2 shows the budget paid for three of the social categories—monks, lay brothers, and cowherds—for bread, wine, and *companagium*. This last term refers to all types of food that accompanied bread: fish, meat, eggs, vegetables. The higher the social category, the lower the percentage of bread and the higher the percentage of *companagium*. The

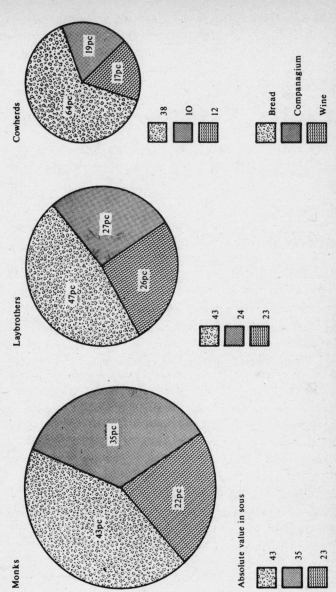

Monks

43pc

35pc

22pc

Absolute value in sous

43

35

23

Laybrothers

47pc

27pc

26pc

43

24

23

Cowherds

64pc

19pc

17pc

38

1O

12

Bread

Companagium

Wine

FIGURE 2. Food Budget for Different Social Categories of the Four Commanderies of the Hospitalers in Provence, 1338[20]

TABLE 2. *Annual Food Expenses for Each Social Category in the Four Commanderies of the Hospitalers*[21]

	Arles	Manosque	Roussillon	Puimoisson
Monks	119s.	104s. 4d.	87s. 8d.	95s.
Clerics	109s.			
Lay brothers	104s.	95s.	77s. 8d.	85s.
Judges, notaries		80s. 8d.		
Servants	84s.	80s. 8d.	64s. 8d	
Cowherds	84s.	56s.	53s. 8d	45s. 6d.

relative importance of wine in all three categories is also remarkable. In Roussillon, 26 percent of the expenditure for cowherds is for wine.

The second group of documents concerns the annual food budgets for the pupils (twelve to eighteen years old) of the Studium Papale at Trets for the scholastic year 1364–65. Figure 3 shows the relative expenses for bread, meat, fish, and eggs, vegetables, fruit, spices, fat and cheese, and wine. The exceptionally high percentage of wine—41 percent—may conceal a bad grape harvest which inflated the price of

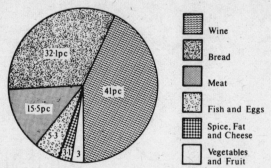

FIGURE 3. *The Diet of Students at the Studium Papale at Trets*[22]

TABLE 3. *Daily Rations for the Studium Papale of Trets,*
1364–65[23]

Nutrient	Grams
Protein	90
Fats	65
Carbohydrates	475
Iron	.01
Calcium	.4
Phosphorus	2.3
Vitamin A	1700 (I.U.)
Vitamin B	.01
Vitamin C	0

Food	Calories	Percent of Diet
Bread	2,080	80
Wine	28	1
Meat	162	7
Cheese	20	1
Vegetables	310	11
	2,600 total	

wine. The percentage spent on vegetables and fruit—3 percent—is low.

The boys have a daily allowance of 0.62 liters of wine.
Soup is served every day: cabbage soup on 125 days in the
year, spinach soup on 41 days, onion soup on 18, chick-pea
soup on 17, lentil soup on 12, and cheese soup on 1, as well as
herb soup, bouillon, etc. Meat is served on 217 days of the
year, with mutton on 160 days, mutton and beef 5 days, mutton
and goat 1 day, pork 1 day, but salt pork 55 days.

The accounts are so detailed as to allow an analysis to
be made of the proteins, calories, vitamins, and mineral elements contained in the boys' food rations (see Table 3).
Stouff comments on these figures:

> The calorific value seems right for boys of fifteen or so.
> The quantity of protein seems low, but it needs to be ad-

justed to include eggs, which were eaten 109 days a year. The quantity of fats is slightly low and would have led to a lack of vitamin D. The carbohydrates are a little high. . . . There is a deficiency of vitamin A, due to the absence of milk products . . . there is a lack of vitamin C, since there were no fresh vegetables, no oranges and little fruit. There is plenty of iron, since spinach soup was served on 41 days, but the balance of calcium to phosphorus, which should be 100 : 100 is 15 : 100. . . . Apart from the deficiencies of vitamins A and C and the imbalance of calcium and phosphorus, the boarders at the Studium could be considered well nourished, with sensible and balanced rations. If they had had a bowl of milk, a pat of butter, and an orange in their daily diet it would have been sufficient and would have satisfied the dietitian of the twentieth century.[24]

The revolutionary development in agriculture and industry, combined with a milder and drier climate and a healthier diet, contributed to the medieval population growth. Other factors led to a higher birthrate and a lower death rate. The birthrate must have increased between the eighth and eleventh centuries as the remaining slave population became serfs and founded families, while the death rate must have fallen with the disappearance of the plague that hit Europe in the seventh century. (The plagues did not come back on a continental scale until the fourteenth century, when the rhythm of their appearance and disappearance was strangely similar to that in the seventh century.) The death rate from invasion and warfare must also have decreased substantially. The Viking invasions were the last ever to be suffered by western Europe. From the eleventh century on it was western Europe that launched invasions. Warfare inside Europe also decreased and was waged only in certain brief periods and in particular regions. Paris, the greatest city in Europe, had more than 200,000 inhabitants who were to live in peace for many centuries.

There was some awareness of the expansion in population, and certain men took the view that the overflow of people could usefully be diverted overseas to serve an ideological goal. Pope Urban II, who preached the First Crusade at Clermont in 1095, proclaimed: "Let none of your possessions detain you, nor solicitude for your family affairs, since the lands which you inhabit, shut in on all sides from the sea and surrounded by mountain peaks, are too narrow for your large population. . . ."[25]

The population of Europe rose from a low 27 million around the year 700 to over 70 million by 1300. Table 4 gives estimates for the increases in the European population figure from 1000 to 1300, with the greatest increase occurring around the year 1200.

The growth of population in England and France was faster than in most other European countries. The relative wealth of statistical data on the English population shows that it nearly trebled between 1068 and 1348, reaching a total between 5 and 6 million (including Scotland, Wales, and Ireland). But the most remarkable figures are those for France, which show that the French population grew to more than

TABLE 4. *European Population Growth, 1000–1300*

Year A.D.	Millions of People	Percent Increase
1000	42	—
1050	46	9.5
1100	48	4.3
1150	50	4.2
1200	61	22.0
1250	69	13.1
1300	73	5.8

20 million (in 1940 the population of France was just double that of medieval France). This suggests why France played such an important role in the medieval period, in the agricultural and industrial revolutions. Her population was nearly one-third that of the whole of Europe.

3

Mining the Mineral
Wealth of Europe

Stone quarrying was by far the most important mining industry in medieval Europe, more important possibly than all the
others combined. The mining of stone in the Middle Ages can
only be compared to the mining of coal in the nineteenth century and the drilling for oil in the twentieth century.

France was richer in building stone than was any other
country in Europe, and during her age of expansion from the
eleventh to the thirteenth centuries more stone was quarried
in France than had been mined throughout the whole history
of ancient Egypt (where the Great Pyramid alone was built
to a volume of 40,500,000 cubic feet).

Today, almost every trace of this upheaval of the land-
scape has disappeared. Of the tens of thousands of open-air
quarries in medieval times, practically all have vanished into
the countryside, including the ones at Berchères-les-Pierres

in the plain of La Beauce, which provided the stone for Chartres Cathedral. Such underground stoneworkings tunneling into the hillsides had their entrances carefully blocked so that mushrooms (which flourished in disused quarries) could be grown, or they were simply overtaken by the spread of the towns. The famous quarries of Les Baux in Provence are a rare exception.*

A medieval underground quarry comprised an intricate web of stone galleries. Their layouts—particularly those found under the streets of Paris—have been the subject of intense study, though less for archaeological or historical purposes than for reasons of safety. Paris is remarkable for being a "hanging town" with 300 kilometers of subterranean galleries (as compared to the 189 kilometers of the Paris *Métro*). The district with the most mines is the Left Bank under the Montagne Sainte-Geneviève, which includes the Jardin du Luxembourg, the Jardin-des-Plantes, and the Butte-aux-Cailles. The Cathedral of Notre-Dame was built mainly from stone quarried from the *faubourgs* Saint-Michel, Saint-Jacques, and Saint-Marcel.

The quarrymen tunneled long parallel and transverse galleries, sometimes on three levels. Vast workshops were cut out of the rock to provide space for roughhewing and to make way for carts pulled by oxen or horses. In order to keep the galleries from collapsing, either natural stone pillars were

* Another is at Saint-Leu d'Esserent, on the river Oise north of Paris, where miners started quarrying in the hillside back in the twelfth century. Through the centuries, the mine went deeper into the hill, until in the twentieth century stone was being mined over a mile from the entrance. The quarrying at Saint-Leu continued without interruption for eight hundred years except during World War II, when the Germans took over the abandoned galleries to build a factory for their secret V-1 rockets. The Allied air force attacked this medieval site with delayed-fuse bombs which pierced the hill and exploded inside the quarry, destroying the rockets, the assembly line, and the Germans working there.

The gallery of a quarry under the streets of Paris. Courtesy Bernard Jourdes.

left *in situ* or other supporting pillars were constructed from rock rubble. In spite of these precautions, quarrymen, like other miners of the time, lived dangerously, and were susceptible to silicosis and illnesses resulting from the damp. Regarded as little more than common laborers, they were not as well looked after or paid as silver or lead miners.

It was, of course, a great economy to have quarries close at hand. According to rough calculations, the cost of carriage by land for a distance of 12 miles was about equivalent to the cost of the stone. The builders had to start by prospecting for stone in the neighboring countryside. They were prepared to try any scheme that would reduce costs—for example, having the stone hand-hewn in the quarries, or having ingenious machines built to load and unload stone. If stone had to be moved any distance, it was always preferable to transport it by water. This was the cheapest method of moving heavy goods in the Middle Ages (as it still is today, even in advanced industrial countries), and canals were built whenever possible for the transport of so heavy and valuable a commodity.

Traditionally, stone has been one of the most significant French exports, with the regional record for achievement going to Caen. Starting in 1066, whole flotillas loaded with Caen stone set sail to English ports. William the Conqueror was aware of its exceptional quality when he chose it to build Battle Abbey. (As recently as 1945, France exported the stone of Caen to England to help in the reconstruction of London.)

The volume of Caen stone imported into England in the twelfth and thirteenth centuries is well documented in the meticulous accounts of the secular and clerical administrators of the day. William of Sens, the French architect, was called upon in 1174 to rebuild the burned-out choir of Canterbury Cathedral: "[He] addressed himself to the procuring of stone from beyond sea"[1]—that is, to acquire Caen stone. In another instance, for the building of Winchester Castle, on September 3, 1272, we read: "And for 1,450 Caen stones . . . £3 7s. 6d."[2] For Westminster Abbey, £10 4s. 8d. was spent in March 1253, for two shiploads of stone from Caen. The builders of the Tower of London similarly spent £332 2s. for seventy-five shiploads. Caen stone bought in 1287 for Norwich Cathedral (some 300 miles away from Normandy) for £1 6s. 8d. cost £4 8s. 8d. landed at the cathedral yard, about 3⅓ times its original purchase price. The freight by ship to Yarmouth was £2 10s. 8d., where it was unloaded onto six barges at a cost of 2s. 2d. The freight up the rivers Yare and Wensum cost another 7s. 2d., and there was a final cost of 2s. for unloading the stone from the barges to the cathedral yard.

The accounts for expenditure on the fabric of Autun Cathedral for 1294–95 include not only wages and the price of transport but the cost of yet another vital raw material needed to build with stone: iron. More than 10 percent of the total cost is absorbed by the expenditure on forges in the quarries and on the building sites.

> To the forge at the quarry, 62 sous
> including our iron   £3 2s.
> To the forge at Autun, for the year   £42 10s. 6d.[3]

The medieval iron industry was fundamental to Europe's prosperity, to bringing so many of its people a new high standard of living. Contemporary writers were fully conscious of the importance of iron, not only for war but for agriculture and building as well. The Franciscan monk Bartholomew wrote in 1260:

> Use of iron is more needful to men in many things than use of gold. Though covetous men have more gold than iron, without iron the commonalty be not sure against enemies, without dread of iron the common right is not governed; with iron innocent men are defended; and foolhardiness of wicked men is chastened with dread of iron. And well nigh no handiwork is wrought without iron, neither tilling craft used nor building builded without iron.[4]

It has been said that the Age of Iron really only began with the Middle Ages. Roman times still depended heavily on bronze, while in the Middle Ages bronze was of only minor importance. Every medieval village had its iron smithy, for now every ox or horse—not only the plow animals of the peasants, but also the horses of the local knight and his entourage—had to be shod with iron shoes. Horseshoes sometimes had to be mass-produced; as we have seen, Richard I ordered fifty thousand from the sixty or so forges set up in the Forest of Dean (which medievalists have called the Birmingham of the Middle Ages).

Armor in the Middle Ages also required more iron. The new methods of shock combat introduced by the Franks in the eighth century made heavy armor important, as did the steel-armed crossbow, which began to be used by infantrymen in the latter part of the tenth century. (The crossbow had such a force of penetration and was so deadly that its use came under discussion in the twelfth century at one of history's first disarmament conferences. In 1139 the Lateran Council voted to prohibit it, but like many later civilian disarmament recommendations this was ignored by the military.)

The increased use of iron in the Middle Ages for agricultural purposes is more difficult to assess. The Celts and the Romans had used iron or pieces of iron to reinforce agricultural implements in earlier periods. But as iron was a rare and costly metal, ten times more expensive in the Middle Ages than now, only the sharp working edge of a spade or other implement would be protected by a piece of forged iron. Still, it is certain that if the plowshare of the medieval heavy plow had not been of metal, or at least partly covered with metal, it would never have been so effective in tilling new arable land in the heavy soil and forests of northern and western Europe.

It is in the realm of building that we have a wealth of evidence—from archaeological and other documents—showing how much more the Middle Ages used iron. Medieval builders were so enthusiastic about this metal that they sometimes employed it rather rashly. In the hope of reinforcing church walls, some master masons embedded iron chains in their stonework. Such was the case at Sainte-Chapelle in Paris, where the chains eventually caused cracks in the masonry walls.

The architect of the remarkable octagonal chapter house of Westminster Abbey, erected between 1245 and 1255, built an iron, umbrellalike structure to prevent the walls of the chapel from falling outward. He embedded iron ties in the walls, as had the architect of Sainte-Chapelle, but in this case he used a series of iron bars to link the iron ties to hooks embedded in the slender central stone column of the chapel. It was remarkably ingenious, but not entirely successful; in the fourteenth century the bars had to be taken down and flying buttresses installed to ensure the continued stability of the chapel walls. Nevertheless, iron bars are still to be seen a few yards away in the Abbey itself, still keeping the walls parallel.

Building accounts are full of exact numbers of iron tools and implements of various types and the prices paid for them. There are clamps, there are rods and locks, but what is most remarkable is the quantity of nails and the enormous number of types used.

In 1390 the stores of Calais recorded 494,000 nails. And in stock at York Castle in 1327 were the following different types of nails[5]:

   220 braggenayl at 15d. the hundred, "by the great hundred"

   100 knopnayl at 6d. the hundred

3,260 doublenail at 4d. the hundred

1,200 greater spyking at 4d. the hundred

5,200 spyking at 3d. the hundred

3,250 thaknail at 3d. the hundred

1,800 lednail at 2d. the hundred

   300 grapnayl at 2d. the hundred

7,760 stotnayl at 2d. the hundred

    1,100 smaller stotnayl at 1½d. the hundred
      300 tyngilnail at 1d. the hundred
   18,600 brodd' at 1d. the hundred

The English clerics who kept building accounts usually included the source of the iron purchased as well as the price per hundredweight. Domestic iron generally came either from the Forest of Dean or from the Weald in Sussex. Most of the imported iron came from Spain, but there was some from Sweden and from Pont de Audemer in Normandy. Imported iron was of much higher quality and therefore considerably more expensive.

The accounts also mention the importation of steel, required to reinforce the workmen's iron tools. At Ely in 1323 we read of "6 sheaves of steel for putting on the iron tools of the masons."[6] Later in the century, at Portchester, there is a reference to the purchase of 94 pounds of Spanish steel, at 1½d. a pound, "for the hardening of the axes and other tools of the masons."[7]

A large share of the credit for the high standard of metallurgy reached in the Middle Ages must go to the engineer who first adapted waterpower to the needs of the iron industry. Waterpower revolutionized the manufacture of metal products as it had revolutionized fulling and other medieval industries. Waterpowered trip-hammers progressively took over the smiths' hard manual work of forging the blooms, and did it far more efficiently since their strokes were much more uniform and the weight of the hammer could be increased considerably. Mechanical hammers for the first stage of the work might weigh from 500 to 1600 kilograms, and "for the later stages there were hammers of 300 kg delivering 60 to 120 strokes a minute, and lighter ones of 70–80 kg delivering 200 strokes a minute."[8] Waterpowered stamping mills were also built to break up the iron ore, but the most significant hydraulic invention was waterpowered bellows, which could produce a draft powerful enough to raise the temperature of the furnaces to some 1500 degrees C, hot enough to liquefy iron ore. For the first time, furnaces were producing molten iron. The casting process had long been used for the more tractable bronze, so with this new discovery it became natural to make iron in the same way. The first known furnace with water-driven bellows is recorded as having been built in 1323, and what is believed to have been the first real blast furnace followed in 1380.

In the Middle Ages it was generally through the movement of workmen from one country to another that technical innovations in metallurgy spread to other ironworking centers. The Cistercians, in their rapid expansion throughout Europe, must also have played a role in the diffusion of new techniques, for the high level of their agricultural technology was matched by their industrial technology. Every monastery had a model factory, often as large as the church and only several feet away, and waterpower drove the machinery of the various industries located on its floor. Some of these factories have survived at Fontenay, Royaumont, and elsewhere. It has been suggested that the forge at Fontenay operated with a waterpowered trip-hammer as early as the twelfth century. This seems plausible, since the Cistercians were always on the lookout for new techniques to increase the efficiency of their monasteries. The Cistercians needed iron for their own use, although in time, as was the case with wool, they began to sell their surplus production. They eagerly accepted any iron-ore deposits offered to them, together with the forges usually close by the deposits. Such acts of donation were nearly always accompanied by a document authorizing the Cistercians to make use of the woods for the working of the furnaces. Without this permission the iron-ore deposits would have been practically useless. The Abbey of Clairvaux, situated in the center of one of the great iron-ore areas of France, gradually took over a large number of the iron-ore mines of the neighboring regions. It went on acquiring iron-ore deposits and forges—either by donations or purchases—until the eighteenth century. From 1250 to the seventeenth century the Cistercians were the leading iron producers of the Champagne region, and by the end of the eighteenth century they owned half of the industrial iron and steel complex of the "Plateau de Langres." But before 1330 they already owned between eight and thirteen iron-producing factories. The map on p. 69 shows some of the iron-ore fields and forges in their possession.

The Clairvaux Cistercians were careful to recover the slag from their numerous furnaces, for they knew it contained a high percentage of phosphates useful for fertilizing their agricultural land.

While there are hundreds of documents referring to the Cistercians working iron-ore deposits all over Europe, there are only a few that refer to them working lead, copper, or zinc ore, and even fewer relating to their working the precious metals of gold and silver. Nevertheless, silver mining made an important contribution to the progress of mining techniques in central Europe from the tenth century onward, and indeed helped to lay the foundation of the metallurgical power of Europe. A leading role in the expansion of these techniques was played by German miners, not only in central Europe but over the rest of the continent as well.

The emphasis on silver mining started with the Carolingians. Having found no substantial gold mines, they decided to develop a monetary system based on the more freely available silver. Later, gold was hoarded by private individuals, but it was not until the great European prosperity of the thirteenth century that gold was coined again—starting in 1253 in Genoa, and in the same year the Florentine gold florin was minted.

In Roman times there were no silver mines, nor indeed any mines of importance, north of the Danube. Tacitus wrote

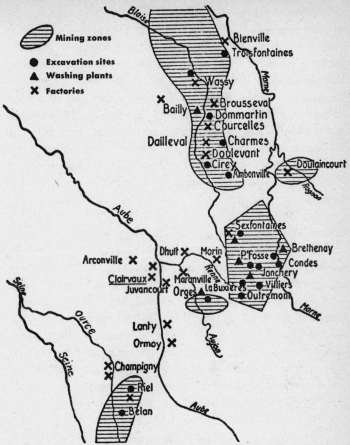

Cistercian iron and steel mines on the Plateau de Langres in Champagne.
Courtesy *Revue d'Historie de la Sidérurgie.*

in A.D. 98: "The gods have denied them [the Germans] gold
and silver, whether in mercy or in wrath I find it hard to say:
not that I would assert that Germany has no veins bearing
gold or silver: for who has explored there?"[9] When the Germans did start prospecting for silver in 968, they found silver-
bearing lead ore on the hill of Rammelsberg above the town

of Goslar in the Harz Mountains—and rich copper ore, too. By the eleventh century mining production there was fully under way. In 1136, when traders carrying rock salt from Halle to Bohemia came across what they thought to be silver-bearing ore washed down the mountains by a spring flood in Saxony, in the region of Freiberg, they picked up ore samples and took them to Goslar to be analyzed. The samples turned out to have a finer grade of silver than the silver ore of Goslar, a discovery that prompted an immediate "silver rush." "As news of this discovery spread, adventurers in considerable numbers, with picks and shovels, hurried to Freiberg. They came in a spirit of adventure not altogether unlike that of the Americans who migrated to California in the gold rush of the mid-nineteenth century."[10] By 1170, mining and smelting at Freiberg were in full swing in a metalworking center of some thirty-thousand inhabitants.

Study of the mining vocabulary used in various countries in Europe shows that to a substantial degree it is of German origin, understandable in that German miners played the leading role in the opening up of new mines and the modernizing of existing ones. In the German movement into eastern and southeastern Europe, miners emigrated with other emigrants into regions held by the Slavs and the Magyars. Colonizing and mining went hand in hand.

> The migration of Germans across the Elbe in the twelfth century was like the rush of Americans after the war of 1812 from the Atlantic States into the Western Reserve and the Ohio Valley. The New East in the Slavic country beyond the Elbe beckoned to the Saxon adventurer as the Indian country beyond the Missouri called to the American pioneer.[11]

They moved into Iglau and then into the Hungarian mines of Zips, Schemnitz, and Kremnitz. Their fame was

Opposite: A scene from the gold and silver mines near Kutna Hora in Moravia, Czechoslovakia. Courtesy Austrian National Library, Vienna.

such that they were called for by rulers from all over Europe (even in Turkey the vocabulary of mining terms today is German). Gold and silver took precedence, but there was interest also in lead, copper, tin, and zinc, and to a much lesser degree in iron, always easily found on the surface in small deposits here and there. German miners in the twelfth century were called in by the rulers of Transylvania, and in the thirteenth century by the rulers of Serbia.

They were not always successful. In 1303 four German miners were called upon by the English Crown to search for minerals in the rich mining area of Flint in Wales. The salaries offered these experts were more than royal. From February 23 to March 2, they were each paid 7s. 6d. a day, while two English miners engaged to help them were paid only 2d. and 3d. They found copper ore which gave promise of a good yield and had it smelted in charcoal furnaces installed for the purpose. But the trial was a bitter disappointment, for the mineral turned out to be worthless copper pyrites.

The great mining interest shown by the rulers of Europe was, of course, due to the substantial financial revenues that mines brought in. Very often such interest raised the question of the ownership of the underground wealth. Was it owned by the territorial or overlord landowner, or by the lord of the soil? In the later Roman empire most of the mines had belonged to the emperor, and on those that were still privately owned a 10 percent tax was levied. The medieval overlords, perhaps with knowledge of this Imperial Roman custom, tried to enforce such regalian rights for their own benefit. The first to do so officially was the Emperor Frederick Barbarossa. In 1157, he distributed the Rammelsberg mines to three monasteries and to the town of Goslar. But the principle of regalian rights was accepted only in some parts of Europe. While in England the Crown was generally able to enforce its control, in France up until the fifteenth century the king did not try to claim regalian taxes from his feudal vassals.

Possibly some of these vassals would have been too powerful for him to risk such claims, but, in fact, no rich gold or silver mines were to be found on French territory. France's wealth lay in her agriculture and in her industry, while the wealth of central Europe lay in her metallurgy. Europe west of the Rhine was relatively poorly endowed with minerals.

In England, however, substantial deposits of silver, lead, and tin did offer some competition to central Europe. The Devon mines produced silver worth £4,046 and about £360 worth of lead in the years 1292–97. After drainage work, the amount of silver produced in 1298 was worth £1,450—nearly double the average production (£800) of the previous years. This increased silver production encouraged the Frescobaldi, Florentine financiers and merchants, to lease the Devon mines from the Crown in the following year. A contract containing eleven clauses was signed, whereby the Frescobaldi were to take over all the ore and pay for each load a maximum of 5s., less if the miners could so agree. And the lessees would pay all costs, besides rendering to the king 20s. per load. The costs were to include the same wages for laborers as were paid before the signing of the contract, or less if the Frescobaldi could get the laborers to agree. The Crown, on the other hand, would reimburse the lessees for the cost of any new adit or machinery they might build. The contract reminds the Frescobaldi that the miners were free workers—that is, free of all tallages and taxes—and that they could not be tried by a local court. Evidently the miners did not accept a reduction in the price for their ore, nor the laborers reductions in their previous salary, because after having purchased 3,600 loads of ore, the Frescobaldi found that they were losing heavily. They did not renew the contract the following year, and the Crown again took over the running of the mines. In 1305 the silver production rose to £1,773, passing the 1298 figure, but by the middle of the century the output had fallen considerably.

Miners were continually prospecting for new ore. While not all new strikes were successful—as we have seen in the 1303 example when the German mining experts found only copper pyrites—there were other times when they turned out to be very profitable indeed. Such was the case when in the 1330s a vein of lead ore was discovered in Somerset on the Mendip Hills, near Priddy. An enthusiastic report was made and we now know that the author's enthusiasm was justified. He is writing to the Bishop of Bath and Wells:

Know, my lord, that your workmen have found a splendid mine of lead on the Mendips to the East of Priddy, and one that can be opened with no trouble, being only five or six feet below the ground. And since these workmen are so often thieves, craftily separating the silver from the lead, stealthily taking it away, and when they have collected a quantity fleeing like thieves and deserting their work, as has frequently happened in times past, therefore your bailiffs are causing the ore to be carried to your court at Wookey where there is a furnace built at which the workmen smelt the ore under supervision of certain persons appointed by your steward. And as the steward, bailiffs, and workmen consider that there is a great deal of silver in the lead, on account of its whiteness and sonority, they beg that you will send them as soon as possible a good and faithful workman upon whom they can rely. I have seen the first piece of lead smelted there, of great size and weight, which when it is struck rings almost like silver, wherefore I agree with the others that if it is faithfully worked the business should prove of immense value to yourself and to the neighbourhood, and if a reliable workman is obtained I think that it would be expedient to smelt the ore where it is dug, on account of the labour of carrying so heavy material such a distance. The ore is in grains like sand.[12]

4

Environment and Pollution

The industrialization of the Middle Ages played havoc with the environment of western Europe. Millions of acres of forests were destroyed to increase the area of arable and grazing land and to satisfy the ever greater demand for timber, the main raw material of the time. Not only was timber used as fuel for the hearths of private homes and for ovens, it was also in one way or another essential to practically every medieval industry. In the building industry wood was used to build timber-framed houses, water mills and windmills, bridges, and military installations such as fortresses and palisades. In the wine industry wood was used for making casks and vats. Ships were made of wood, as was all medieval machinery such as weavers' looms. Tanners needed the bark of the trees and so did the rope makers. The glass industry demolished the woods for fuel for its furnaces, and the iron industry needed charcoal for its forges. By 1300, forests in France covered only about 32 million acres—2 million acres less than they do today.

There is a remarkable document from 1140 which provides evidence of this onslaught on the medieval forests. Suger, France's first great nationalist prime minister (who said of the English "that they were destined by moral and national law to be subject to the French and not contrariwise"[1]), wrote in one of his books of his difficulty in finding the 35-foot beams that he desperately needed as tie beams for the roof of the central nave of the Abbey of Saint-Denis, which he was having rebuilt. He had been told by all his master carpenters that it was absolutely impossible to find such large beams any longer in the area around Paris and that he would have to go far afield for that sort of timber. But Suger was not a man to take no for an answer:

> On a certain night, when I had returned from celebrating Matins, I began to think in bed that I myself should go through all the forests of these parts. . . . Quickly disposing of other duties and hurrying up in the early morning, we hastened with our carpenters, and with the measurements of the beams, to the forest called Iveline. When we traversed our possession in the Valley of Chevreuse we summoned . . . the keepers of our own forests as well as men who knew about the other woods, and questioned them under oath whether we would find there, no matter with how much trouble, any timbers of that measure. At this they smiled, or rather would have laughed at us if they had dared; they wondered whether we were quite ignorant of the fact that nothing of the kind could be found in the entire region, especially since Milon, the Castellan of Chevreuse . . . had left nothing unimpaired or untouched that could be used for palisades and bulwarks while he was long subjected to wars both by our Lord the King and Amaury de Montfort. We how-

ever—scorning whatever they might say—began, with the courage of our faith as it were, to search through the woods; and towards the first hour we found one timber adequate to the measure. Why say more? By the ninth hour or sooner, we had, through the thickets, the depths of the forest and the dense, thorny tangles, marked down twelve timbers (for so many were necessary) to the astonishment of all. . . .[2]

The Forest of Yvelines toward which he had "hastened" had once covered an immense area to the southwest of Paris. It now covers only 15,500 hectares (38,750 acres).

Suger must have ridden well over 50 kilometers that morning to reach his final destination. He had left the area of Saint-Denis, a few kilometers to the north of Paris, and had ridden to the southwest of Paris by the upstream sections of the River Yvette, which flows in the Vallée de Chevreuse, now a popular excursion spot. Finally he had reached the Forest of Yvelines probably somewhere south of the source of the Yvette.

The past is still very much present in today's forest. Stags are hunted twice a week, and the names of villages such as Les Essarts-le-Roi are constant reminders of the clearing of the medieval forests (*essarts* were areas of forest land cleared and made into pasturage or arable land). Richard Fitz Nigel, treasurer to the King of England, writing in the 1170s (a period when there seems to have been extensive clearing), shows clearly the concern felt at the time for forests cleared without the ground being prepared properly for agriculture. "If," he says, "woods are so severely cut that a man standing on the half-buried stump of an oak or other tree can see five other trees cut down about him, that is regarded as waste. Such an offense," he goes on to say, "even in a man's own woods, is regarded as so serious that even these men who are free of taxation because they sit at the king's exchequer must pay a money penalty all the heavier for their position."[3]

Whatever Fitz Nigel's concerns, the fact remains that medieval man brought about the destruction of Europe's natural environment. He wasted its natural resources, and very soon felt the consequences of his destructive activities, the first of which was the considerable rise in the price of timber as a result of its increasing scarcity. At Douai, in northern France, in the thirteenth century wood had already become so scarce and expensive that families from the lower income groups could not afford to buy a wooden coffin for their dead. They had to rent one, and when the ceremony at the cemetery was over, the undertaker would open the coffin, throw the corpse into the earth, and bring back the coffin to use again.

Owing to the difficulty of finding suitable large timber, men looked for new technical solutions to building and construction problems. For example, in the famous sketchbook of Villard de Honnecourt, the thirteenth-century architect and engineer, who was working in the north of France not very far from Douai, there is a design for a bridge. The author of the drawing states proudly that it is built with short timber only twenty feet long: "How to make a bridge over water with twenty-foot timber."[4] On another page is a drawing of a floor, under which is written: "How to work on a house or tower even if the timbers are too short."[5] The lack of long beams had a considerable influence on the techniques of timber-framed building, and carpenters created a revolutionary timber-framed house with many shorter timbers.

A few figures from building accounts serve to show how quickly medieval man could destroy his environment. An average house built of wood needed some twelve oaks. In the middle of the fourteenth century, for the building operation at Windsor Castle, a whole wood was bought and all the trees felled—3,004 oaks. This was still not sufficient, for some ten years later 820 oaks were cut in Combe Park and 120 in Pamber Forest, bringing the total for this one castle up to 3,944 oaks. The *Times* of London reported on August 24, 1971, that only 300 to 400 oaks were still standing in Robin Hood's famous Sherwood Forest. The article was headed: "Hearts of Oak grow Faint in Sherwood as Age, Thirst and Pollution take Toll." But the greatest toll was taken in the Middle Ages.

The building of thousands of furnaces in hundreds of medieval forests to satisfy the extensive demand for iron was a major cause of deforestation. Iron ore, unlike gold ore, is practically never found in its natural state except in meteorites, and it requires a special fuel to smelt and reduce it. From the very beginning, the fuel used was charcoal, the black porous residue of burned wood. This absolute reliance on charcoal made it essential for iron smelters up to the late eighteenth century to build their furnaces in the forests, where wood for the making of charcoal was directly at hand.

The extent of the damage caused by iron smelters to forests can be appreciated when one realizes that to obtain 50 kilograms of iron it was necessary at that time to reduce approximately 200 kilograms of iron ore with as much as 25 steres (25 cubic meters) of wood. It has been estimated that in forty days, one furnace could level the forest for a radius of 1 kilometer.

It is not surprising to hear that certain authorities took measures to halt or at least slow down the massacre of the forests. It was in their financial interest. In the forest of Dean by the opening decades of the thirteenth century, the Crown was restricting the right of working solely to the royal forges in the Forest, and in 1282 a report was made by the regarders of the Forest on the wastage of timber caused by the sixty or so forges located there. In the Dauphiné in 1315 the representatives of the Dauphin were greatly alarmed at the widespread destruction of the woods of that region. They formally accused the iron-producing factories of being directly responsible for this disaster and recommended that forcible measures should be taken to arrest the situation.

There were objections in 1255 when two limekilns in the Forest of Wellington consumed five hundred oaks in one year, and on the territory of Colmars in the Basses-Alpes water-powered saws were forbidden at the end of the thirteenth century. In 1205 exploitation of the woods belonging to the monks of Chelles in France was regulated, and in the same year the commune of Montaguloto in Italy required every citizen to plant ten trees annually.

In England, the royal forests, which covered quite an extensive area of the kingdom, were protected by the much-hated forest law (laid down to protect the hunting grounds of the Norman conquerors rather than for any ecological reasons). Nevertheless, encroachments were made regularly on the woodlands in the royal forests, and kings in financial difficulties had to accept vast disforestations. In 1190, the first year of Richard I's reign, the knights of Surrey offered him 200 marks that "they might be quit of all things that belong to the forest from the water of Wey to Kent and from the street of Guildford southwards as far as Surrey stretches."[6] In 1204 the men of Essex offered King John 500 marks and 5 palfreys for the disforestation of "the forest of Essex which is beyond the causeway between Colchester and Bishops Stortford." In the same year the men of Cornwall were prepared to pay as much as 2,200 marks for the disforestation of the whole of Cornwall, while the men of Devon offered 5,000 marks for the disforestation of the whole of Devon.

The decreasing availability of timber and the progressive rise in the price of wood led England to import timber from Scandinavia. The first fleet of ships loaded with Norwegian fir trees sailed into Grimsby harbor, on the east coast of England, in 1230. And in 1274, the master carpenter of Norwich Cathedral went to Hamburg to buy timber and boards. During this same period a substitute fuel for wood was found—coal.

Some of the great European coalfields of the nineteenth and twentieth centuries were first mined in the thirteenth century: in Belgium those of Liège, Mons, and Charleroi, and in France those of the Lyonnais, Anjou, and Forez. A charter of the Priory of Saint-Sauveur-en-Rue in the Forez mentions coal as early as the year 1095.

In England the vast coalfields that were to play such a decisive role in the Industrial Revolution of the eighteenth and nineteenth centuries appear in innumerable documents of the thirteenth and fourteenth centuries: those of Newcastle-upon-Tyne, and also those in the Midlands, in Derbyshire, and Nottinghamshire, as well as the Shropshire coalfields which later enabled Abraham Darby in 1709 to launch the second Industrial Revolution by using coke to reduce iron ore. The Scottish and Welsh coalfields were also already fully active.

Coal in France was called *terre houille* or *charbon de roche*, and in England the terms "pit coal" and "sea coal" were common, the latter from the fact that coal was originally worked and picked up on the beaches of maritime counties such as Durham or Northumberland.

As early as 1226, we find in London a Sea Coal Lane, also known as Lime Burners Lane. The lime-burning industry was one of the first to convert to the use of coal, along with the iron industry. Brewers, dyers, and others followed. In 1243 the first recorded victim of coal mining, Ralph, son of Roger Ulger, drowned in an open pit. At first coal was mined in shallow pits, usually 6 to 15 meters (20 to 50 feet) deep, but sometimes, as in the French coal mines of Boussagues in the Languedoc, there were already underground galleries. In Newcastle there were such extensive diggings around the city that it was dangerous to approach it by night, lest one fall and break one's neck in the open trenches. Here and in many other places, the medieval environment was already an industrial environment.

So great was the desire for money that in 1278 one man

even dug a trench across a highway—for which he was fined—and a number of people were arrested for stealing a barge loaded with coal. Coal mining was a profitable industry, and cities such as Newcastle increased their income sharply toward the end of the thirteenth century. Coal also began to be exported. As early as 1200, Bruges was importing English coal, and we know that in 1328 a ship from Pontoise loaded with wheat returned to France with a shipload of Newcastle coal.

With the burning of coal, western Europe began to face atmospheric pollution. The first person recorded to have suffered from medieval pollution was a Queen of England, Eleanor, who was driven from Nottingham Castle in 1257 by the unpleasant fumes of the sea coal burned in the industrial city below. Coal smoke was considered to be very detrimental to one's health, and up to the sixteenth century coal was generally used as a domestic fuel only by the poorer members of society, who could not afford to buy wood. Medieval coal extracted from the surface was of inferior quality, with more bitumen in it than the coal mined today. As it burned, it gave off a continuous cloud of choking, foul-smelling, noxious smoke. The only good domestic coal was that extracted from the coalfields bordering the Firth of Forth, which was burned by the Scottish kings, and the coal extracted at Aachen in Germany, which was used to make fires in the town hall and in the mayor's chambers.

By the last decades of the thirteenth century, London had the sad privilege of becoming the first city in the world to suffer man-made atmospheric pollution. In 1285 and 1288 complaints were recorded concerning the infection and corruption of the city's air by coal fumes from the limekilns. Commissioners of Inquiry were appointed, and in 1307 a royal proclamation was made in Southwark, Wapping, and East Smithfield forbidding the use of sea coal in kilns under pain of heavy forfeiture.

As the King learns from the complaints of prelates and magnates of his realm, who frequently come to London for the benefit of the Commonwealth by his order, and . . . of his citizens and all his people dwelling there . . . that the workmen [in kilns] . . . now burn them and construct them of sea-coal instead of brush wood or charcoal, from the use of which sea-coal an intolerable smell diffuses itself throughout the neighbouring places and the air is greatly affected to the annoyance of the magnates, citizens and others there dwelling and to the injury of their bodily health.[7]

The proclamation does not seem to have been very successful. Complaints continued and a commission of oyer and terminer was appointed, with instructions "to inquire of all such who burnt sea-coal in the city, or parts adjoining and to punish them for the first offence with great fines and ransoms, and upon the second offence to demolish their furnaces."[8] The commission was no more successful than the proclamation, and London remained a polluted town.

The bad reputation of sea coal continued throughout the ages. In the fifteenth century Enea Sylvio Piccolomini, who later became Pope Pius II, wrote when visiting Scotland, "this kind of stone being impregnated with sulfur or some fatty matter is burned instead of wood, of which the country is destitute."[9] Sea coal was still unpopular in the sixteenth century when the Venetian envoy Soranzo wrote an account of England in which he says: "In the north towards Scotland they find a certain sort of earth, almost mineral, which burns like charcoal and is extensively used by blacksmiths, and but for a bad odour which it leaves would be yet more employed as it gives great heat and costs but little."[10] The London Company of Brewers offered in 1578 to burn wood instead of sea coal in the brew-houses nearest to the Palace of Westminster because its members understood that the Queen "findeth hersealfe greately greved and anoyed with the taste and smoke of the sea-cooles."[11]

> Even late in Elizabeth's reign the more old fashioned and dainty ladies would not go into a room where sea-coal was burnt or eat meat cooked with that fuel; but that by that time it was in fairly common use in less fastidious circles is evident from the speech which Shakespeare puts into Dame Quickly's mouth: "Thou didst swear to me upon a parcel-gilt goblet, sitting in my Dolphin Chamber, at the round table, by a sea-coal fire, upon Wednesday in Whitsun week."[12]

While Londoners were choked with noisome fumes, tens of thousands of villagers throughout Europe were deafened by the din of the village forges. An anonymous fourteenth-century poet expressed his anger at the iron industry and its workers, whose activities kept him awake at night:

> Swart smutted smiths, smattered with smoke,
> Drive me to death with din of their dints;
> Such noise on nights ne heard men never,
> What [with] knaven cry and clattering of knocks!
> The crooked caitiffs cryen after col! col!
> And blowen their bellows that all their brain bursteth.
> Huf! puf! saith that one; haf! paf! that other;
> They spitten and sprawlen and spellen many spells.*
> They gnawen and gnashen, they groan all together,
> And holden them hot with their hard hammers.
> Of a bull-hide be their barm-fells†
> Their shanks be shackled for the fiery flinders;
> Heavy hammers they have that hard be handled,
> Stark strokes they striken on a steely stock,
> Lus! bus! las! das! snore they by the row,

* Tell many tales.
† Leathern apron.

Such a doleful a dream the devil it to-drive!
The master loungeth a little, and catcheth a less,
Twineth them twain and toucheth a treble°
Tik! tak! hic! hac! tiket! taket! tyk! tyk!
Lus! bus! lus! das! . . . Christ them give sorrow!
Many no man for brenn-waters† on night have his rest.[13]

In the towns people suffered also from industrial water pollution. Two industries in particular were held responsible in the Middle Ages for polluting the rivers: the slaughtering and the tanning industries, especially tanning. Municipalities were always trying to move the butchers and the tanners downstream, outside the precincts of the town.

The slaughtering and quartering of livestock in the Middle Ages was generally done on the butcher's premises. A French parliamentary decree of September 7, 1366, compelled Paris butchers to do their slaughtering and cleaning alongside a running stream beyond the city. This decree was certainly necessary, as some 250,000 head of livestock were slaughtered each year in Paris. The author of the *Menagier de Paris* worked out that 269,256 animals had been slaughtered in 1293: 188,522 sheep, 30,346 oxen, 19,604 calves, and 30,784 pigs. Quite enough to pollute the Seine.

The Paris authorities tried to limit the degree of this pollution not only by restricting the slaughtering of animals within the precincts of the city but also by imposing restrictions on the tanners, who dressed ox, cow, and calf hides, and the tawers, who dressed the skins of deer, sheep, and horses. "In 1395 the king's representative at the *Châtelet* wanted to compel the tawers who were dressing their leather on the banks of the Seine, between the Grand-Pont and the Hôtel

° The master pauses, catches up a smaller hammer, and intertwines (or perhaps separates) the bass of the sledgehammer with his own lighter treble.

† For the hissing of the steel in the trough of water.

du duc de Bourbon to move downstream, because industry corrupted the water of the riverside dwellers, both those lodging in the Louvre and those lodging in the Hôtel du duc de Bourbon."[14]

Tanning polluted the river because it subjected the hides to a whole series of chemical operations requiring tannic acids or lime. Tawing used alum and oil. Dried blood, fat, surplus tissues, flesh impurities, and hair were continually washed away with the acids and the lime into the streams running through the cities. The water flowing from the tanneries was certainly unpalatable, and there were tanneries in every medieval city.

In 1425, in Colchester in Essex, there are reports of the grievous complaints of the ale manufacturers against the tawers for "impayring and corrupcion" of the waters used by the ale makers for their ale. The word "pollution" did not yet exist, but the medieval words are just as expressive.

> Grevous compleynt [was made] that mochel people of the same ton brewen hure [their] ale and maken hure [their] mete with water of the ryver of the said toun, the which said ryver ther ben certeyn persones dwellying upon, as Barbers [Tanners] and White Tawyers, that leyen many diverse hides . . . [to the] impayring and corrupcion of the said water of the rever biforesaid, and in destruction of the ffysche therynne [and] to gret harmyng and noissaunce of the said people.[15]

Documents in the archives of the city of Marseilles show that the municipality diverted the river Jarret to ensure the irrigation of the gardens of the city suburbs and provide running water for the tanning industry. When the municipal statutes were reviewed in 1253, the *prud'hommes* were recommended to keep watch over the water of the Jarret, so that any used in this way should not be allowed to flow into the harbor.

Many local authorities took measures to combat the pollution of their cities, but in 1388 the English Parliament sitting in Cambridge passed the first nationwide antipollution act. It concerned not only the pollution of the air but also of the waters. It forbade throwing garbage into rivers or leaving it uncared for in the city. All garbage had to be carried away out of town. Otherwise, the law proclaimed, "the air . . . is greatly corrupt and infect and many Maladies and other intolerable Diseases do daily happen. . . ."[16] If the authorities of the cities—mayors and bailiffs—did not take the necessary measures to enforce this antipollution act, the citizens were invited to bring their complaints to the chancellor, a high government official, who would summon the municipal authorities, and if these were found guilty they would be punished.

However effective these various antipollution measures were, medieval people usually preferred to rely on wells for drinking water. Sometimes they repaired the Roman aqueducts, which were often in a half-ruined state, and occasionally they built new ones. Sometimes they brought water considerable distances in underground conduits. Just about a century after the Norman Conquest, in 1167, the monks of the Cathedral Priory of Canterbury, who had obtained a grant of land containing the springs, installed a very elaborate and complete system of water supply, of which a most interesting contemporary plan has fortunately survived. The water was carried by an underground pipe and, after entering the city walls, flowed into a whole series of pipes. One pipe fed water to the infirmary hall; another went to the refectory, the scullery, and the kitchen; another carried water to the baker's house, the brewer's house, the guest hall, and the bathhouse; and a pipe ran into a tank beside the prior's chambers and fed his water tub. Waste from the water tub and from the bathroom flowed into the main drain, flushing the rere-dorter or *necessarium.*

Numerous documents of the period mention the existence of private and public baths as well as private and public toilets.

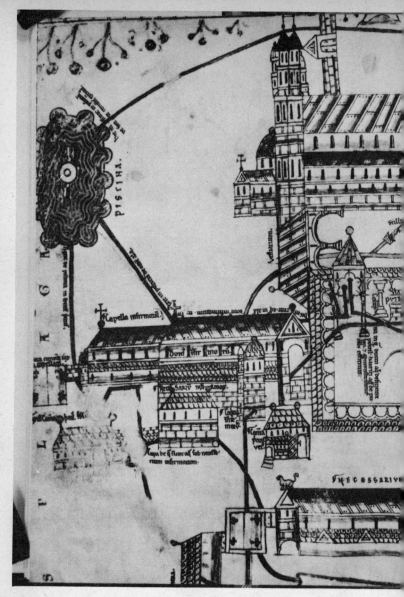

The underground water system at Canterbury. The *necessarium* is the long building in the lower middle of the drawing. Courtesy of the Master and Fellows of Trinity College, Cambridge, Eng.

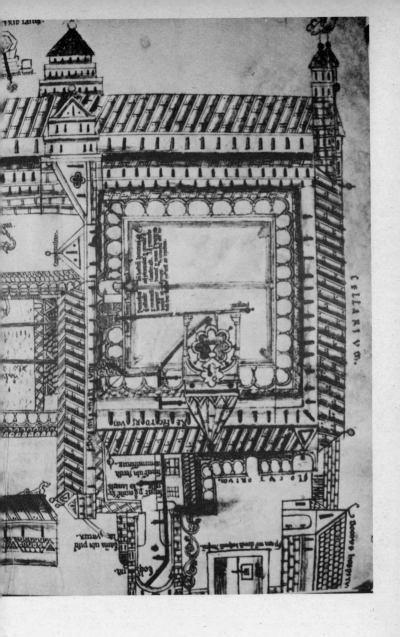

Twelfth-century painting of life in a bathhouse. Courtesy Municipal Library, Leipzig.

If there was medieval pollution, there was also medieval hygiene. But the medieval pollution must have increased still more with the breaking down of medieval hygiene. The standards of hygiene in the twelfth and thirteenth centuries were relatively high, but progressively the authorities worried about the "permissiveness" they discovered in the many public baths, and the incidence of the Black Death certainly hardened this attitude. By the seventeenth century a palace like Versailles was built practically without any bathrooms or public toilets.

In the thirteenth century there were no less than thirty-two public baths in Paris, for men and women. According to the professional statutes (relating to more than one hundred professions) recorded in 1268 by the provost of Paris, Etienne Boileau, the owners of the bathhouses were allowed to ask two prices at the entrance: 2d. for a steam bath and 4d. for a bath in a tub. In the linen inventories of private houses, mention is sometimes made of a piece of linen to be laid on the bottom of the wooden tub as a protection against splinters. In the statutes, the owners of the bathhouses made a reservation for the future: if the price of wood or coal (another example of the use of coal in the Middle Ages) should go up, the prices of the steam and hot baths would be raised accordingly. The owners were to protect their establishments materially and morally by making sure that men such as lepers could not enter and that men with a bad reputation would be kept out. The bathhouse was not to be used as a house of prostitution or as a *bordel*—the Old French word used is *bordiau*. (Interestingly, the medieval word in English for bathhouse was *stew*, which has come down to the English today as a synonym for brothel.) Miniatures of the period show that the bath was indeed a place where people gossiped, ate, and soaked socially, often with a companion of the opposite sex. One of Boccaccio's ladies prepares a tub bath for her lover, and when he does not show up she thriftily takes it herself.

One entertained one's friends in one's *baignerie*, generally situated near one's bedroom.

On the manuscript page where the provost of Paris had had transcribed the statutes of the bathhouse owners—the Etuviers—a few lines were added at a later date which show that the authorities were getting increasingly worried about hygiene, or the way hygiene was put to use by lovers. From then on a bathhouse proprietor had to decide if he wanted to run a bathhouse for women or for men. He was not allowed to accommodate both sexes in the same establishment. The author of these lines went on to relate what happens when the bathhouses are mixed. "Shameful things. Men make a point of staying all night in the public baths and women at the break of day come in and through 'ignorance' find themselves in the men's rooms."[17] This prudish attitude toward the growing permissiveness brought the bathhouses into financial difficulties, and they finally had to close one after another. At Provins, for example—where pressure very likely came from the local church authorities—the *bains-neufs* in 1309 were rented at 209s., in 1315 at 100s., and in 1320 at only 60s. Hygiene thus disappeared from Western society, not to reappear for half a millennium.

5
Labor Conditions in
Three Medieval Industries

Having considered some of the effects of the medieval industrial revolution on the environment, let us now examine in some detail the effect of the growth of technology on the work force in three major industries: mining, textiles, and construction.

Involved as they were in the dynamics of increasing production, it was inevitable that the entrepreneurs of the Middle Ages developed new attitudes toward their workmen, and created new regulations accordingly. The miners were the most privileged group of workers, no doubt a reflection of the high regard given to the products of the tin, lead, and silver mines, and the substantial revenues accruing from them.

It is astonishing to study the range of rights that miners enjoyed. They were allowed to take timber from the neighboring woods for use in their mines. Sometimes when wood was scarce, they could even prevent the landowner from cutting his own wood until they had obtained a sufficient supply for their furnaces. They were permitted to prospect anywhere except in churchyards, gardens, orchards, and highways, and were even allowed to divert streams and were given the right of access to the nearest highway.

John de Treeures complained that:

> fully sixty tinners have entered on his demesne and soil, which bears wheat, barley, oats, hay and peas, and is as good and fair as any soil in Cornewaille, and have led streams of water from divers places to Treeures over part of his said demesne and soil, so that, by reason of the great current of water they have obtained and the steep slope of the land there, all the land where they come will go back to open moor, and nothing will remain of all that good land except great stones and gravel.[1]

Those who objected to such violations rarely got satisfaction. In central Europe the overlords or the lords of the soil wisely set up a mining administration independent of local authorities, headed by a *Bergmeister*, and then let the miners run their own mines. They had their own law courts, in which twelve or fourteen miners sat as judges. This was to prevent local authorities from intervening arbitrarily in mining disputes, thus risking a stoppage of mining operations, which would be against the financial interests of the overlords or lords of the soil.

This type of legislation seems to have been also adopted in England. In the great lead-mining centers of England, in Derbyshire, Alston Moor, and the Mendip Hills, in the royal silver mines of Devon and in the iron-producing Forest of Dean, we find that there were mining law courts, and in many of these the chief official turns out to be none other than the

German *Bergmeister*, spelled in Britain as bermaster, bar-master, bermar, or barmar. In Derbyshire the law courts themselves were known as berghmotes or barmotes.

The miners were exempted from ordinary taxes and tolls, and from military service. They were offered, when necessary, land to build their cottages on. They were entitled to a measured plot of ground on which to search for ore, and the interest of their concessionary was to be permanent, assignable, and transmissible.

In Germany, besides all these rights, a still higher honor was offered to the mining classes. If a group of miners proved successful, a "mine city" soon arose—such as, among others, Freiberg, Goslar, Iglau, Kutna Hora, and Joachimstal—and the last stage in freeing the miners from the feudal laws was to give such a community the status of a freemen's city. The inhabitants, at least those who were bona fide miners, then enjoyed all the privileges of town hall as well as those of the mines, including free brewing and baking, free transportation of goods, the removal of the burdensome guild regulations, which hindered the miners in their occupation, and finally freedom from any military service. One of the most ancient mining codes is that of Iglau in Bohemia, issued in 1249, which contains the following articles:

In God's Name, amen. We Wenczlaw, by God's grace King of Bohemia and of Moravia, offer to all who see this letter our eternal greeting etc.

Statutes of the Mines and Mountains
I 1. We lay down, make and wish: whatever the licensers with the advice of the assessors in Iglau have conceded or given to anyone in the mines or in the galleries under their seal and that of the licensers, that shall be firm and fixed without any denial.
2. And where a mine or gallery has been discovered

or worked, then shall a man have possession of 4½ *lehen**
of the roof and 1 *lehen* of the floor, height and depth in
equal measure.

3. For the man who discovers a new mine shall be measured 7 *lehen*, and on both sides 1 *lehen* for the lord king
and 1 for the citizens.

4. The discoverers of the mine shall give to those who
have measured the mine 7 short shillings.

5. Whoever works in the gallery called a *stoll*, and finds
metal, from that same place where he has found metal
shall be measured for him 7 *lehen* and the right of other
mines.

II 6. If it should be however that someone with agreement or knowledge of the judge and of him who licenses
the mine should begin to work in the gallery and finds
metal, from that same place shall no one hinder him for
3½ *lehen* before him or behind him. . . .

VII 15. If, as has been mentioned before, a man with
the consent of the judge and the assessors and of him
who licenses the mines starts a gallery and another comes
before him beyond the correct measure of 3½ *lehen* with
another gallery or with some digging, and finds metal
first, witnesses shall be called to this and the matter
examined; whoever was the first receives the measure of
7 *lehen*.

VIII 16. We wish also that every discoverer of a new
mine who first presents the seam and the metal in the correct way to the judge or to him who licenses the mines,
no one should dare to work before him or behind him to
the measure of 1 *lehen*; whoever acts against this, he
shall be deprived of all gain and the first shall remain
with all his right and justice.

IX 17. What the licensers with knowledge of the assessors of Iglau dispose and decide with the mining laws,
that shall be held firm and fixed.[2]

---

* A *lehen* was a measurement of length equal to 7 fathoms (approximately 42 feet).

Other mining codes have also survived, from Freiberg, Kutna Hora, and Schemnitz. It is now thought that the common archetype of these laws and customs of medieval mining was originally drawn up in the region of Goslar. "Other Goslar legislation radiated towards the North up to Sweden, towards the East, in Saxony around Freiberg, and from there towards the South, from Iglau towards the Hungarian mines. These old German regulations seem to have influenced certain Italian and French legislation (in particular those of Massa and the mines of the Lyonnais)."[3]

It is not certain what influence, if any, was exercised on the German miners by the famous tin-mining industries—called stannaries—of Devon and Cornwall, which were already fully active in the Bronze Age. This western promontory of England may possibly have been the Cassiterides, or Tin Islands, where the Phoenicians replenished their stocks of tin. It is even possible that the free miners of these stannaries in some way affected the German mining laws and customs, as they certainly seem to have had a part in unearthing the German tin mines. The thirteenth-century chronicler Matthew Paris wrote that in 1241 German tin was discovered by a Cornishman who had fled to Germany, and that this brought about a fall in the price of tin, due to overproduction.

Tin prices fluctuated according to demand throughout the centuries. Tin was used in the Middle Ages not only with copper to make bronze—for church bells, and later for cannons—but also, alloyed with lead, in the manufacture of pewter mugs and plates, an important English export industry of the time. Tin production also fluctuated considerably. There was an exceptional rise between the years 1156 and 1171, when production practically quintupled, going from approximately 70 tons to nearly 350 tons. In 1198 King Richard I, realizing how profitable the stannaries were, decided to reorganize the industry to favor the free miners and thereby encourage them to increase production. He summoned to his assistance juries drawn from the miners, and in 1201 King John followed suit and confirmed the ancient privileges of "digging tin and turfs for smelting it at all times, freely and peaceably and without hindrance from any man, everywhere in moors and in the fens of bishops, abbots, and counts . . . and of buying faggots to smelt the tin without waste of forest, and of diverting streams for their works, and in the stannaries just as by ancient usage they have wont to do."[4]

King John proclaimed that the miners would henceforth be free from the jurisdiction of all the local magistrates and coroners and would be answerable only to the wardens and bailiffs of the newly founded mine law courts: "We have granted likewise, that the chief warden of the stannaries and his bailiffs through him, have over the aforesaid tinners, plenary power to do them justice and to hold them to the law. . . ."[5]

A few years later this very favorable charter yielded substantial results. Production rose to some 500 long tons in 1212, and 600 long tons in 1214. In 1237, production reached 700 long tons. The rise in production also, of course, increased the tax yield. In 1214, the coinage duty tax produced £799, a remarkable sum when one considers that the combined revenues of Devon and Cornwall without mining revenues amounted only to some £500. In 1306 the coinage duty rose to £1,726 9s. 4d. In addition to this the Crown had an excellent source of revenue in their option on all tin mined in Devon and Cornwall.

The exceptional privileges granted to those who chose to become miners provoked the anger of many manorial lords. Unwilling to see their peasants joining the much freer and more lucrative mining profession, the lords frequently fought back, but in the end were always defeated, and the miners retained their rights. In fact, the free miners not only always took advantage of their privileges but often overstepped their rights. Complaint followed complaint. Miners were even accused of digging on church land in 1237. In 1318, an inquiry revealed that the Devon miners did not even hesitate "to seize and beat up the king's bailiffs . . . and hold them in prison pending the payment of a ransom. . . ."[6]

There is an extraordinary contrast between the rights and privileges of medieval miners and the conditions prevailing for workers in the great medieval textile industry. While the miners were freemen, the textile workers of the industrial cities in Flanders and in Italy formed a real proletariat bound to a capitalist system.

Up to the second half of the thirteenth century, the great center of the European textile industry had been in the densely populated cities of Flanders, in what is now Belgium and northeast France, in Flemish towns such as Ypres, Ghent, and Bruges, and in French towns such as Arras, Saint-Omer, and Douai. Then the Flemish merchants began to run into a succession of economic and social difficulties. They had become increasingly dependent for their raw material—wool—on England, where the best sheep in Europe were raised, and each year they used to cross the Channel to buy an adequate supply. But then a whole chain of events made their purchases more expensive and wool scarcer in Flanders. In desperate need of money, Edward I decided to put a tax on wool, and in 1275 the first export duty was levied. Before the end of the century the original tax of 6s. 8d. per sack had been raised sharply. The price of wool for the manufacturers in Flanders was further increased at the beginning of the fourteenth century when the king of France, Philip the Fair, devalued the currency to help overcome his financial difficulties.

The Flemish industry was even harder hit by the economic sanctions Edward I enforced on Flanders, intending to create political and economic difficulties for the King of France, with whom he was in dispute. Occasionally, these sanctions amounted to a complete embargo on the export of wool, bringing the industry to a near standstill and causing massive unemployment and misery. The great wool famine of 1297 was particularly disastrous, with starving workmen having to roam the country in search of food. Edward I's economic tactics proved successful when the Count of Flanders turned against the King of France and signed a treaty of alliance with England.

Strikes became a regular occurrence in the late thirteenth century and "culminated in a general revolt of the workers against the capitalist entrepreneurs, who had dominated the cloth industry in Flanders and who also dominated the politics of the towns."[7] The earliest strike is recorded as breaking out in Douai in 1245, and in 1274 the weavers and fullers of Ghent left the city in a body to go to the neighboring duchy of Brabant. The commotions in Flanders reached a climax in 1280. That summer the textile workers rose in arms in Ypres, then in September in Bruges, and in October again in Douai. Plundering and massacre were followed by harsh repression. Textile workers were banished or emigrated of their own free will, taking their knowledge and experience to the expanding textile industries of England and Italy, where the workers were granted immunity from taxes. As early as 1271 Henry III decreed that "all workers of woollen cloths, male and female, as well of Flanders as of other lands, may safely come into our realm, there to make cloths,"[8] and he granted them freedom from taxation for five years.

The fact that England's main raw material, wool, was exploited in the twelfth and thirteenth centuries primarily by the Flemish makes it reasonable to describe England as a "developing" country and Flanders as an advanced industrial country. Due to a number of factors, however, this situation was reversed in the following centuries, and England took the lead in world textile manufacturing. To start with, Edward's tax export levy gave English textile manufacturers the opportunity of buying wool at a much lower price than that paid by

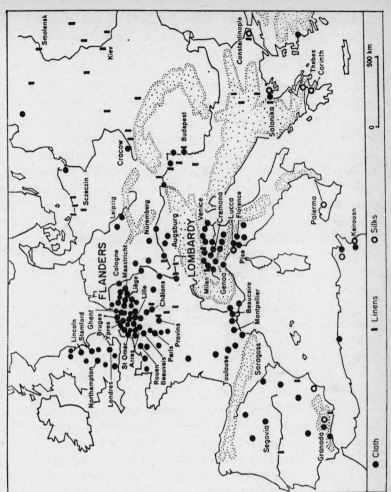

The textile cities of Europe. Courtesy Armand Colin.

● Cloth ▬ Linens ○ Silks

the Flemish manufacturers. The English industry was further helped by the influx of textile specialists emigrating from Flanders and by the introduction of the spinning wheel and the fulling mill. "Both inventions made possible a considerable increase in production without a corresponding increase in the labour force involved."[9] Statistics showing the number of sacks of wool and lengths of cloth exported annually are revealing. The number of sacks decreases, while the number of lengths of cloth increases. Whereas in the early fourteenth century England exported 35,000 sacks per annum, she was exporting only 19,000 by the end of the century, and no more than 8,000 in the mid-fifteenth century. On the other hand the number of lengths of cloth exported annually rose from 4,000 in the year 1347–48, to 16,000 in the 1360s, and to 54,000 in the mid-fifteenth century.

The decline of the once all-powerful textile manufacturing industry of Flanders in the last decades of the thirteenth century was hastened by the intervention of Italian, and in particular Florentine, bankers in the English wool market. In order to gain control of this valuable raw material, they brought into play all their recently acquired financial power.

By the beginning of the fourteenth century, commercial and banking techniques in Florence had reached a high level of efficiency. Italian merchant capitalists were introducing rational methods of business practice: letters of payment, which could be cashed abroad for the convenience of travelers, clergy, or merchants; nonnegotiable bills of exchange; double-entry bookkeeping. The Frescobaldi—whom we met in a previous chapter leasing the Devon mines from the Crown —the Bardi, and the Perruzzi, who had settled in England to collect the papal taxes and were now loaning vast sums of money to the English King, were the most active. By buying up the Cistercian wool production a year or two ahead, they displaced the Flemish merchants, who did not have the capital to compete with them.

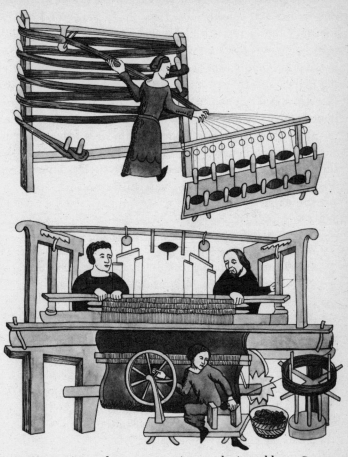

A woman warping, and two men weaving on a horizontal loom. Courtesy Archives Communales, Ypres.

The impact of the financiers on the Florentine textile industry was also considerable, since up to the second half of the thirteenth century it had manufactured only cheap cloth made from second-grade wool. It had also specialized in dyeing and finishing northern cloth. But now the manufacture of high-quality cloth took precedence, reaching a peak in the first decades of the fourteenth century. By 1338 Florence was importing 10,000 lengths of cloth while manufacturing 80,000.

The banking and commercial techniques of the merchant capitalists of Florence effectively enslaved the majority of the thirty thousand textile workers of the city. Describing such medieval conditions, Arnold Hauser in *The Social History of Art* wrote that

> The raising of the output demanded a more intensive exploitation of the available labour, a progressive division of labour and the gradual mechanization of labour methods, by which is to be understood not merely the introduction of machines, but also the depersonalization of human work, the valuation of the worker purely in terms of the output achieved. Nothing expresses the economic philosophy of this new age more trenchantly than precisely this materialistic approach, which estimates a man according to his achievement and the output according to its value in money—the wage—which, in other words, turns the worker into a mere link in a complicated system of investments and financial yields, of risks and of profit and loss, of assets and liabilities.[10]

The division of labor was far-reaching. The manufacture of a piece of cloth in medieval Florence necessitated no less than twenty-six different operations, each performed by a specialist. The assembly-line system of today is criticized in that the workman is only a cog, an element separated—in effect, alienated—from the final, complete product. The Florentine textile workers were alienated, too, and for the same reasons. And they had the added frustration of the entrepreneurs' refusal to let them form an association. Their bosses knew only too well what power such organizations could offer, for their own power was itself largely founded on the associations or guilds of the Florentine ruling classes.

In order to hold this urban proletariat in check, the fourteenth-century Florentine industrialists were perfectly prepared to introduce some of the more reprehensible methods later adopted by nineteenth-century British industrialists. One of these was the truck system, which consisted in granting advances in goods or money to be repaid later in work, the goods themselves being, of course, generally overvalued. This chained the workman to his employer.

The only way the Florentine textile manufacturer could increase his margin of profit was by lowering the wages of his workmen. He had no control over the price of the raw material he bought from the importers, who were the merchant bankers, and no control either over the market price of the cloth, which was fixed by the authorities. The cost of labor amounted to 60 percent of the cost of the finished product. The workmen could not appeal any decision relating to their wages. They had no rights. The inspectors who came to visit them regularly did not do so to listen to complaints, but to check on any breach in the regulations. The guilds had their own police officers and their own jails for dealing with any recalcitrant workers. The textile industry was thus run methodically and efficiently—but only for the benefit of the businessmen, a tiny minority who formed only 2 percent of the population, or 5 to 10 percent if one includes all the members of their families.

The numerous constraints and restrictions imposed on the textile workers in relation to mobility and wages contrast with the freedom of the building workers, who could move from one building site to another and were free to decline any wage offer. An analysis of medieval building accounts and of the reports that often accompanied them does not show a picture of a God-fearing medieval working class. The documents reveal strikes, workers beating up other workmen for accepting lower wages, malpractices, thefts, and absenteeism.

In the twelfth century, masons working on the church of the monastery of Obazine in France threw down their tools in anger one morning and hurled abuse at the Abbot because he had thrown away a pig they had killed and which they had been looking forward to eating. The Abbot was a vegetarian!

At Westminster in January 1331, "the masons would not work on Monday or Tuesday because they were in arrear of their wages since Christmas, and they thought they would lose their wages, until the Lord Treasurer promised that they should be fully paid for time past and future and then they began to work on Wednesday."[11]

In 1339, four carpenters were charged with intimidating "foreign" carpenters who were willing to work in the city of London for less than 6d. and an afterdinner drink. They did, in fact, beat up one of them, John de Chalfhonte, who had accepted a lower rate. The *Chanson des Quatre Fils Aymon*, written at the end of the twelfth or the beginning of the thirteenth century, tells the story of a repentant nobleman, Renaud de Montauban, who asked permission from the master of Cologne Cathedral to work as a laborer on the building site— he was subsequently killed by hammerblows from the workmen because his wages undercut theirs.

The most damning report of working practices prevailing on a medieval building site must be that made on the management of the works at York Minster, from January 9 to 12, 1345. There were absenteeism, stolen and misappropriated building materials, quarreling among the workmen, refusal to work, unfit workmen, building defects, and rotting machinery. The full text of this remarkable report reads (quoting first the evidence of the Master of the Works):

He says that he believes that the masons have received salaries more than were due and too excessive. Wages used to be paid by the fortnight but payment is now put off for a month or even more. Orders given that in future payment shall not be delayed beyond a fortnight at most. He says that once he paid Roger de Hirton, mason of the fabric, his wages for almost a fortnight, when he was absent all the time and had done no work. Also concerning money paid for drink. Also there was often removal of timber, stone and lime, and knows not where it went. The roofing of the church and the stonework suffer injury through lack of care. . . . The wardens of the work and also the workmen, though they seemed to be capable, often quarrelled, so that the work was often delayed and is endangered. The outer pilasters which are called "botraces" have for the most part perished for defect of covering. Also W. the carpenter is an old man and cannot work at high levels. It is ordered that another young man be employed in his place, and that the other old man shall supervise defects.

The master of the masons appeared 11 January. He says that there are many of the masons who go against his orders, and also workmen who are not capable or fit for their work, and that some are so disobedient that he cannot restrain or punish them properly. Also that timbers, stone, lime, cement and so forth have frequently been made away with; and that there has been much misappropriation of stone from the quarry, and that almost nothing fit for work is brought in. For lack of proper care and of roofing there is such a quantity of water that lately a lad has almost been drowned; and these defects arise from the lack of lead roofing. Also he says that he cannot look after the work, workmen and other things as he ought, because he is interfered with by the Mayor, and he cannot view defects because Sir Thomas de Ludham alone has the keys to the doors of the fabric.

11 January. Will. de Wrsal, under-master of the

works, says that the chief defect that he knows is that
the cranes at the west end of the church are rotten and
worthless. The master of the carpenters says that he does
not know any maladministration by the chamberlain except that he occasionally gives away a stone, and he
thinks that he receives money for the gift. Also he thinks
that the chamber which Richard de Melton made beside
the church is useless and very injurious to the work and
ought to be removed.[12]

A literary text, the *Contrefait de Renard*, written between
1319 and 1328, tells the story of how workmen only work when
the foreman is present, but as soon as he has his back turned
they sit down and rest or go to have a drink at the local tavern.
And on every possible occasion they claim a raise in their
salaries. Workmen were reasonably sure to work only on taskwork, which means they were paid for the job done rather
than by the day. When one sees how easily money was wasted,
one can appreciate how much more profitable taskwork must
have been for those who had to pay for the building expenses.
On the one hand, taskwork deprived the local official of the
opportunity to adjust the accounts in his own favor, and on
the other it discouraged absenteeism. The arrival and de-
parture of the workmen were carefully noted by the cleric,
so that he could pay the correct wages due them.

Robert of Oxford	He was absent 3 days in Whit-sun week	2s 3½d[13]
Philip of Dilwyn	Came in the 5th week on Wednesday, departed on the following Friday, returned in the 11th week.	2s 3½d[14]

But large buildings could not be constructed by taskwork
(although Henry III, having difficulty financing Westminster

Abbey, encouraged his master masons to put out to task certain small jobs in the Abbey), and absenteeism generally flourished. It was certainly not overwork that caused absenteeism, because the English workman of the thirteenth century had more official days off in the year than the English workman of the 1970s. Medieval workmen had sometimes up to a fortnight at Christmas, a week at Easter, and a few days off in Whitsun week, plus the feast days, which were numerous at the time. The regulations at York Minster in the fourteenth century even provided half-holidays, with work ceasing at noon on the vigils of feast days and on Saturdays. Over the year, the men worked an average of approximately 5½ days a week, though it must be said that on these days they worked from dawn to dusk, with breaks only for meals. In summer they would work 12¼ hours, and in winter 8¾ hours. The substantial difference in the length of the working days resulted in the authorities' paying summer and winter wages, the latter being some two-thirds of the summer wages. In some cases there were four wage rates, for summer, autumn, winter, and spring.

Building accounts of the Middle Ages reveal a remarkable wage structure. It is immediately evident that there was no overall organization of masons. Except for London, where there was an attempt in the thirteenth century to enforce a control of wages, there was no wage control elsewhere of any sort. The masons were free to ask any price for their professional skills, and the would-be employer was free to refuse the masons' demand. As a result we find in the accounts an extraordinary disparity in salaries. At Caernarvon Castle, in 1304, there were fifty-three masons on the payroll in receipt of seventeen different rates of pay.

One of the reasons for this situation was that the main employers of the building trade were opposed to letting the working class unite and confront them with a powerful organization capable of making firm demands for increased pay.

Actually, such an organization was never a serious threat, as the building workers were part of a floating proletariat who were continually moving from one building site to another. It was only in large towns like London that the masons were a stable enough population to associate and try to enforce some wage control. But then there was another problem: when associations or guilds did come into existence, protected by the municipalities, they were not associations of the working class but of men who had risen from the working class and were now in a small way privileged capitalists. As a French author has written, the guilds and corporations were syndicates of bosses exploiting a monopoly.

Though the masons could not present a united front to the employers, they were relatively well paid. They were highly skilled workmen who were in demand, and the employers had to take this into consideration. On an average they received 4d. a day. The layer who only laid the stones got perhaps 3½d., the hewer who cut the stone 4d., and the freestone mason perhaps 4½d. At the lower end of the scale, the laborer who dug the foundations or carried the stones was paid only 1½ or sometimes 2d. At the higher end of the scale, the master mason or architect could receive 12d. a day, or in some cases up to 2s. a day. And the architect, often under contract to the Crown or the Church, had other privileges attached to his professional status. While the masons were only paid for the days they worked on the building site (or exceptionally for alternate feast days as well), the architects were often paid for every day of the week. And they were offered robes and sometimes houses where they could live with their families during the time they were under contract. An architect could live well. One of the ways he could substantially increase his income was to act as an expert on a committee. He would receive a large sum to make up for the days he was absent from the building site for which he was responsible.

Is it possible to measure the standard of living of the

ordinary mason? In a week he would receive some 20d. It has been calculated that his weekly wage—workmen were paid at the end of each week, as is still the custom in England—was approximately three times the price of food. It is interesting to compare the builders' wages with the mean purchase prices of livestock. In the twelfth century in England pigs were worth from 8d. to 1s., sheep 4d. to 6d., cows from 2s. 4d. to 3s. 4d. The mason's 4d. a day must have allowed him to live decently if he was a bachelor or married with one child. Two, three, or four children would have made his 4d. rather inadequate. But in many cases a mason must have had further means of livelihood. He may often have had a small agricultural holding which his wife would look after while he was on a building site. And we know that some masons supplemented their earnings by renting out carts for the transport of stone. Some even had quarries.

But while the masons could generally live decently, the laborers who were only receiving 1½ d. or 2d. a day, and that not always on a regular basis, must have always had a difficult time making ends meet. It can only be presumed that the laborers, who were nearly always local people—statistics show that on many of the large building sites 95 percent of the laborers were of local origin, while the same proportion, 95 percent of the masons were from other parts of the country— worked on the land when they were not employed on the building sites.

One other question demands an answer: how does the standard of living of the masons of the twelfth century, thirteenth century, and first half of the fourteenth century compare with that of subsequent centuries? The Black Death, by reducing the population by 30 percent or more, naturally created a shortage of both unskilled and skilled labor. All labor was able to get higher wages. The English Parliament endeavored to check these wage increases by publishing a first Statute of Labourers in 1349, which was reissued in 1351

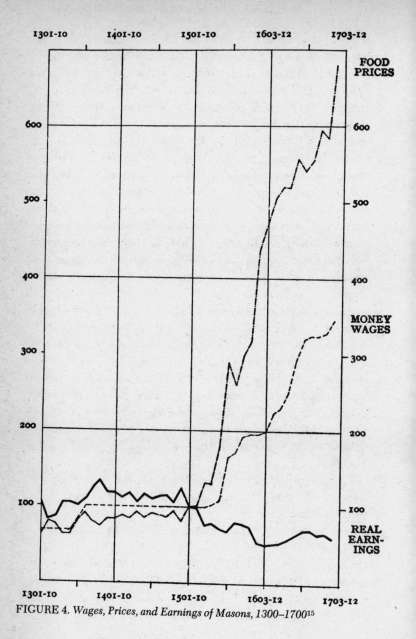

FOOD
PRICES

MONEY
WAGES

REAL
EARN-
INGS

1301-10   1401-10   1501-10   1603-12   1703-12

FIGURE 4. *Wages, Prices, and Earnings of Masons, 1300–1700*[15]

with a special clause concerning the building trade. Stiffer penalties were prescribed in the statute of 1360. The building trade was to accept the pre–Black Death wages. But the Statute of Labourers was ignored. The existing 6d. daily wage was maintained until the 1540s, when it rose to 10d. By the beginning of the seventeenth century the masons' daily wage had risen to 16d., and to 18d. by the end of the century.

As the wages rose some 42 percent between 1350 and 1510, and food prices seem to have risen by only 33 percent, there was an increase in the real wages of the masons for this period. But in the sixteenth century there was a sharp reversal of this trend, with wages not keeping up with the substantial increases in the price of food. If a figure of 100 is taken for the real weekly earnings of the masons for the decade 1500–1510, these earnings fell to an average of 61.2 in 1541–92, and to 45.3 in 1593–1662. So it would seem that the real wages of masons in the seventeenth century were only half those of the masons of the first half of the fourteenth century.

Projected onto a graph, these figures show that the mason, who was one of the highly skilled workmen of the medieval industrial revolution, had a standard of living considerably superior to the masons of the seventeenth and eighteenth centuries.

6

Villard de Honnecourt: Architect and Engineer

At the higher end of the wage scale, there was a small group of professional men who not only earned a considerable income, but had the benefit of a whole series of privileges attached to their professional status. They were the architect-engineers, so called because in the thirteenth and fourteenth centuries there was "neither the specialization nor the separation of functions that is reflected in our design and operational personnel today: the architect, the structural engineer, the various mechanical engineers, and the general contractor, together with his team of sub-contractors. The medieval master builder was really a master of all phases of the work, familiar with each operation and constantly in immediate touch with it."[1] They were as much engineers as architects, and it was not until the Renaissance that this role and status were to change.

We have seen that architects lived well. Often they were

in such demand that they could impose their own terms. In 1129, Raymond, the master of the works of Lugo Cathedral, obviously worried about inflation, had a clause included in his contract with the Archbishop that if the value of money were to fall, he would be paid principally in kind, and receive per year 6 silver marks, 36 lengths of cloth, 17 loads of wood, and as many shoes and gaiters as he needed, and per month 2s., plus 1 measure of salt and 1 pound of candle wax. He was a wise man. Other architects were not as financially acute as Raymond and died in debt.

When John of Gloucester, the King's mason, died in 1260, he owed the King no less than 80 marks or £53 6s. 8d., though he owned "an estate at Bletchingdon, Oxon., . . . a house in Bridport, Dorset, and two in Oxford . . . a house and curtilage in Westminster."[2] The King continually bestowed privileges and presents on John of Gloucester. He exempted him from certain taxes, ordered that he should be paid double his salary when traveling for business, offered him casks of wine and each year two furred robes of good squirrels for himself and two more for his wife, Agnes.

James of Saint George, who was in charge of the great chain of ten new fortresses built in north Wales between 1277 and 1295, was on October 20, 1284, granted the huge allowance of 3s. a day for life, or £54 15s. 0d. a year. Later he was offered to hold during his lifetime a manor stated to be worth £25 16s. 6d. One can reckon that he was receiving in all some £80 a year—an extraordinarily high income when one considers that at that time possessions of "£20 worth of land entitled or even compelled a landed proprietor to become a knight."[3] It was also agreed that an allowance of 1s. 6d. a day should be paid to his wife, Ambrosia, should she survive him. This was four or five times the average daily wage of a highly skilled workman. In the old texts, James of Saint George is called *le machoun*, or sometimes *machinator*, sometimes also *ingeniator*. Besides being the architect who presumably drew up the plans of castles like Caernarvon, Conway, or Beaumaris, he is designated by these professional names as a construction engineer, a maker of war machines. The expression *ingeniator* was generally reserved for architects who specialized in building military installations. Though the architects who built cathedrals or parish churches were not usually designated as *ingeniatores*, they were nevertheless as much engineers as their colleagues who specialized in military structures.

These architect-engineers fulfilled one of the ambitions of the medieval citizen, which was to have a more outstanding building than any in the neighboring city, with a higher vault, a higher spire. Men of those years were out for world records, a spirit that ended when the vault of the choir of Beauvais Cathedral—156 feet 6 inches, the height of a fourteen-story high-rise building—crashed to the earth in 1284.

The medieval record was set by the Strasbourg spire, which rose to 466 feet—the height of a forty-story skyscraper. No stone building of the following six centuries ever approached this. Engineers had to introduce iron and steel structures to surpass it, a feat that did not occur until the building of the Eiffel Tower in the last quarter of the nineteenth century.

Although buildings in New York and now Chicago far surpass these heights, it was only in the 1960s that a building in London—the Post Office Tower (619 feet)—overtook medieval Strasbourg. Saint Paul's, which dominated the London skyline until the recent postwar period, is only 365 feet to the top of the cross, and a guidebook to London still marvels at the Victoria Tower of the Houses of Parliament, which "soars to the height of 340 feet, that is 20 feet higher than the Clock Tower." At 320 feet the roof bar of the London Hilton Hotel skyscraper is dwarfed by Strasbourg. Medieval men did not, like most contemporary Europeans, consider that high-rise building was aesthetically deplorable.

It was probably the engineering feats of these architect-

Schematic diagram of a cathedral. Courtesy Oxford University Press.

engineers that made them the heroes of the Middle Ages, the equivalent of our astronauts or Olympic gold medalists. No homage was too great for them, and no modern architect or engineer has been revered as were the great medieval architects.

A medieval architect, finding himself in New York and having heard that some of the most famous architects of the twentieth century—Gropius, Saarinen, Mies van der Rohe—had built tinted glass skyscrapers between 60th Street and Grand Central Terminal reminiscent of the stained glass buildings of the French thirteenth century, would be amazed to discover that these great men were only honored with inscriptions engraved in small characters and placed rather unobtrusively on a wall or column of the building, and that on Mies van der Rohe's Seagram Building there is no inscription at all.

In medieval times, especially in the thirteenth century, such great architects would have been honored with monumental inscriptions, or with inscriptions placed in such a central position that the general public could not fail to notice them.

A 25-foot-long inscription in large raised letters forming

a band at the base of the south transept of Notre Dame de Paris honors the architect-engineer who built this transept. It reads: "Master Jean de Chelles commenced this work for the Glory of the Mother of Christ on the second of the Ides of the month of February, 1258."

In the central section of the nave of many medieval cathedrals, a vast labyrinth was inlaid in stone on the floor, stretching across the whole width of the nave. The only one extant today is in Chartres Cathedral and measures 59 feet in diameter. In the Middle Ages these mazes were thought to represent the pilgrimage route to the Holy Land. This symbolic relationship was so firmly rooted in the belief of the time that to crawl on one's knees over the maze carried with it a measure of grace. On entering the cathedral, the faithful went to the labyrinth and fell on their knees. They followed the maze to the center where there lay a circular or octagonal plaque in metal or marble which depicted not, as one would expect, Christ, the Virgin Mary, the saints, or high dignitaries of the Church, but the architect-engineers responsible for the building of the cathedral. Alongside these portraits were their names, dates, and the part that each played in the raising of the great church.

In the labyrinth of the Cathedral of Reims, now destroyed but known to us from an early engraving, four of the architects were depicted in the four corners. Jean d'Orbais, in the top right-hand corner, began the choir in 1211. Jean le Loup, holding a square rule in the top left-hand corner, finished the choir and the transept and began the facade; he died in 1247. Gaucher de Reims, in the lower left-hand corner, continued the facade from 1247 to 1255. Bernard de Soissons, in the lower right-hand corner, is seen drawing a rose window on the floor with a large compass. He built the great rose window of the west front between the years 1255 and 1290. Robert de Courcy, who started the building of the twin towers in 1290, is the architect represented in the place of honor, the center of the labyrinth, and may have been the one responsible for having the plaque incised with the portraits of his predecessors.

Another great honor that was bestowed on such medieval master masons was to be allowed by the church authorities to be buried in the church that they had built, with their wives beside them if they so wished. The epitaph of Pierre de Montreuil is one of the most remarkable because of the academic title he was honored with: *Doctor Lathomorum*—Doctor of Masons. "Weep, for here lies buried Pierre, born at Montreuil, a pattern of character and in his life a Doctor of Masons. May the King of Heaven lead him to the skies: he died in the year of Christ, the thousandth, two hundredth, with twelve and fifty four."

The change in the status of the architect had been noticed by the middle of the thirteenth century. The very high fees and honors that the architect-engineers received, and sometimes bestowed upon themselves, provoked jealousy and criticism. Nicolas de Biard, a Dominican preacher, spoke out against them:

> The master masons, holding measuring rod and gloves in their hands, say to others: "Cut here," and they do not work; nevertheless they receive the greater fees, as do many modern churchmen. Some work with words only. Observe: in these large buildings there is wont to be one chief master who orders matters only by word, rarely or never putting his hand to the task, but nevertheless receiving higher wages than the others. So there are many in the church who have rich benefices, and God knows how much they do; they work with the tongue alone, saying "This should you do" and they themselves do nothing.[4]

This passage also reveals the feeling of a university-trained man—a man trained in the liberal arts—who resents a manual worker, a technician—a man trained in the mechanical arts. He resents the man's acting as an intellectual, working "by words only." When *Doctor Lathomorum* was inscribed on his tomb, Pierre de Montreuil was given intellectual status by the award of this university "degree" to which he was not entitled.

What were these great men of the time like? Fortunately, there is one about whom we know a great deal. Villard de Honnecourt was born at the turn of the thirteenth century and was active professionally between 1225 and 1250. He came from the little village of Honnecourt near Cambrai, in Picardy in the north of France. Villard's fame is due to the chance survival of his sketchbook, just as the fame of Vitruvius, the Roman architect of the time of Augustus, rests on his *Ten Books on Architecture*. Vitruvius's writings must have been known to Villard, and the two men have much in common. Villard's sketchbook is in the Bibliothèque Nationale in Paris and is composed of thirty-three parchment leaves inscribed both recto and verso. Originally there were more parchment leaves, but unfortunately they were "borrowed"— possibly by Villard's colleagues, pupils, or later followers— and never returned.

When only a boy, Villard was sent to work on the building site of the Cistercian monastery of Vaucelles—now completely destroyed—in the Escaut valley, only a two-hour walk from his native village. There he drew the ground plan of the choir of the church, a most unusual plan for a Cistercian church. When archaeological excavations were made, it was discovered that Villard's plan was very precise. It may have been the first drawing of his sketchbook.

From Vaucelles he moved to Cambrai, only half a day's walk away and one of the important textile cities of the north of France. There he worked in the lodge of the cathedral, destroyed at the end of the eighteenth century, and copied into his sketchbook, from the architectural drawings lying around in the tracing house, "the plan of the apse and the choir of our Lady of Cambrai as it is now, rising from the ground."[5] He also drew "the inner and outer elevations, as well as the design of the chapels, the walls and the flying buttresses."[6] Though these last drawings are on some of the "borrowed" parchments, we do know what the elevations of the chapel should have looked like, because when Villard went to Reims, a cathedral he greatly admired, he drew "the elevation of the chapels of the Church of Rheims from the outside" and added "if those at Cambrai are done properly they will look like this."[7]

These elevations were the work of Jean d'Orbais, whose portrait Villard would not have seen, as it was incised in the labyrinth only at the end of the century. Perhaps Villard discussed the elevations and plans of Cambrai with Jean Le Loup, who was in charge of the Reims building site at the time of his visit. Under a drawing of a church with a double ambulatory, Villard noted that he had discussed the plan with an architect named Pierre de Corbie. It seems to have been customary for architects to work together.

Elsewhere in his sketchbook Villard drew a church with a double row of the cathedral's flying buttresses. Flying buttresses were one of the great "inventions" of the medieval architect-enginer. They were an ingenious and revolutionary building technique, conceived to help solve the technical problems created by the desire to give maximum light to the churches while raising the vaults higher and higher. These technical solutions must have amazed men of the time as they still amaze visitors today.

Gothic churches were full of "inventions." Another example can be found in the complex systems of passageways—horizontal and vertical—that were built into the fabric of great cathedrals. Early Romanesque churches had no such system. At Beauvais there were passageways at no less than five levels, and at Chartres there were no less than nine stair-

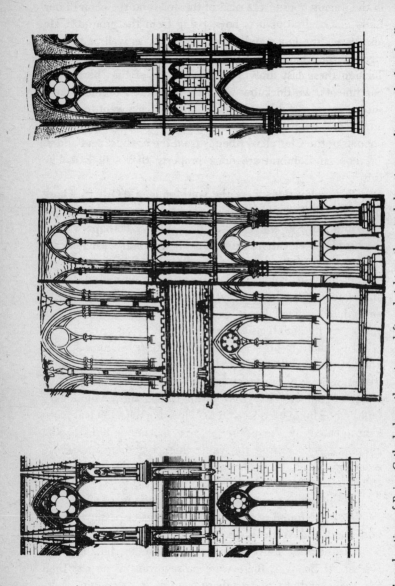

Two elevations of Reims Cathedral: on the extreme left and right are the actual elevations, as they were built and still exist today, and in the center are the respective "modernized" versions by Villard de Honnecourt. Courtesy Hans Hahnloser.

cases or vices. The schematic diagram reproduced is that of a great church with passageways at three levels interconnected with spiral stairs. The reasons for building these passageways inside and outside the walls were several. In case of fire it was easy and quick to reach the place where flames had broken out, and the surveillance and maintenance of the roof coverings and of the stained glass windows were facilitated. The vices, built inside the masonry and very economically made in that they were practically prefabricated, played a further role which is often not noted. As the building went up, the vices followed, and therefore could be used to bring men and materials up the stairs to the level reached by the walls. These vices allowed the builders the economy of not erecting extensive scaffolding inside and outside the building. "They, as much as any factor, made possible the freeing of the ground floor . . . for they incorporated stable and enclosed means of access, without temporary ladders or stagings, to the higher portions of the work where alone the localized scaffolding occurred."[8]

Villard was well aware of the enormous importance of the passageways. Having drawn in his sketchbook two further elevations of Reims, he appended two long texts in which he described where the passageways were, to "allow circulation in case of fire."

> Consider well these elevations. Before the roof of the side-aisles there must be a passageway over the entablature and there must be another at the top in front of the windows, with low crenelations, as you see in the picture before you. On the tops of the pillars, there should be angels, and, in front, flying buttresses. Before the great roof, there must also be passageways and crenelated entablature, to allow circulation in case of fire. And on the entablature there must be gutters to carry off the water. I say the same for the chapels.[9]

123

While sometimes Villard chose to draw buildings or parts of buildings primarily for technical reasons, he would also draw them for aesthetic reasons, because he liked them. In Reims, for example, he drew a bay of the nave because "I liked it." In the same text he informs us that he has "been invited to go to Hungary," a major event in his life: "This is one of the windows of Rheims, in the area of the nave, as it stands between two pillars. I had been invited to go to Hungary when I drew this; which is why I liked it all the more."[10]

What is remarkable in this drawing, made around the year 1230, is that Villard did not copy the Reims window exactly. Consciously or unconsciously, he "modernized" the window, which had been designed around 1211. He drew it as it would have been built twenty years later.

He modernized Laon as well. He drew one of the towers of the cathedral, for which he confessed his proud admiration. Oxen peer out from the sides, and the spot from which tourists today generally photograph or film the same view, a window in the adjacent tower, is probably the very spot from which Villard de Honnecourt made his drawing over seven hundred years ago. In Chartres he altered the west stained glass rose window in the same spirit and while he was in the cathedral he drew the labyrinth which is still inlaid in the nave, but he reversed it. Unfortunately, the plaque, which might have given us the names of the architects, has disappeared, and Villard's drawing does not include any inscription.

He visited Lausanne when he was on his way to Hungary. It was, of course, a journey he was never to forget, and of which he was very proud. To make sure that no one consulting his sketchbook would forget it either, he mentions his sojourn in this faraway land in various passages. It was not unusual for the French architect-engineers of the time to be sent to distant and what we would now call "underdeveloped" countries—that is, underdeveloped when compared to the France of the thirteenth century, with its relatively advanced

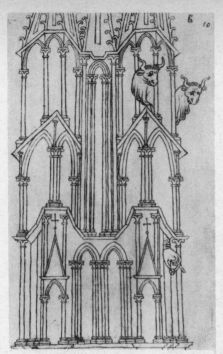

The Tower of Laon, as seen by Villard (*left*) and as it is today (*right*).
Courtesy Hans Hahnloser.

technology (much as American engineers have been called on
in the twentieth century to build bridges, steel mills, or hydro-
electric plants in various countries considered underdeveloped
when compared to the United States). Etienne de Bonneuil,
for example, signed a contract on August 30, 1287, in front of
the provost of Paris to go to the distant and then underdeveloped country of Sweden:

> We—Renaut le Cras, Provost of Paris—make known that
> before us appeared Etienne de Bonneuil, to be master
> mason and master of the church of Uppsala in Sweden,
> proposing to go to said country as he had agreed upon.
> And he acknowledged having rightfully received and

125

obtained payment of forty Paris livres from the hands of Messrs Olivier and Charles, scholars and clercs at Paris, for the purpose of taking with him at the expense of the said church four mates and four yeomen (*bachelers*), seeing that this would be to the advantage of said church for the cutting and carving of stone there. For this sum he promised to take said workmen to said land and to pay their expenses. . . . And should it happen that said Etienne de Bonneuil or the mates whom he has consented to take with him to the land of Sweden should perish on the sea on their way, owing to storms or in some other manner, he and his companions and their heirs shall be clear and absolved of the entire above mentioned sum of money.[11]

When Villard heard that he had been invited to work in Hungary, he must have started adding drawings to his sketchbook so that he would have more models to draw upon for his work there. He may have been invited by the Cistercians, who were then expanding in Hungary, or possibly through the connection with his home town of Elizabeth of Hungary, sister of the reigning monarch, who had made a personal endowment to the Cathedral of Cambrai shortly before her death in 1231. She was canonized in 1235, and Villard may possibly have built the church dedicated to her at Košice now in Czechoslovakia.

Villard reached Hungary around 1235. The pages relating to his stay there have, all but one, been lost. The only drawing relating to Hungary is of little interest, a church pavement. He wrote: "Once when I was in Hungary, where I remained for a long time, I saw the paving of a church with this design."[12]

He returned to France sometime around the year 1240, before the Tartar invasion of 1241, and went home to Picardy where he is presumed to have worked on the Collegiate Church of Saint-Quentin. There he converted the sketchbook that he had made for his own personal use into one available to his pupils and colleagues. He added explanatory notes alongside some of his sketches and wrote a few lines introducing himself and explaining what was to be found in his book:

> Villard de Honnecourt greets you and begs all who will use the devices found in this book to pray for his soul and remember him. For in this book will be found sound advice on the virtues of masonry and the uses of carpentry. You will also find strong help in drawing figures according to the lessons taught by the art of geometry.[13]

We know that following his death at least two successive generations studied his sketchbook, for modern scholars have recognized that other drawings were added later in the thirteenth century. They are anonymous and are attributed now to Magister I and II.

None of the drawings relating to the mechanical devices is by either Magister I or II. They are the work of Villard alone. The most remarkable in this series is that relating to a perpetual-motion mechanism. It reflects the general passionate interest of medieval men in natural sources of energy. They were power-conscious to the point of fantasy, always looking for sources of power beyond hydraulic, wind, and tidal energy. "They were coming to think of the cosmos as a vast reservoir of energies to be tapped and used according to human intentions . . . without such fantasy, such soaring imagination, the power technology of the Western world would not have been developed."[14]

It does not really matter that the perpetual-motion devices conceived in the thirteenth century could not work. We know now that it is impossible to create such a device. What is important is that in the thirteenth century there were engineers and scientists endeavoring to build perpetual-motion machines for practical purposes. Villard de Honnecourt was not alone for, as he writes: "Often have experts striven to make

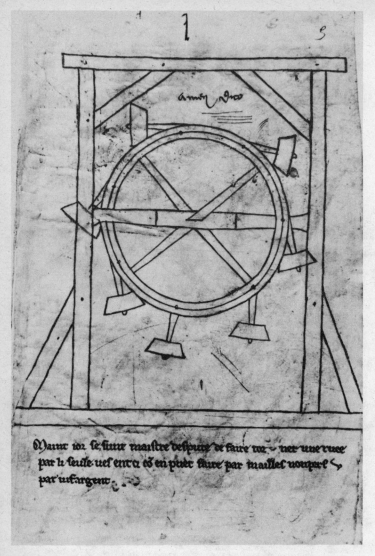

Villard's perpetual motion wheel. Courtesy Bibliothèque Nationale, Paris.

a wheel turn of its own accord. Here is a way to do it with an uneven number of mallets and with quicksilver,"[15] and later in the century, in 1269, Peter of Maricourt, one of the great scientists of his age, confirms in his epoch-making book on magnetism the general interest of men of the time in this problem. He wrote: "I have seen many men floundering exhausted in their repeated efforts to invent such a wheel."[16]

Villard hoped that with mallets or bags filled with mercury assembled so as to swing freely "there will always be four on the downward side of the wheel and only three on the upward side; thus the mallet or bag will always fall over to the left as it reaches the top, ad infinitum."[17] But Villard's hopes were unfounded. The idea of perpetual motion had originated, it seems, in India in the twelfth century, in keeping with traditional Indian cyclical philosophy. The Hindu astronomer and mathematician Bhaskara in about 1159 described two *perpetuum* wheels, one made of light wood with hollow rods half filled with mercury or quicksilver, the other with the rim of a wheel scooped out and filled half with water and half with mercury. The Arabs picked up the idea, and an Arabic treatise is known to have contained six gravitational perpetua mobilia; one is Bhaskara's wheel with the hollow rods and two others are Villard de Honnecourt's wheels of pivoted hammers and of pivoted quicksilver.

It is probably through the Islamic world that western Europe got involved in perpetual motion, but with the difference that Europe, given its interest in mechanization, would try to use perpetual motion as a practical source of energy. For example, the relatively widespread use of the compass in the thirteenth century led certain scientists to wonder if magnetism could not be used like gravity to produce a perpetuum mobile. Peter of Maricourt came up with two devices. The first was a magnetic perpetual-motion machine, which he presented in a diagram, and the second he described as:

A globular lodestone which, if it were mounted without friction parallel to the celestial axis, would rotate once a day. Properly inscribed with a map of the heavens, it would serve as an automatic armillary sphere for astronomical observations and as a perfect clock, enabling one to dispense with all chronometers.[18]

Villard's wide interest in an unlimited source of energy and in various types of machines makes him an archetypal engineer of the medieval industrial revolution. On the back of one of his sketchbook parchments he represented no less than five mechanisms, four of which have real technological interest. The fifth drawing is a crossbow fitted with a sort of pinhole sight under which Villard wrote: "How to make a crossbow which never misses."[19] The drawings are sometimes difficult to interpret, since Villard neglected to draw in certain details of their mechanisms.

In the top left-hand corner, Villard drew a waterpowered saw, the first ever to be represented. Of it he wrote: "How to make a saw operate itself."[20] This has been described as the "first industrial automatic power-machine to involve two motions: in addition to the conversion of the wheel's rotary motion into the reciprocating motion of sawing, there is an automatic feed keeping the log pressed against the saw."[21] Beneath the water-driven saw is what is thought to be the earliest representation of clockwork. The mechanism is linked by a spindle to the statue of an angel placed on the roof of a great church, above the apse—there was such an angel over the east end of Chartres Cathedral before the fire of 1836—to make it rotate slowly, following the path of the sun in the sky. Villard wrote: "How to make an angel keep pointing his finger towards the sun."[22]

The drawing represents a vertical axis or spindle supported by a frame which also carries a horizontal axis,

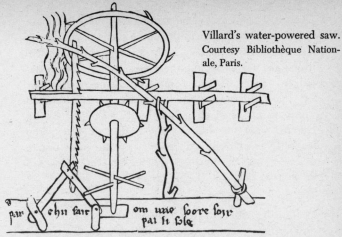

Villard's water-powered saw.
Courtesy Bibliothèque Nationale, Paris.

par celui fait om une poore lon
pai li sole

upon which is a wheel. A cord has a weight suspended from it and is passed over a guide pulley, thence horizontally to the vertical shaft about which it is coiled twice; thence it passes to the horizontal shaft, round which it is coiled three times and is finally carried over another guide-pulley and its end hanging vertically down carries a second weight apparently less than the first. The descent of the heavier weight will cause the vertical spindle and the horizontal axis to revolve, so as to cause the statue to perform a single revolution in twenty-four hours.[23]

Before the end of the century, the medieval engineer was to perfect this mechanical escapement and build the weight-driven mechanical clock that would play such a decisive role in Western civilization.

In the bottom left-hand corner is an eagle stuffed with ropes and pulleys. Villard wrote beside this drawing: "How to make the eagle face the Deacon while the Gospel is read."[24] This is a gadget. Villard seems to have adored gadgets. On another page he depicted two others: a hand warmer, which he suggests for a bishop to use at High Mass, and a Tantalus cup.

If you wish to make a hand warmer, you must first make a kind of brass apple with two fitting halves. Inside this brass apple, there must be six brass rings, each with two pivots, and in the middle there must be a little brazier with two pivots. The pivots must be alternated in such a way that the brazier always remains upright, for each ring bears the pivot of the others. If you follow the instructions and the drawing, the coals will never drop out, no matter which way the brazier is turned. A bishop may freely use this device at High Mass; his hands will not get cold as long as the fire lasts.[25]

The system described in detail by Villard was later adapted to keep mariners' compasses level and barometers vertical.

The second gadget is the well-known Tantalus cup.

It consists of a bird which sits on top of a tower in the middle of a wine-cup, and when wine is poured it seems to drink it up. The mechanism is explained in the accompanying (modern) drawing. The cup is hollow at the base, and has a tube rising inside the tower to a point just below the rim of the cup. The bottom of the tower is perforated to allow wine to flow into it. When the level of the liquid rises in the cup it overflows inside the tower (unseen) into the hollow base. Air is forced up into the bird and out through its beak, producing a bubbling sound as if it were drinking. Villard's drawing is misleading since it shows the bird's beak considerably higher than the rim of the cup.[26]

In fact, this gadget is of considerable antiquity. It is found in the twelfth problem of the *Pneumatics* of Hero of Alexandria, who was living in the first century A.D. and whose work is known to have been translated into Arabic and then into Latin. The fact that Villard's explanation of the mechanism is incomplete and the drawing inexact shows that he never had a

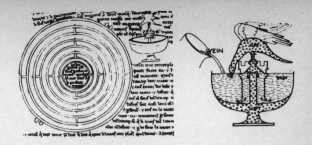

Top right: A Tantalus cup, drawn from an Alexandrian model, and immediately to its left Villard's incorrect drawing of the gadget. *Below:* Medieval hand warmer like the one drawn and described by Villard (see also sketch *above left*). Courtesy Hans Hahnloser.

Tantalus cup in his hands, but copied it, incorrectly, from one of the Latin manuscripts of Hero of Alexandria.

Villard was also, like many architect-engineers of his time, a military engineer capable of building machines of war. He devoted two pages of his sketchbook to details of a powerful catapult. One page is unfortunately missing, but the remaining parchment page was covered by Villard with his drawing. The caption reads:

> If you wish to build that strong engine called the catapult, pay close attention. Here is the base as it rests on the ground. In front are the two windlasses and the double rope by which the pole is hauled down, as you may see on the other page. The weight which must be hauled back is very great, for the counterpoise is very heavy, being

133

a hopper full of earth. This is fully two fathoms long, eight feet wide and twelve feet deep. Remember that before the bolt is discharged, it must rest on the front stanchion.[27]

Villard may also have been a bridge builder, for he drew a very complex mechanism for sawing timber under water. "By this means," he wrote, "one can cut off the tops of piles under water so as to set a pier on them."[28]

Classical mechanical treatises were quite freely available in the Middle Ages. We know of seven tenth-century manuscripts of Vegetius's military treatise which had been written in the fourth century A.D., nineteen from the twelfth and thirteenth centuries, and no less than one hundred from the fourteenth and fifteenth centuries. Vitruvius's famous book, which contains such a wealth of information on Roman technology, was also available in many cultural centers of western Europe and was copied over and over. We still possess fifty-five Vitruvius manuscripts ranging from the tenth to the fifteenth centuries.

The rediscovery of a Vitruvius manuscript in 1414 by the humanist Poggio in the monastery of Saint Gall led the Renaissance to believe that the Middle Ages had been unaware of the great Roman architect. In turn, the writings of Renaissance scholars led most of posterity generally to believe that they alone had rediscovered the classical world, and that the Middle Ages had been ignorant of Roman culture. Though medievalists have been fighting against this unfounded legend, most people are still influenced by the Renaissance humanists.

Villard's sketchbook is only one of the documents that prove how actively Rome was still present in the Middle Ages. A substantial number of his drawings were inspired by Roman statues or monuments. On one page he drew two foliate heads of bearded men, clearly classical figures, and on another, two foliate heads and two male nudes, one with a chlamys around

his shoulders and the other with a Phrygian cap. On one remarkable page he drew an enigmatic, classically inspired nude
holding a vase of flowers. And on another he copied a Roman
monument above which he wrote: "I once saw the sepulchre
of a Saracen which looked like this."[29] The drawing takes up
a whole page of the sketchbook.

Vitruvius must have had some influence on the choice
and diversity of the subjects treated in Villard's sketchbook.
Like the other architects of the Roman world, Vitruvius was a
man of the mechanical arts—that is to say, a man who probably had no formal education, and who may have had to work
on technical problems while still a young man in order
to earn his living. He resented what he saw as the lack of
esteem architects enjoyed, as opposed to "educated" Romans,
those who had been fortunate enough to study what were
later known as the liberal arts. He recommended that architects, in order to attain this social and intellectual consideration, should be interested in a multitude of subjects seemingly
unrelated to architecture.

> Let them be educated, skilful with the pencil, instructed
> in geometry, know much history, have followed the phi-
> losophers with attention, understand music, have some
> knowledge of medicine, know the opinions of the jurists
> and be acquainted with astronomy and the theory of the
> heavens.[30]

Although Vitruvius did not himself quite reach the standard he recommended—even his Latin was not of the highest
quality—he did cover quite a wide range of subjects, for which
posterity has been indebted to him. Without his intellectual
ambition we would be unaware of much Hellenistic and
Roman technology. Even the subtitles of his Book X must
have made interesting reading for a medieval architect and
engineer like Villard de Honnecourt: Machines and Imple-

ments; Hoisting Machines; Engine for Raising Water; Water Wheel and Water Mills; The Water Screw; The Pump of Ctesibus; The Water Organ; The Hodometer; Catapults. Rivaling Vitruvius, Villard himself drew hoisting machines, water-driven apparatus, and catapults.

Villard also observed nature and animals—he was to draw some 163 animals. He drew insects (a grasshopper, a dragonfly, a bee), a snail, birds, wild animals (a hare and a wild boar), and domestic animals (a cat, a dog, horses). He also drew animals that he saw in menageries—a bear, lion cubs, a lion. For a while he became interested in the training of lions. He drew a lion tamer, who with two dogs on a lead faces Leo the lion, and he described a very "unusual" way of training these lions.

> I want to describe how a lion is trained. The lion's trainer has two dogs. Whenever he wishes the lion to obey his command and the lion growls, he beats his dogs. This puzzles the lion so much that, when he sees the dogs beaten, his own spirits are dampened and he does what he is ordered. If he is angry, there is no use trying for he will do nothing either with good or bad treatment. . . .[31]

Villard's interest in nature extended to medicinal recipes, possibly inspired by Vitruvius's writing: "The architect should also have a knowledge of the study of medicine. . . ." One of Villard's recipes—for curing wounds—is particularly interesting in view of the fact that one of its ingredients is hempseed, familiar today as *Cannabis Sativa*. It is for this reason worth quoting it in full:

> Remember well what I have to tell you. Take the leaves of red colewort and of avens. Take also an herb called tansy and some hempseed. Crush these four herbs together in equal quantities. Take of madder twice as much

as each of the other and crush it. Then put these five herbs in a pot, infusing them in white wine the best you can procure and taking care that the mixture is not too thick to drink. Do not drink too much at a time, an eggshell will contain enough for a dose, provide it be full. It will cure any wound that you may have. Clean your wound with a little tow [tow is the residue of the stalks of hemp], put upon it a leaf of the red colewort and drink the potion morning and night, twice a day. It is best prepared with a new sweet wine, if it be of good quality. It will ferment with the herbs. If your infusion be made with old wine, leave it two days before you drink it.[32]

It is also quite possible that Vitruvius's chapter I of Book III on symmetry and proportion led Villard to superimpose geometrical shapes on men and animals. These diagrammatic figures, the most frequently reproduced of Villard's drawings, have provoked certain modern art historians to label Villard de Honnecourt as the forerunner of cubism (which certainly he was not). On the top row of the page devoted to these exercises, he has superimposed a square on a man's face. The face is divided into three equal lengths, exactly the proportions Vitruvius recommends:

If we take the height of the face itself, the distance from the bottom of the chin to the under side of the nostrils is one third of it; the nose from the under side of the nostrils to a line between the eyebrows is the same; from there to the lowest roots of the hair is also a third comprising the forehead.[33]

On the same page he has drawn a castellated tower and wall, the head of a horse, four other human heads, a greyhound, an extended left hand, a grazing sheep, a spread eagle, and two intersecting ostriches. Clearly, he used geometrical forms in different ways. First he superimposed geometric shapes such

"Diagrammatic figures" by Villard. Courtesy Bibliothèque Nationale, Paris.

as the square, the rectangle, and the triangle on the head of a horse and on that of a man; then he drew a pentagram on the face of a bearded man in the top right-hand corner of the page, and a triangle on the face of a bearded man on the middle of the left-hand side. Villard wanted to show that one can use the same figure for two dissimilar heads, and two quite dissimilar geometrical figures for two almost similar heads. It was believed for many years that this method provided the beginner with easy proportions for sketches. But more recently scholars have shown that "this method of using geometrical forms is chiefly for the purpose of transferring small drawings from the parchment to the sculptor's stone block, the mural painter's wall, or the glass designer's table."[34] In other words, he used geometrical overlays—such as a network of squares on a man's face—as a means of reproducing a drawing to any desired scale. At the foot of one page the following text was written: "Here begins the method of drawing as taught by the art of geometry, to facilitate working."[35] On another page Villard drew four masons revolving in a holy cross, three fishes with one head, a helmeted head, a squared face, four workmen in isometric elevation, and the head of a wild boar in profile. Villard wrote: "On these four pages are figures of the art of geometry, but to understand them one must be careful to learn the particular use of each."[36]

Twice on the four pages of the sketchbook devoted to these diagrammatic figures, Villard used the word "geometry." Another page was inscribed "All these devices were extracted from geometry"[37] and the two following pages (possibly filled in by Magister II) are devoted to a series of diagrams representing various geometrical devices related to construction for stone cutting, mensuration, and carpentry. These seem to have been copied from a handbook of practical geometry, of a type that circulated quite freely in the thirteenth century. The captions in the top row read from left to right: "How to measure the diameter of a column, only part of which is

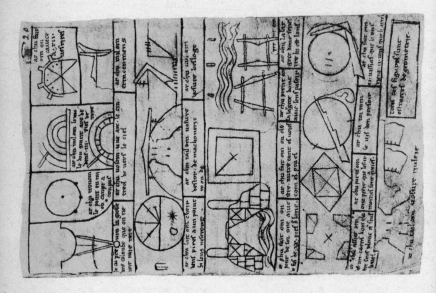

"Practical geometry" by Villard. *Top row:* How to measure the diameter of a column only part of which is visible; how to find the midpoint of a drawn circle; how to cut the mold of a three-foot arch; how to arch a vault with an outer covering; how to make an apse with twelve windows; how to cut the springing stone of an arch. *Second row:* How to bring together two stones if they are not too far apart; how to cut a voussoir for a round building; how to cut an oblique voussoir. *Third row:* How to make a bridge over water, with twenty-foot timbers; how to lay out a cloister with its galleries and courtyard; how to measure the width of a watercourse without crossing it; how to measure the width of a distant window. *Fourth row:* How to place the four cornerstones of a cloister without plumb line or level; how to divide a stone so that each of its halves is square; how to shape the screw of a press; how to make two vessels so that one holds more than the other. *Bottom row:* How to cut a regular voussoir. Courtesy Bibliothèque Nationale, Paris.

visible—How to find the mid-point of a drawn circle—How to cut the mould of a three foot arch"; in the third row: "How to make a bridge over water with twenty foot timbers [the bridge mentioned in chapter 4]—How to lay out a cloister with its galleries and courtyard—How to measure the width of a water course without crossing it—How to measure the width of a distant window"; in the fourth row: "How to place the four corner stones of a cloister without plumb line or level—How to divide a stone so that each half of its halves is square," etc.[38]

There are two drawings on this page that at first do not seem any more remarkable than the twenty or so others—the two squares in the third and fourth rows—but in point of fact they are related to an artful method of building—doubling a square and taking the elevation from a plan—which was to be one of the famous secrets of fifteenth-century masons.

In 1459, the master masons from such cities as Strasbourg, Vienna, and Salzburg met to codify their statutes. They laid down, among other decisions, that "No worker, no master, no wage earner, will divulge to anyone who is not of our guild and who has never worked as a mason, how to take the elevation from a plan."[39] The secret was not published until 1486, when the German architect Mathias Roriczer came out with a book *On the Ordination of Pinnacles* with drawings astonishingly similar to those in Villard's sketchbook.

But what was meant to be a secret in the fifteenth century was certainly no secret in the thirteenth century. The amazing thing about this doubling of squares is that it is to be found in Vitruvius where Villard de Honnecourt, Magister II, and others must have read it; and Vitruvius tells us that he learned it from Plato, who gave the solution in his *Meno*, in a dialogue between Socrates and a slave. Vitruvius wrote: "In this way Plato demonstrated the doubling by means of lines."[40]

Villard de Honnecourt's sketchbook is astonishingly similar to Leonardo's famous notebooks. This is by no means fortuitous. Both men, though separated by 250 years and living in two different historical periods, the Middle Ages and the Renaissance, received roughly the same education, that of the mechanical arts. Both men belonged to a tradition where notebooks such as theirs were common and circulated quite freely. No less than 150 manuscripts of this type, ranging from the end of the fourteenth century to the very first years of the sixteenth century, have been recorded. If Leonardo never had the opportunity of consulting Villard's sketchbook, we know that he consulted many manuscripts of engineers of the fourteenth and fifteenth centuries. In fact, a French scholar has recently shown that a great many of the inventions attributed to Leonardo da Vinci are to be found in one form or another in the manuscripts of engineers such as Konrad Kyeser (born in 1366), Roberto Valturio (born in 1413), and Francesco di Giorgio (born in 1439). Leonardo even annotated one of Francesco di Giorgio's manuscripts. Like Villard, Leonardo of course knew Vitruvius; in fact, he had a copy of his treatise in his library.

But while Villard accepted his status as a man of the mechanical arts, Leonardo repudiated it in dramatic fashion. In all the books that have been written about Leonardo, including Freud's psychoanalysis of some of his paintings, one salient fact has not been stressed sufficiently: Leonardo's greatest problems were caused by the contempt in which he was held by the humanists. Having lacked the opportunity of attending a university to study the liberal arts, he had learned no Greek and very little Latin. This was to prove a major stumbling block in his life. The Renaissance humanists, who were his contemporaries, glorified the great culture of classical antiquity, but to him that culture was largely a closed book. He was probably never truly accepted in a humanist milieu, where discussions would often be carried on in Latin. Certainly his name is never associated with the famous Neoplatonist circle of his home town, Florence—with Lorenzo Il Magnifico and the philosophers Ficino, Landino, Poliziano, and Pico della Mirandola. Thus, time and time again in his writings Leonardo returns to the scorn of the humanists: "Because I am not a literary man some presumptuous persons will think that they may reasonably blame me by alleging that I am an unlettered man. Foolish men! . . . They will say that because I have no letters I cannot express well what I want to treat of."[41] He questions the right of these literati to judge him: "They go about puffed up and pompous, dressed and decorated with the fruits not of their own labours but those of others, And they will not allow me my own. And if they despise me, an inventor, how much more could they—who are not inventors but trumpeters and declaimers of the works of others—be blamed."[42]

We have in these passages—and in others where Leonardo is outraged because the intellectuals consider him merely a manual worker, a technician—remarkable proof of the gulf that has always existed, wider at some times than at others, between the literary intellectual and the technologist, between what C. P. Snow, that rare combination of both types, has appropriately called the Two Cultures.

> Two groups comparable in intelligence, identical in race, not grossly different in social origin, earning about the same incomes, who do not communicate at all, and have so little in common that instead of going from Burlington House or South Kensington [London's shrines to science] to Chelsea [her home of the arts] one might have crossed an ocean . . . because after a few thousand Atlantic miles one found Greenwich Village talking precisely the same language as Chelsea and both having about as much com-

munication with M.I.T. as though the scientists spoke nothing but Tibetan.[43]

Our own Western society, with its present hostility to technology and science, has failed to solve this major human problem. In the Communist world the Soviet Union has tried to bridge the gap but has failed hopelessly. Only China still seems to have a chance. By systematically sending all candidates for university studies onto the land or into industry, China may at last produce a new, unified type of man. But how much time will the experiment be given?

The classical world never really tried to create such a man. Medieval Christianity did at least make the attempt. We see it in Villard, and in at least two of his thirteenth-century contemporaries: Peter of Maricourt and Roger Bacon. Maricourt's attempt fell far short, but Bacon, a true man of the liberal arts, came close to bridging the gap. He drew up a plan for a vast educational reform of Christianity based on the importance of experimental science, mathematics, and language. His ideas, however, were too revolutionary for the authorities, and in about 1277 his movements seem to have been restricted. But not before he had written numerous books, works that show both a university training and a knowledge of the mechanical arts from Greek, Roman, and Arabic times. In particular, there is a famous passage which reads like the letter Leonardo wrote to the Duke of Milan to offer him his services.

Machines of navigation can be constructed, without rowers, as great ships for river or ocean, which are borne under the guidance of one man at a greater speed than if they were full of men. Also a chariot can be constructed, that will move with incalculable speed without any draught animal. . . . Also flying machines may be constructed so that a man may sit in the midst of the machine

The Almighty as an architect-engineer. Courtesy Austrian National Library, Vienna.

turning a certain instrument, by means of which wings artificially constructed would beat the air after the manner of a bird flying. Also a machine of small size may be made for raising and lowering weights of almost infinite amounts—a machine of the utmost utility. . . . Machines may also be made for going in sea or river down to the bed without bodily danger . . . and there are countless other things that can be constructed, such as bridges over rivers without pillars or any such supports. . . .[44]

Leonardo must have read this text on flying machines for Bacon is specifically referred to in one of Leonardo's notebooks, now in the British Museum—and Bacon may have prompted him to draw such a machine.

The greatest homage the Middle Ages offered the architect-engineer was to represent the Almighty, in thirteenth- and fourteenth-century miniatures, as an architect-engineer Himself, measuring the universe with a large compass. It is as if today, in a film on the Almighty, God were to be represented programming a computer.

7

The Mechanical Clock:
The Key Machine

The men of the Middle Ages were so mechanically minded they could believe that angels were in charge of the mechanisms of the universe: a fourteenth-century Provençal manuscript depicts two winged angels operating the revolving machine of the sky.

The spirit of inventiveness that accompanied this outlook was only possible because medieval society believed in progress, a concept unknown to the classical world. Medieval men refused to be tied down by tradition. As Gilbert de Tournai wrote: "Never will we find truth if we content ourselves with what is already known. . . . Those things that have been written before us are not laws but guides. The truth is open to all, for it is not yet totally possessed."[1] And Bernard, master of the episcopal school at Chartres from 1114 to 1119, said: "We are as dwarfs mounted on the shoulders of giants,

"Two winged angels operating the revolving mechanisms of the sky."
Courtesy British Museum, London.

so that although we perceive many more things than they, it is not because our vision is more piercing or our stature higher, but because we are carried and elevated higher thanks to their gigantic size."[2]

The attitude exemplified by Gilbert de Tournai and Bernard of Chartres led men to accept inventions as something normal and to assume that new inventions would always be forthcoming. The surgeon Theodoric wrote a treatise in 1267 in which he remarked that for the extraction of arrows "every day a new instrument and a new method is invented."[3] A sermon in 1306 given at Santa Maria Novella in Florence by the Dominican Fra Giordano of Pisa sang the praises of the recent invention of eyeglasses. Fra Giordano said:

> Not all the arts have been found; we shall never see an end of finding them. Every day one could discover a new art. . . . It is not twenty years since there was discovered the art of making spectacles which help one to see well, an art which is one of the best and most necessary in the world. And that is such a short time ago that a new art which never before existed was invented. . . . I myself saw the man who discovered and practised it and I talked ˙with him.[4]

The ambition of inventors was unlimited, their imagination boundless, but of all the extraordinary machines they conceived and sometimes built, one above all symbolizes the inventiveness of the age: the mechanical clock.

Though Lewis Mumford's theory of the origin of the mechanical clock—that it was created in the Benedictine monasteries—is disputed today, his views on the role of the clock in the evolution of Western Europe are still very relevant:

> The clock, not the steam engine, is the key machine of the modern industrial age . . . at the very beginning of modern technics appeared prophetically the accurate automatic machine. . . . In its relationship to determinable quantities of energy, to standardization, to automatic action, and finally to its own special product, accurate timing, the clock has been the foremost machine in modern technics: and at each period it has remained in the lead: it marks a perfection towards which other machines aspire.[5]

Before Giovanni di Dondi built his highly complex mechanical clock in Italy in the fourteenth century, possibly the most complex astronomical clock ever built had been that of Su Sung in China in the eleventh century. Both were in their time and for many centuries the most advanced scientific and engineering machines existing anywhere in the world. Su Sung and Giovanni di Dondi each wrote in minute detail how to build and maintain their wonderful clocks, and the writings of both have survived, although in both cases the machinery was so complicated that later generations found them difficult to repair. For both these inventors of genius we know dates of birth and death, and all the titles and official positions with which they were honored during their lifetimes. In the case of Su Sung, however, posterity was frustrated by governmental policy. Astronomical instruments—and, one presumes, the secrets of their construction—were closely guarded by official Chinese astronomers, because:

> In ancient and medieval China the promulgation of the calendar by the emperor was a right corresponding to the issuing of minted coins with image and superscription in western countries. It had always been one of the most important duties of the ruler of the vast agrarian culture-area of the "black-haired people." Acceptance of the calendar was equivalent to recognition of imperial authority. Owing to this close association between the calendar and State power, any imperial bureaucracy was likely to view with alarm the activities of independent investigators of the stars, or writers about them, since they might secretly be engaged upon calendrical calculations which would be of use to rebels planning to set up a new dynasty.[6]

The Peking imperial court monopoly of astronomical clocks strictly limited the number of scientists and engineers with knowledge in this sphere. When in 1126 the Sung dynasty was

A modern drawing of the astronomical clock tower built by Su Sung and his collaborators at K'ai-feng in Honan province, the capital of the empire in A.D. 1090. The clockwork, driven by a waterwheel and fully enclosed within the tower, rotated an armillary sphere on the top platform and a celestial globe in the upper story; puppet figures meanwhile gave notice of the passing hours and quarters by signals of sight and sound. Courtesy John Christiansen.

chased from Peking by the Chin Tartars and took refuge in the south, they left Su Sung's clock behind and were subsequently unable to duplicate it because of their lack of specialists. Su Sung's son was called in but he, too, was unable to help. Meanwhile, in the north, the Chin Tartars had kept the Peking specialists on hand and so were able to use the clock, as were the Yüan dynasty, who overthrew the Chin Tartars in 1279. But the Ming dynasty, who overthrew the Yüan in 1368, were uninterested in any automata and either destroyed the famous clock or let it fall to pieces. No more is heard of it; its technicians apparently dispersed. Thus in an amazingly short time a great body of scientific and technological knowledge that had been built up for over a millennium was lost so completely that when, in 1600, the Jesuit scholar and scientist Matteo Ricci was invited to Peking and brought with him the most up-to-date European mechanical clocks, he found that "there was extremely little to show that mechanical clocks had ever been known in China . . ." and "there was no one who could explain Chinese mathematics, astronomy or other sciences to the Jesuit missionaries."[7] By an extraordinary coincidence the greatest Chinese astronomical clock had disappeared just four years after the birth of the greatest European astronomical clock.

Giovanni di Dondi's clock, although not the first to do so, used a verge and foliot escapement fitted to a weight-driven mechanism in place of a waterwheel linkwork escapement fitted to a waterpowered mechanism. Earlier medieval engineers, while generally disposed toward hydraulic power, had realized that waterpowered clocks could not progress beyond a certain point—in winter in northern Europe they froze and stopped—and so they had worked toward building a mechanical clock.

The search for a solution to the technical problems got under way in the second half of the thirteenth century. Robert the Englishman wrote in 1271:

Clockmakers are trying to make a wheel which will make one complete revolution for every one of the equinoctial circle, but they cannot quite perfect their work. . . . The method of making such a clock would be this, that a man make a disc of uniform weight in every part so far as could possibly be done. Then a lead weight should be hung from the axis of that wheel, so that it would complete one revolution from sunrise to sunrise, minus as much time as about one degree rises according to an approximately correct estimate.[8]

Only five or six years later, in a book written at the court of Alfonso X of Castile, a weight-driven clock is illustrated with an astrolabe as its dial and with an escapement produced by a revolving drum that leaked mercury. Mercury had taken the place of water, an idea that must have been borrowed from the Hindu astronomer and mathematician Bhaskara's perpetual-motion mercury wheel of about 1150, known in Europe through Arabic treatises. This relatively simple machine has in common with Su Sung's complex mechanism the fact that neither had the function we would normally expect of clocks. They did not primarily tell time, but rather were built to forecast the movements of the sun, the moon, and the planets. Remarkably enough, the time-telling clock which dominates our lives was only a by-product of the astronomical clock.

This is quite apparent in Giovanni di Dondi's masterpiece of 1348–64. His treatise describes how he provided dials for the five then-known planets, the sun, and the moon. But although his clock also had a time-telling mechanism, there was no horary dial. For Dondi that was only an ordinary or "common" clock, and the mechanism of the common clock was in his view already so well known that he did not bother to draw in the details of these train bars, adding that "if the student of the ms. cannot complete this clock for himself he is wasting his time in studying the ms. further."[9] This is very unfortunate, for we would otherwise have had detailed four-teenth-century drawings relating to the mechanisms of two inventions of the first importance, the weight-driven mechan-ism and the mechanical escapement mechanism.

That weight-driven clocks with a mechanical escapement system should have been so common in the middle of the fourteenth century suggests that the mechanism must have been invented many decades previously. Modern horologists have tended to consider, in the absence of any written or visual document, that the mechanical clock was created some-time in the early part of the fourteenth century, but recently an English horologist, Alan Lloyd—who succeeded in recon-structing a working model of Dondi's astrarium, later pur-chased by the Smithsonian Institution in Washington*— suggested that the mechanical clock was invented sometime between 1277 and 1300, which seems a reasonable hypothesis. Robert the Englishman's text of 1271 shows that clockmakers were then making great efforts to solve the mechanical prob-lems involved. It may well be that Bartholomew the Orologist of Saint Paul's Cathedral, mentioned in 1286, was responsible for a mechanical clock, and that the great new Canterbury clock of 1292 was of the same type, as well as the first public clock built in Paris in 1300 by Pierre Pipelart (which cost £6).

The first literary reference to what undoubtedly seems a mechanical clock is a famous passage of Dante's *Paradiso*, Canto X, written between 1316 and 1321:

> As clock, that calleth up the spouse of God
> To win her Bridegroom's love at matin's hour,
> Each part of other fitly drawn and urged,
> Sends out a tinkling sound, of note so sweet,
> Affection springs in well-disposed breast;
> Thus saw I move the glorious wheel; thus heard

* A second replica is now in the London Science Museum.

*Voice answering voice, so musical and soft,
It can be known but where day endless shines.*[10]

In an illuminated manuscript of the second half of the fourteenth century there is a schematic representation of the first documented astronomical clock, and standing beside and pointing to it is the inventor, the Abbot of Saint Albans, Richard of Wallingford. This remarkable and controversial man is the same Abbot Richard who in 1331 took the unprecedented step of seizing the millstones of the townsmen of Saint Albans and paving his courtyard with them.

Though Richard was orphaned at the age of ten, his father had been a smith, and it was perhaps in his father's forge that he acquired an interest in mechanical inventions, for smiths were naturally called upon to make clocks, or any mechanical device. The Prior of Wallingford took care of the young orphan and eventually sent him to study at Oxford. He then entered the Abbey of Saint Albans and was elected Abbot in 1326. His passion for inventions later brought him into conflict with some of his own monks and earned him a rebuke from King Edward III.

Among his achievements were the introduction of new trigonometrical methods, the creation of a very complex and extremely costly astronomical clock, and the invention of two astronomical instruments—one which he called the *Albion*, and the other a *Rectangulus*. The *Albion* was a mechanical contrivance for finding the positions of the planets, basically an equatorium. It was one of the most influential astronomical computing devices of the Middle Ages, and its fame is demonstrated by the fact that there are thirty complete texts or fragments of Richard's treatise still extant. The *Rectangulus*

consisted of four brass rules hinged to one another and mounted by a swivel joint on the top of a pillar. The lowest rule (I) was engraved with a scale. The uppermost rule (IV) was provided with pin-hole sights and a plumb-line which would have reached the divided scale on rule I. Rules II and III were hinged in the manner shown in the figure and could be inclined to make any desired angle with rule I, which must have remained in a horizontal plane.[11]

Richard of Wallingford's treatise is sufficiently detailed for us to reconstruct his *Rectangulus* six hundred years later. He divided his treatise into two parts: the construction and the use of the instrument. Some of the surviving manuscripts have working drawings, and one of them has "a scale divided in sixes, instead of a scale divided in fives, on the lowest rule—the difference between duodecimal and decimal systems had been realised."[12] Thomas of Walsingham, the Saint Albans chronicler, vividly describes the difficulties encountered by the Abbot when building his clock—difficulties that were to be encountered by many later inventors:

He made a noble work, a horologium, in the church, at great cost of money and work; nor did he abandon finishing it because of its disparagement by the brethren, although they, wise in their own eyes, regarded it as the height of foolishness. He had, however, the excuse that he originally intended to construct the horologium at less expense, in view of the great and generally recognised need for repair of the church, but that in his absence and as a result of interference by some brethren and the greed of the workmen it was begun on a costly scale and it would have been unseemly and shameful not to have finished what had been put in hand. Indeed, when on a certain occasion, the very illustrious King Edward the Third came to the monastery in order to pray, and saw so sumptuous a work undertaken while the church was still not rebuilt since the ruin it suffered in Abbot Hugo's time, he discreetly rebuked Abbot Richard in that he neg-

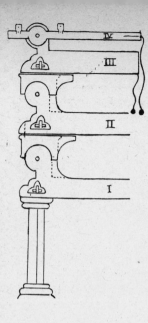

Wallingford's *Rectangulus*

Working drawings for the construction of the *Rectangulus*

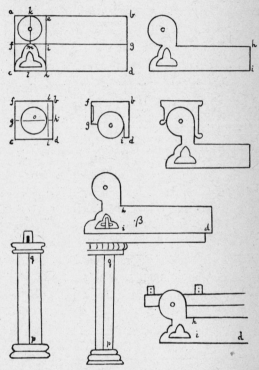

Lowest rule of the *Rectangulus* with scale in sixes.
All courtesy of the President and Fellows of Corpus Christi
College, Oxford.

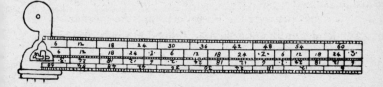

lected the fabric of the church and wasted so much money on a quite unnecessary work, namely the above mentioned horologium. To which reproof the Abbot replied, with due respect, that enough Abbots would succeed him who would find workmen for the fabric of the monastery, but that there would be no successor, after his death, who could finish the work that had been begun. And, indeed, he spoke the truth because in that art nothing of the kind remains, nor was anything similar invented in his lifetime.[13]

The antiquary John Leland, visiting the abbey over two hundred years later, in about 1540, admired the clock, which he believed to be unequaled in all Europe. "One may look," he wrote, "at the course of the sun and moon or the fixed stars or again one may regard the rise and fall of the tide." He also mentioned that Richard of Wallingford had written a book describing its "remarkable mechanism."[14] This book remained lost until 1965, when Dr. J. D. North drew the attention of scholars to a manuscript in the Bodleian Library which he thought might be Richard's own treatise.

The text includes four or five illustrations. Three of these illustrations show trains of gears or other mechanical linkages; one of them is a sectional view through the "dial," the indexes, and the rotating lunar globe of an elaborate astronomical clock. The text describes the representation by wheel work of the motions of various heavenly bodies, including the calculation, with the aid of tables provided, of the number of teeth required on the gear-wheels. It also tells how to make the clock ring a bell.[15]

Astronomical clocks like those of Richard of Wallingford and Giovanni di Dondi again raise the fascinating problem of the relationship between the liberal arts and the mechanical arts. While men in the Middle Ages trained in the liberal arts had no say in mechanisms powered by hydraulic energy, they had a great deal of say in the mechanisms of astronomical clocks. Here was a case where academic science and technology worked hand in hand. This close collaboration between astronomers of the liberal arts and technologists of the mechanical arts is exceptional in history. Not until the second half of the nineteenth century were science and technology to be seen consistently working closely together.

Richard of Wallingford spent over nine years at Oxford studying philosophy, theology, and scientific subjects, and Giovanni di Dondi went to Padua where he studied medicine, astronomy, philosophy, and logic. He lectured on medicine in Florence and on astronomy in Padua. He was a personal friend of Francesco Petrarch, who left him fifty ducats to buy a gold ring to wear in his memory, and who wrote of Dondi: "Master John de Dundis, natural philosopher and easily the leader of astronomers, called 'of the clock' on account of that admirable work of the planetarium which he made, which the uneducated people think is a clock. . . ."[16]

Giovanni di Dondi must have been helped considerably in the building of his astrarium by his father, Jacopo, who like him was a professor of medicine and who also designed an astronomical clock. Born about 1293, Jacopo's first success as an inventor was to extract salt from hot mineral springs near Padua. The results of that invention, however, were not altogether happy, for Jacopo soon had to write "a brief treatise in four chapters to defend against rivals and invidious detractors his recent invention. . . . [he] denies the accusation that his salt in the course of time produces lung complaints because of the sulphur it contains . . . his family have used his salt for more than three years and are in good health."[17] On August 20, 1355, the Prince of Carrara awarded Jacopo di Dondi an exclusive privilege to extract salt from the springs and to sell it freely without taxation.

Jacopo's interest in astronomy led him to correct existing

astronomical tables. Writing in about 1424, Prosdocimo de Baldomandi of Padua stated that "the tables of planetary motion of Jacobus de Dondi of Padua, extracted from the Alfonsine tables, are easier and more convenient to use than the Alfonsine tables and equally well, perhaps better, verified and corrected. . . ."[18]

The astronomical clock that Jacopo is thought to have designed was constructed by a young Paduan called Antonio, presumably a young man of the mechanical arts. It was installed in March 1344 on the tower of the Palazzo Capitano in Padua. It included a 24-hour chapter ring, a calendar dial, and the signs of the zodiac, and it was equipped with a striking mechanism. Destroyed in 1390, it was reconstructed in 1434, possibly with the original dial. Jacopo's epitaph refers to his clock: "Yet, indeed, dear reader, know that it is my invention that, from afar, shows at the top of the lofty tower the time, and the changing hours which you count."[19]

As a widower, Jacopo lived in his son's house in Padua from 1348—the year the work on Giovanni's astrarium began —to his death in 1359, and he must have played an important part in its planning; but his son's detailed manuscript—which runs to some 130,000 words—makes no mention of Jacopo's role. In it Giovanni tells us why he designed the clock, how to make it, how to set the dials and read them, how to maintain the mechanism in running order, and, if necessary, how to repair it.

The Dondi clock was famed throughout Europe. Philippe de Maisières, a personal friend of Giovanni, wrote in about 1385 that it is "such a great marvel, that the solemn astronomers come from far regions to see [it] in great reverence. . . ."[20] Dondi's manuscript with its 180 or so accompanying diagrams was copied over and over again, and there are eleven known surviving copies in European libraries. While most contemporary clocks were of iron, Dondi's was made of brass and bronze, and his description of his horological masterpiece is so detailed—he even specified the thickness of the sheets to be employed, the length of studs, and where to drill holes—that Alan Lloyd was able to make his twentieth-century model an exact replica of the fourteenth-century clock. When we compare Dondi's drawings with the Smithsonian reconstruction, the six hundred years' distance in time seems to vanish. Dondi's mind and skill are revealed to be as complex and sophisticated as those of a present-day computer technician.

To start with, Dondi sketched the seven-sided framework of his astrarium. In the upper part were to be installed the seven dials of the Primum Mobile, the moon, and the five planets then known—Venus, Mercury, Saturn, Jupiter, and Mars. In the lower part were to be fitted the 24-hour dial, the dial for the fixed feasts of the church, the dial for the movable feasts, and the dial for the nodes.

The next drawing, the earliest known representation of a mechanical clock, showed the clock movement, though omitting the details of the bearings (which he thought too well known for him to trouble to draw them). Nevertheless, he did give the details of the clock train:

> Hour circle revolution in 24 hours, 144 teeth, pinion of 12 carrying a wheel of 20 meshing with a wheel of 24 on the great wheel. Thus the barrel rotates 10 times in 24 hours. Great wheel 120 teeth mesh with a pinion of 12 carrying a second wheel of 80, which therefore revolves 100 times a day. The second wheel meshes with a pinion of 10 carrying the escape wheel of 27 teeth, which therefore makes 800 revolutions a day, each calling for 54 oscillations of the balance, i.e. 43,200 a day or 2 second beat. This is the standard beat.[21]

As the Italian hours were then calculated on a single daily cycle, starting at sunset, Dondi built a 24-hour dial. There were wings, or scales, on which were engraved tables

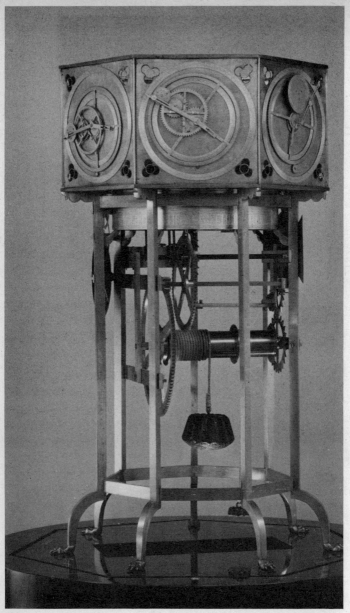

Smithsonian reconstruction of the astrarium. Courtesy Smithsonian Institution, Washington, D.C.

Detail of the reconstructed astrarium. Courtesy Smithsonian Institution, Washington, D.C.

divided on each side into months and days. With these tables, the rising and the setting of the sun could be determined for every day of the year. Dondi started his 24-hour cycle at noon, not at sunset, as he considered noon to be a more reliable point from which to base astronomical calculations. The hour dial revolved counterclockwise, so that readings had to be taken from the left-hand edge of each hour division.

For his annual calendar dial for the fixed feasts, he made a large circular band with 365 teeth cut in the upper edge, corresponding to the number of days of the year. On the outside of the band he engraved the length of each day of the year in hours and minutes, the dominical letter, the day of the month, and the name of the saint to be commemorated. The day was always visible through an opening in the dial plate.

The calendar of the movable feasts required such a complex mechanism that it was not until the middle of the nineteenth century, half a millennium later, that such a calendar was again included in an astronomical clock—by Jean-Baptiste Sosime Schwilgué in the third Strasbourg clock of 1842. (In fairness, it should be pointed out that the introduction in 1582 of the Gregorian calendar in place of the Julian calendar made the calendar of movable feasts even more complicated to represent than was the case for Dondi.) There are five movable ecclesiastical feasts, with Easter Day the most important. Once Easter Day was fixed, the other movable feasts would fall automatically into place. To find Easter Day, Dondi built three linked chains, the top chain having twenty-eight links corresponding to the twenty-eight years of the solar cycle, the second chain with nineteen links corresponding to the lunar cycle, and the bottom chain with fifteen links corresponding to a cycle used in Roman times. While the calendar of the fixed feast days was placed under the dial of Venus, the perpetual calendar of movable feasts was placed under the dial of Mercury. (The Venus dial was copied by Leonardo da Vinci. He must have done it directly from the clock itself, rather than from any contemporary manuscript, for his drawing includes certain details that are not illustrated in any of the known diagrams. Leonardo also sketched the astrarium's dial of Mars.)

The dials of Mercury and of the moon have the most complex mechanisms. The Mercury dial includes oval wheels, one of which has internally cut teeth. This may well be the first application of such a technique. "For Mercury there is, beyond the correction at leap year, provision for a secondary correction after 144 years by setting the wheel M forward 1 tooth. In the argument of Mercury there is an annual deficit of $42'5''$, so that the dial should be set forward $\frac{2}{3}°$ annually with a residual correction of $1°$ in 29 years."[22] Dondi's drawing shows the lunar dial to consist of an upper oval wheel with an unequal number of teeth in equal-sized sectors. On a seven-sided frame is a skew gear, possibly the first in Western technology. The dial allowed for the moon's elliptical orbit; the next clock with such a movement was made by Thomas Mudge nearly four hundred years later, in about 1755–60.

The complexity of Dondi's astrarium was such that when it broke down around 1440 there was great difficulty in getting it repaired. Eventually, a man to fix it was found far away, a certain Guillelmus Zelandenus—a native of Zeeland—who had settled in France, in Carpentras. But again in the years 1529–30, when the Emperor Charles V saw Dondi's astrarium in Pavia, it was in disrepair. This is the last we hear of the famous clock. Not until 1561 was another comparable astronomical clock built.

The mechanical clocks in the great cities of fourteenth-century Europe made a significant contribution toward shaping the modern Western world. On churches and on town halls the clocks struck equal, or equinoctial, hours, and this in itself was a historical revolution in the measuring of time, with far-reaching intellectual, commercial, and industrial consequences.

Egyptian, Greek, Roman, Byzantine, and Islamic water

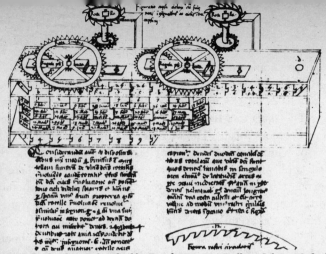

Perpetual calendar, as sketched by Dondi. Courtesy Bodleian Library, Oxford.

Smithsonian reconstruction of the perpetual calendar. Courtesy Smithsonian Institution, Washington, D.C.

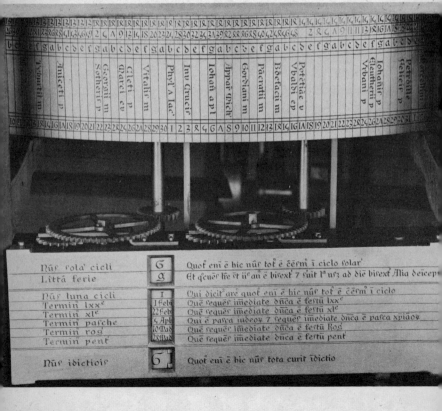

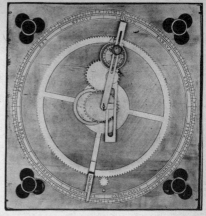

Smithsonian reconstruction of the Dial of the Moon. Courtesy Smithsonian Institution, Washington, D.C.

Smithsonian reconstruction of the Dial of Venus. Courtesy Smithsonian Institution, Washington, D.C.

Dondi's drawing of the lunar dial. Courtesy Science Museum, London.

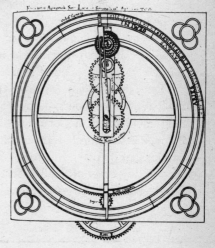

clocks had indicated unequal, or temporal, hours—in all these civilizations the day was divided into hours of light and hours of darkness, generally periods of twelve hours each. The hours were counted from sunrise to sunset and from sunset to sunrise, so that the length of a daytime hour differed from that of an hour of the night—except at the equinoxes—and both varied according to the season of the year. The variation in the length of the day was greater in the higher latitudes. In northern Egypt, for example, on a latitude of 30 degrees north, the period from sunrise to sunset varies only between 10 and 14 hours, whereas in London, on a latitude of 51½ degrees north, it varies between 7¾ hours and 16½ hours. Thus, "London hours" vary from approximately 38 minutes to 82 minutes. The water clocks that preceded the equinoctial mechanical clocks had an attendant who each morning would divide the day into twelve hours and then set his clock to enforce this division of time. Until the fourteenth century Europe lived not only with these temporal hours but also with canonical hours, which governed life in the monasteries. The monastery bells were rung seven times in twenty-four hours.

The first clock recorded as striking equal hours is that of the church of Saint Gothard in Milan. According to a chronicler in 1335, the church had "a wonderful clock, with a very large clapper which strikes a bell twenty-four times according to the twenty-four hours of the day and night and thus at the first hour of the night gives one sound, at the second two strikes . . . and so distinguishes one hour from another, which is of greatest use to men of every degree."[23] In Padua, Jacopo di Dondi's public clock of 1344 "through days and nights tells the twenty-four hours automatically."[24] Public clocks also rang equal hours in Genoa in 1353, in Florence in 1354, in Bologna in 1356, in Ferrara in 1362. And in 1370 there was a public clock on one of the towers of the Royal Palace in Paris, now on the corner of the boulevard du Palais and the quai de l'Horloge. King Charles V was so enthusiastic about this striking clock that he had two others built, one at the Hôtel Saint Paul and the other at the Château de Vincennes. He also wished all the citizens of Paris to regulate their private, commercial, and industrial life to the tempo of the authoritarian equinoctial hours, and ordered all the churches in Paris to ring their bells when the royal clocks struck the hour.

By making the churches ring their bells at regular sixty-minute intervals, Charles V was taking a decisive step toward breaking the dominance of the liturgical practices of the Church. The Church would bow to the materialistic interests of the bourgeois and turn its back on eternity.

> the regular striking of the bells brought a new regularity into the life of the workman and the merchant. The bells of the clock tower almost defined urban existence. Time-keeping passed into time-saving and time-accounting and time-rationing. As this took place, Eternity ceased gradually to serve as the measure and focus of human actions.[25]

This shift in attitude of the Church in western Europe—the Church of Rome—goes a long way toward accounting for what we have called the medieval industrial revolution. It signaled an acceptance of new technology and a readiness to compromise with new ideas. In the Greek Orthodox Church, there was no acceptance of new technology and no readiness whatsoever to compromise with new ideas. A remarkable demonstration of the strict observance of tradition in the Orthodox Church is given by the fact that until the twentieth century Orthodox priests never allowed a mechanical clock to be installed in an Orthodox church. For them it would have been blasphemy; for them the mathematical division of time into hours, minutes, and seconds had no relationship with the eternity of time. But the Church of Rome had no such objection to clocks being installed on the facades or towers of their churches, and today there are tens of thousands of mechanical church clocks in western Europe.

The same contrast can be applied more broadly to West and East. What is most remarkable in this connection is the different way time has been judged or measured in the two parts of the world. Until very recently the East had not systematically adopted our equinoctial time, but used a method of time measurement dating back several millennia. That they adopted our way of measuring time so late has, at least in the majority of Eastern countries, handicapped their economic and industrial development, and it must also be pointed out that the reason it was adopted was because the European middle classes, in particular the Italian middle class, considered it expedient to their own trading purposes. The rational outlook of the merchants and bankers was fundamental to the installation of mechanical clocks in the West. With their capitalistic mentality they had observed the value of time. They already knew that "time is money."

8

Reason, Mathematics,
and Experimental Science

Giovanni di Dondi, the horologist; Villard de Honnecourt,
the architect-engineer; Walter of Henley, the agronomist—
all had one thing in common: a rational outlook on life.
This does not mean that they were men in advance of their
time or that they reasoned like men of the twentieth century. Their society professed a faith, and they would not have
been able to imagine that one day men would be living in
Europe without such a faith. Nor was any of them aware that
he was contributing, each in his own way, to the creation of
a new world, different from any that had existed before. From
the first quarter of the twelfth century to the last quarter of
the thirteenth century—until the year 1277, to be precise—
there was a sustained effort to marry reason and faith. During
these exceptional 150 years, before the Church had begun to

dictate rigid dogmas, men learned how to reason and dispute intellectually, and this intellectual freedom helped lay the foundations of modern science.

Gerbert of Aurillac, elected Pope under the name of Sylvester II (999–1003) was the first to set Europe on the path of science—he revived the use of the abacus, developed Boethius's treatises on arithmetic and music (using a monochord), and wrote a treatise on astronomy.

Lanfranc and his disciple Saint Anselm, both Archbishops of Canterbury in the eleventh century, led the field in the application of reason to faith. Saint Anselm wrote: "It seems to me negligent, if after we have been confirmed in the faith, we do not strive to understand what we believe."[1]

Peter Abelard (c. 1079–1142) led Europe on the path of formal and philosophical logic. Abelard had the sad privilege of becoming twice famous in his lifetime, and for quite different reasons. In his youth he was the most renowned logician and dialectician in Europe, and he was also renowned for having been castrated by Heloise's uncle. In common with many other couples at this period, Abelard and Heloise had no use for marriage—as Heloise wrote to her lover, if they married he would not be able to meditate amid the noise of the servants and the cries of the babies. It was fine for the rich to marry, for they had enough room to isolate themselves. Still, a son was born to them, whom they called Astrolabe, an act that could almost be taken to herald the coming scientific age.

Abelard held that it was only through intellectual inquiry that we can investigate truth. In a treatise entitled *Sic et Non* (*Yes and No*) he collected all the contradictory statements he could find in the Scriptures and the Fathers on 158 points of Christian doctrine. He laid down the principles by which the arguments should be weighed, but he did not venture to offer any solutions himself. His aim was not to invite skepticism, but to sharpen the tool of inquiry, "for by doubting we are led to questions, by questioning we arrive at the truth."[2]

A contemporary French medievalist has written:

> Abelard was primarily a logician and, like all great philosophers, he introduced a method. He was the great champion of dialectic. With his "Logic for Beginners" (*Logica ingredientibus*) and especially with his *Sic et Non* of 1122 he gave to the western mind the first "discourse on method." With striking simplicity he demonstrated the need to resort to reason.[3]

Abelard distinguished clearly between empirical knowledge of a fact and rational knowledge of the cause of that fact:

> Some sciences are concerned with action, others with understanding; that is, some consist in constructing things, others in analyzing compound things. For many people are practised in action but have little scientific understanding; they have tested the healing powers of medicines and are good at healing because of their experience alone, but they do not know much about the natural causes. For they know the herbs are useful for healing, and of which diseases, because they learn this by experience, but the reason why the herbs have this power they do not study; they know the powers of herbs and the nature of infirmities because they are practised in the practical science, but they are not instructed in the theoretical (but beasts and all the other irrational animals are very sound in practice but are ignorant of nature and causes, as for example the dog brings about its own cure by licking its wound. Bees, also nature has taught with wonderful subtlety to make honey, which is beyond human skill). Many people on the other hand have understanding but not practical ability and these can impart knowledge to others but cannot put it into practice themselves.

The man of understanding is he who has the ability to grasp and ponder the hidden causes of things. By hidden causes we mean those from which things originate, and these are to be investigated more by reason than by sensory experiences. . . . Whence Virgil's judgment: Happy the man who has been able to discern the cause of things.[4]

Abelard has generally been regarded as the first European intellectual, and quite rightly so. It was part of his nature to be in constant opposition, always prepared to attack ideals and refute social and intellectual tradition. His reliance on reason could not help but bring him into conflict with a mystic like Saint Bernard of Clairvaux, who said of Abelard that "he deems himself able by human reason to comprehend God altogether."[5]

Abelard represented the new trend of thought, at odds with Saint Bernard's belief that one could find more in forests than in books, that nature could reveal more than any teacher. Saint Bernard's anti-intellectualism derived from a need to defend his mystical faith against the massive invasion of books from the classical world, works translated from Greek and Arabic in the frontier towns of Christendom, mainly in Sicily and Spain. This influx of books may not have had the impact that was to follow the spread of printing, but it exerted a strong influence on Europe's ways of thinking in the twelfth and thirteenth centuries, and it helped to increase its population of students. It also gave rise to what has been called the "renaissance of the twelfth century," when medieval Europe fell under the spell of the classical world.

There was, however, one fundamental difference between this earlier renaissance and the later, more famous, one. While the latter was primarily concerned with literature and art, the twelfth-century renaissance was primarily taken up with philosophy and science. Scholars all over Europe were desperate to make all known scientific and technical books available in translation. Inasmuch as a major part of Greek scientific literature had been translated into Arabic—and often annotated with Arabic commentaries—scholars like the Englishman Adelard of Bath or the Italian Gerard of Cremona, men eager to make this vast store of knowledge available to Europe, learned Arabic. At Toledo, in Spain, translators were organized into teams that included Christians, Jews, and Moslems. They produced Latin translations not only of Greek works but also of original works by Arab scholars, particularly in the fields of medicine, astronomy, arithmetic, algebra, and trigonometry.

Prior to the twelfth century, Europe had been acquainted with very few scientific works from the classical world, partly because of the Romans' disinterest in theoretical science. They had themselves produced few writings of value and only occasionally translated Greek scientific literature into Latin. The following scientific works were among the few available to medieval Europe prior to the great influx of translations: Plato's *Timaeus* (the first forty-three chapters), some logical works (*Logica Vetus*) of Aristotle, Lucretius's *De Rerum Natura*, Vitruvius's *De Architectura*, Seneca's *Quaestiones Naturales*, and Pliny's *Historia Naturalis*. From the late Roman period there were works by Macrobius, Martianus Capella, and Boethius.

Table 5 lists some of the authors translated in the twelfth and early thirteenth centuries, along with the titles of their works, the names of the Latin translators, the languages of the original, and the places and dates of the Latin translations. The table, though by no means exhaustive, should demonstrate the importance of the translation boom during this period. It was the work of these translators that made possible the rise of modern science, for it was they who made accessible this vast body of knowledge to the humanists of the twelfth and thirteenth centuries in the schools and universities of

TABLE 5. *Principal Sources of Ancient Science Translated in the Middle Ages*[6]

ARABIC SOURCES FROM ABOUT 1000

Author	Work	Latin Translator	Place and Date of Latin Translation
Al Khwarizmi (9th century)	Liber Ysagogarum Alchorismi (arithmetic)	Adelard of Bath	c.1126
	Astronomical tables (trigonometry)	Adelard of Bath	c.1126
	Algebra	Robert of Chester	Segovia, 1145
Rhazes (died c.924)	De Aluminibus et Salibus (chemical work)	Gerard of Cremona	Toledo, 12th century
pseudo-Aristotle	De Proprietatibus Elementorum (Arabic work on Geology)	Gerard of Cremona	Toledo, 12th century
Alhazen (c.965–1037)	Opticae Thesaurus	unknown	End of 12th century
Avicenna (980–1037)	Physical and philosophical part of Kitab al-Shifa (commentary on Aristotle)	Dominicus Gundissalinus and John of Seville	Toledo, 12th century
Averroës (1126–98)	Commentaries on Physica, De Caelo et Mundo, De Anima and other works of Aristotle	Michael Scot	Early 13th century
Leonardo Fibonacci of Pisa	Liber Abaci (first complete account of Hindu numerals)	unknown	1202

GREEK SOURCES FROM ABOUT 1000

Hippocrates and school (5th, 4th centuries B.C.)	*Aphorisms* Various treatises	Burgundio of Pisa Gerard of Cremona and others from Arabic translation	12th century Toledo, 12th century
Aristotle (384–322 B.C.)	*Meteorologica* (Books 1–3) *Physica, De Caelo et Mundo, De Generatione et Corruptione*	Gerard of Cremona from Arabic translation	Toledo, 12th century
	Meteorologica (Book 4) *De Animalibus* (*Historia animalium, De Generatione Animalium*, translated into Arabic in 19 books by El-Batric, 9th century)	Henricus Aristippus Michael Scot from Arabic translation	Sicily, c.1156 Spain, c.1217–20
Euclid (c.330–260 B.C.)	*Elements* (15 books, 13 genuine)	Adelard of Bath from Arabic translation	early 12th century
	Optica and Catoptrica	unknown	Probably Sicily, c.1254
Archimedes (287–212 B.C.)	*De Mensura Circuli*	Gerard of Cremona from Arabic translation	Toledo, 12th century
Hero of Alexandria (1st century B.C.?)	*Pneumatica*	unknown	Sicily, 12th century
Galen (A.D. 129–200)	Various treatises Various treatises	Burgundio of Pisa Gerard of Cremona and others from Arabic translation	c.1185 Toledo, 12th century
Ptolemy (A.D. 2nd century)	*Almagest*	Gerard of Cremona from Arabic translation	Toledo, 1175
	Optica	Eugenius of Palermo from Arabic translation	c.1154

Europe. They deserve our respect—quite as much as the over-praised humanists of the fifteenth century.

Scholars in search of scientific knowledge who were not prepared to wait for the translations to reach them could go to Toledo, one of Europe's most famed cities for the teaching of the arts of the quadrivium: arithmetic, music, geometry, and astronomy: "In our times it is in Toledo that the teaching of the Arabs, which is nearly entirely devoted to the arts of the quadrivium, is offered to the crowds. I hastened there to listen to the teachings of the wisest philosophers of this world."[7] This writer, Daniel de Morley, had no qualms about admiring the teaching of the infidel Arabs or trusting the evidence of the pagan philosophers of the past: "No one should be disturbed if when talking of the creation of the world, I invoke the evidence not of the Church Fathers but that of Pagan philosophers, for even if they are not counted among the faithful, certain of their teachings, as long as they are in good faith, must be incorporated in our teaching."[8]

Twelfth-century humanists often admired classical antiquity just as enthusiastically as did humanists of the fifteenth century. Peter of Blois wrote: "One only passes from the darkness of ignorance to the enlightenment of science if one rereads with ever increasing love the works of the ancients. Let the dogs bark, let the pigs grunt! I will nonetheless be a disciple of the ancients. All my care will be for them and each day the dawn will find me studying them."[9]

Such admiration for the culture of antiquity did not, however, diminish the humanists' belief in the progress of knowledge. Bernard of Chartres, of the Cathedral School of Chartres, the first humanist center, expressed this belief in the famous text already quoted: "We are dwarfs on the shoulders of giants . . . so . . . we perceive more things than they do. . . ." In Chartres, study of the seven liberal arts, the trivium—grammar, rhetoric, dialectic—had priority, but study of the quadrivium—geometry, arithmetic, music, and astronomy—was also considered essential. The natural sciences did receive a due measure of attention. William of Conches, for instance, "attempted to reconcile the atomic theory of Democritus and the Epicureans with the physical theories of the *Timaeus*,"[10] and Chartres was deeply influenced by the teaching of Plato, in particular the scientific ideas contained in the *Timaeus*.

The first attempt to explain the universe in terms of natural causes was associated with the school of Chartres. Thierry of Chartres (died *c.* 1155), having tried to find a rational explanation of the Creation, declared that it was impossible to understand the story of Genesis without the intellectual training provided by the quadrivium, that is, without the mastery of mathematics, "for on mathematics all rational explanation of the universe depended."[11] And William of Conches defended the use of reason against the opponents of natural science, who

> since they themselves are unacquainted with the forces of nature, in order that they may have all men as companions in their ignorance, wish them to investigate nothing but to believe like rustics. We, on the contrary, think that a reason should be sought in every case, if one can be found.[12]

In answer to those who believed that God could find a way of reconciling the elements fire and earth, William replied, "We do not place a limit upon divine power, but we do say that of existing things none can do it, nor in the nature of things can there be anything that would suffice."[13] In another passage he was again provoked to violent indignation by men who said "we do not know how this is, but we know that God can do it." "You poor fools," he retorted, "God can make a cow out of a tree, but has He ever done so? Therefore show some reason why a thing is so, or cease to hold that it is so."[14]

The historical importance of texts such as those of William of Conches and other humanists of the twelfth century lies in the fact that they furthered the demythologizing of nature that Christianity had begun. As the Christian faith spread through the Middle East and the Mediterranean, it destroyed the belief of the classical world that there were gods residing in nature. This Christian demythologizing was one of many factors behind the technological creativity of the period we have been studying. The historian Lynn White has written that

> In 1056 Robert Forbes of Leyden and Samuel Sambursky of Jerusalem simultaneously pointed out that Christianity, by destroying classical animism, brought about a basic change in the attitude toward natural objects and opened the way for their rational and unabashed use for human ends. Saints, angels and demons were very real to the Christian, but the *genius loci*, the spirit inherent in a place or object, was no longer present to be placated if disturbed.[15]

It is a remarkable fact that at the instigation of the Cathedral School of Chartres, the seven liberal arts were carved in stone, personified and holding their attributes, on the Royal Portal of the Cathedral. Beneath each of the arts, an author was represented who by his thought and writings had made an important contribution to the substance of that art. Thus, seven authors of the past, mostly pagan, were placed on a cathedral portal. The man considered responsible for this was Thierry of Chartres, then chancellor of the school.

For the most part the thinkers exemplifying the liberal arts have been identified according to Thierry's *Heptateuchon*. The principal authors whose works he had chosen for the Handbook were Priscian for Grammar, Aristotle for dialectic, Cicero for rhetoric, Boethius for arithmetic and Ptolemy for astronomy. Geometry is probably not represented on the portal by any of the various writers whose treatises Thierry had selected, but by the author on whose concepts these treatises are based, namely Euclid. Music is most likely accompanied by Pythagoras, for she displays those instruments that, according to tradition, enabled the Greek philosopher to develop his theory of intervals.[16]

The decision of the cathedral school to have the seven liberal arts represented in stone was in keeping with the school's policy of bringing together men of the liberal arts and men of the mechanical arts, the intellectuals and the highly skilled workmen, science and technology. The quadrivium was the common ground on which they could meet.

The progress of reason and science moved from Chartres to Paris, and then to Oxford. One of William of Conches's pupils, John of Salisbury, who in 1176 was elected Bishop of Chartres, in 1164 wrote a letter to his close friend Thomas à Becket in which he enthusiastically described the intellectual atmosphere of Paris:

> I made a detour through Paris. When I saw the wealth of goods, the cheerfulness of its population, the regard the clerks enjoy, the majesty and glory of the Church, the various occupations of its philosophers, full of admiration I thought I saw angels ascending and descending Jacob's ladder which was touching the sky. Enraptured by this happy pilgrimage, I had to confess "the Lord is in this place, and I knew it not." And this phrase of a poet comes to my mind: "Happy exile it is for the one who has this city for abode."[17]

Paris was compared to Athens by another scholar, Bartholomew, the English monk and encyclopedist of the first half of the thirteenth century:

Just as the town of Athens in olden times was the mother of the liberal arts and of letters, the nurse of philosophers and all manner of science, such is Paris in our day, not merely for France, but for all Europe. In her role as Mother of Wisdom, Paris welcomes all comers from every country in the world and helps them in all their needs and governs them in peace.[18]

The introduction of Aristotle's works, accompanied by various Arabic commentaries, particularly those of the great philosophers Avicenna and Averroës, presented the newly founded University of Paris with a more or less complete system of scientific thought. Aristotle's dialectic came to be accepted as the basis of science and reason. Thus the university had to try to reconcile—and this was a far more complicated task of synthesis than any that had yet been attempted in western Europe—Aristotelianism and Christianity, to make them a unity which could embrace the totality of truth, human and divine. Faith had to be married to reason, philosophy to theology, the faculty of the arts to the faculty of theology. Many famous medieval thinkers—Alexander of Hales, Albertus Magnus, Thomas Aquinas—tried to realize this synthesis, but all attempts failed. The thirteenth century witnessed a number of condemnations, which were largely disregarded. The teaching of Aristotle was prohibited in Paris in 1210 and 1215 and in Toulouse in 1245. In 1263, Urban reiterated condemnations directed at the Averroists. The Bishop of Paris, Etienne Tempier, in 1270 condemned 13 propositions taught at the Faculty of the Arts.

The theologians and the Pope, who considered that the endeavors to reconcile Christianity with Aristotelianism were becoming a real danger to the Christian faith, demanded more forceful action, and on March 7, 1277, Tempier condemned this time not 13 but "219 execrable errors which certain students of the Faculty of the Arts have the temerity to study and discuss in the schools." In so doing he slowed the progress of science and reason in Paris—the Athens of the thirteenth century.

While the main studies in the Paris Faculty of Arts were those of the trivium, in which Aristotelianism was dominant, in Oxford the quadrivium and Neoplatonist ideas were more important. This accounts for the progress of science at Oxford, and of experimental science in particular. Although certain propositions were condemned at Oxford, this did not have the same effect on the development of scientific theory as did the condemnations of 1277 in Paris.

A single name, Roger Bacon (c. 1214–92), has invariably been associated with the origins of experimental science at Oxford University. He was thought to be a unique genius, a man on his own, a man ahead of his time. But as in the case of Leonardo, we know now that the legends were exaggerated and that Bacon, like Leonardo, was indeed a man of his time. Just as scholars have shown us Leonardo's precursors, the last half-century of research by historians has demonstrated that however remarkable Bacon was, and there is no question of his genius, he was in many ways only a follower. The man who was Bacon's master was Robert Grosseteste (c. 1175– 1253).

Grosseteste was born of probably humble parents at Stratbrook in Suffolk. Educated at Oxford, and possibly in Paris, he was the first chancellor of Oxford University, and first lecturer to the Oxford Franciscans in 1224. Though Bishop of Lincoln from 1235 until his death, he retained his interest in the welfare of the university. He had a very good knowledge of Greek and did much to encourage the study of the language, attracting Greeks to Oxford and arranging for grammars to be brought from Greece and other lands. He himself translated Aristotle's *Nicomachean Ethics*, together with the

The earliest known illustration of a reader wearing spectacles. Courtesy Bibliothèque Nationale, Paris.

commentaries of Eustratios, Metropolitan of Nicaea (*c.* 1050–1120), and he added many notes on Greek lexicography and syntax.

His literary activity was tremendous. He wrote commentaries on the *Physics* of Aristotle. His treatise on the compotus (*c.* 1232) includes a discussion of the reform of the calendar, which was to be cited repeatedly by subsequent writers. His *Compendium Sphaerae* contains the first mention of the trepidation of the equinoxes in a non-Moslem work, and he knew, of course, that the earth was round. In his treatise on the sphere he declared that the sphericity of the earth, as of all the stars and planets, was proved both by natural reason and astronomical experience—in the case of the earth, by the observation of the sky by men in different locations. But Robert Grosseteste's importance lies mostly in his insistence on basing natural philosophy upon mathematics and experimentation. He believed that it was impossible to understand the physical world without mathematics, an opinion based on his metaphysical conception of the nature of reality. He held light to be the first corporeal form, believing that the characteristic property of light was its ability to propagate itself instantaneously in straight lines in all directions without loss of substance, and that in this way light had generated the universe. At the beginning of time God had created uniform matter out of nothing; light, created by autodiffusion, had then produced the dimensions of space and all beings. On these grounds, Grosseteste believed that the study of optics was the key to understanding the physical world.

The study of optics led Grosseteste to suggest the use of lenses for purposes of magnification:

> For this branch of Perspective thoroughly known shows us how to make things very far off seem very close at hand and how to make large objects which are near seem tiny and how to make distant objects appear as large as we choose, so that it is possible for us to read the smallest letters at an incredible distance or to count sand, or grain, or grass, or any other minute objects.[19]

If this text does not actually prove that magnifying lenses of some sort had already been discovered, at least it points the way to the microscope and the telescope. And as I mentioned in an earlier chapter, the invention of eyeglasses for nearsightedness was made in the 1280s in Italy. The inventor may well have known of Robert Grosseteste's writings on lenses.

Jean de Meun, the French poet who wrote the last part of *The Romance of the Rose*, in about 1270, had probably read Grosseteste's treatises on optics.

> *One may learn the cause*
> *Why mirrors, through some subtle laws,*
> *Have power to objects seen therein—*
> *Atoms minute or letter thin—*
> *To give appearance of fair size,*
> *Though naked unassisted eyes*
> *Can scarce perceive them. Grains of sand*
> *Seem stones when through these glasses scanned.*

The poet adds that with these glasses one can read letters from such a distance that one would not believe it unless he had seen it. Then he concludes:

> *But to these matters blind affiance*
> *No man need give: they're proved by science.*[20]

Jean de Meun also mentions other scientific observations made by Grosseteste in the field of optics. The poet writes of burning glasses, of various types of mirrors, and of rainbows:

> *Only he who's learned the rule*
> *of optics in some famous school*
> *Can to his fellow explain*
> *How 'tis that from the sun they gain*
> *their glorious hues.*[21]

For Robert Grosseteste, the mathematical laws of geometrical optics were the foundation of physical reality, essential to the understanding of nature.

Roger Bacon, Grosseteste's successor, was born into a well-to-do English family, who seem to have given substantial financial support to some of his experiments. He was educated at Oxford and Paris before joining the Franciscan Order, and he followed the path begun by Robert Grosseteste, whom he admired but had probably never met, in the fields of optics, mathematics, and experimental science. In his *Opus Majus*,

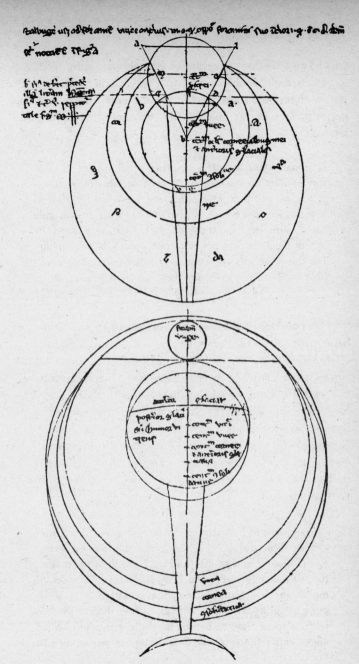

Roger Bacon's diagram of the curvatures of the refracting media of the eye. Courtesy British Museum, London.

part of an ambitious program of educational reform of Christendom which he dispatched to Pope Clement IV in 1268, Bacon described some of the experiments Grosseteste had performed, such as magnifying writing with appropriate lenses:

> If a man looks at letters or other small objects through the medium of a crystal or of glass or some other transparent body placed above the letters and if it be shaped like the lesser segment of a sphere with the convex side towards the eye, and the eye is in the air, he will see the letters much better and they will appear larger to him. For this reason this instrument is useful to old people and people with weak eyes, for they can see any letter however small if magnified enough.[22]

Bacon's imagination sometimes ran away with him, and being often short of money he was not always able to prove his theories. Some of the lenses and parabolic mirrors he discussed would have been very expensive to manufacture. He believed, for example, that Julius Caesar had "erected very large mirrors, in order that he might see in advance from the shore of Gaul the arrangement of the cities and camps of England," and that in his own times "similar mirrors might be erected on an elevation opposite hostile cities and armies, so that all that was being done by the enemy might be visible."[23] He wrote that:

> The wonders of refracted vision are still greater. . . . From an incredible distance we might read the smallest letters and number grains of dust and sand owing to the magnitude of the angle under which we viewed them . . . a child might appear a giant and a man a mountain . . . a small army might appear very large and situated at a distance might appear close at hand, and the reverse. So also we might cause the sun, moon, and stars in appearance to

descend here below, and similarly to appear above the heads of our enemies, and we might cause many similar phenomena, so that the mind of a man ignorant of the truth could not endure them.[24]

Bacon also gave a lengthy description of the eye and drew a geometrical diagram of the various curvatures of the ocular media: "the eye of a cow, pig and other animals can be used for illustration, if anyone wishes to experiment."[25] His descriptions of the anatomy of the vertebrate eye and the optic nerves were the best that had been written up to that time.

For Bacon the "gate and key" to all sciences was mathematics. He thus shared the Platonists' conviction that mathematics was of transcendental importance and of practical utility in almost every study. For example, only by mathematics could "the manifest and palpable errors" of the Christian calendar be corrected, errors that were bringing great discredit upon the Church. Here Bacon was following Grosseteste's lead, though his investigation of these errors was more thorough and arrived at a more accurate solution than any previously reached. Bacon was ashamed that the outside world had such contempt for the mathematics of western Christendom: "Unbelieving philosophers . . . Arabs, Hebrews and Greeks, who dwell among Christians, as in Spain, Egypt, parts of the East, and in many other regions of the world, abhor the folly which they behold in the arrangement of the chronology followed by the Christians in their festivals."[26]

The Julian calendar, named after Julius Caesar, under whose reign the calendar year had been reformed, assumed that the true length of the year was 365¼ days.

This fourth is summed up through four years, so that in leap years it is reckoned as one day more every fourth year than in ordinary years. But it is clearly shown by all computers ancient and modern, and rendered certain by astronomical proofs that the length of the solar year is not so great, nay, less. This deficiency is estimated by scientists to be about one hundred and thirtieth part of one day. Hence at length in 130 years there is one day in excess. If this were taken away the calendar would be correct as far as this fault is concerned. Therefore, since all things that are in the calendar are based on the length of the solar year they of necessity must be untrustworthy, since they have a wrong basis.

In the second place, there is another great error, namely regarding the determination of the equinoxes and solstices. For this error arises not only from the length of the year but has in itself grave errors. . . . At the beginning of the Church the winter solstice was placed on the eighth day before the Calends of January on the day of our Lord's nativity and the vernal equinox on the eighth day before the Calends of April. . . . For this year [1267] the winter solstice was on the Ides of December, twelve days before our Lord's nativity and the vernal equinox on the third day before the Ides of March. . . . This fact cannot only the astronomer certify, but any layman with the eye can perceive it by the falling of the solar ray now higher, now lower, on the wall or other object, as any one can see.

But the third disadvantage is a far greater one. For as we have shown, the truth is that, without error, Easter ought to be celebrated on the Sunday after the fourteenth moon which is found either on the equinox, or after the vernal equinox. . . . Since the true equinox mounts more and more in the calendar, about the fourteen hundred and eighty-first year it will be on the fifth day before the Ides of March. . . . But this is a most serious disadvantage; because thus not only Easter, but Lent and all the movable feasts will recede in a shocking fashion from their positions and the whole order of the ecclesiastical office will be confused. . . . In the real Lent meats will be eaten for many days. . . .

But a greater disadvantage comes from the beginning of lunation as given by the golden number in the calendar. For any one can see with the eye, if he looks at the sky, that the new moon occurs as a matter of fact three or four days before it is marked in the calendar and every seventy-six years the beginning of lunation recedes from its place in the calendar sixteen minutes of one day and forty seconds and this is more than a fourth of one day and nearly a third of a day, because sixteen minutes and forty seconds are six hours and forty minutes of one hour. In every 304 years it recedes from the place of first lunation in the calendar one day and six minutes of a day and forty seconds. After 4256 years the moon according to the calendar will be called new when it is full of light. After 7904 years there will be an error of one whole lunation, with the exception of a small part, namely thirty-eight minutes and thirty seconds. This error can reach to one hundred lunations, and then again the first error will return, so that successive ones may follow in order, and thus these errors roll around forever. Skilful astronomers have no doubt that all these statements are facts. Moreover, every computer knows that the beginning of the lunation is in error three or four days in these times and every rustic is able to view this error in the sky.[27]

Roger Bacon's appeal to Pope Clement IV to reform the scandalous errors of the Julian calendar went unheeded, but the considerable work he had done in this field was not completely lost, for some 150 years later Cardinal d'Ailly drew up a further report on the matter for the Council of Constance (1414–18) which made direct use of Bacon's work, as well as that of Grosseteste. But even d'Ailly's report produced no practical results, and in the course of the centuries the errors became more and more apparent, until by the end of the sixteenth century there was a discrepancy of ten days. At last Gregory X decided to act in 1582, more than three centuries

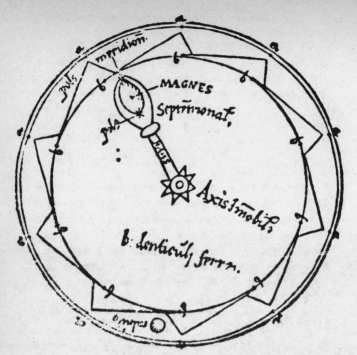

Peter of Maricourt's original drawing of his magnetic *perpetuum mobile*.
Courtesy British Museum, London.

after Grosseteste and Bacon had appealed for change. It was
decided that October 5, 1582, would become October 15,
1582, and that the last year of a century would not be a leap
year, except when the date is divisible by 400. He thus
created the Gregorian calendar, by which we still live.

Roger Bacon was also following Grosseteste's lead when
he devoted a chapter of his *Opus Majus* to experimental
science: "There are two modes of acquiring knowledge—
namely by reasoning and experience. Reasoning draws a conclusion and makes us grant the conclusion but does not make
the conclusion certain, nor does it remove doubt, so that the
mind may rest on the intuition of truth when the mind discovers it by the path of experience."[28]

192

Bacon did not, however, always apply to himself the principles of experimental science he laid down in his *Opus Majus*—as, for instance, when he wrote of the "windows of refracted vision." He seems, too, to acknowledge that the greatest experimental scientist of his time was Petrus Peregrinus, more commonly known as Peter of Maricourt, to whom he referred with enthusiasm as "Dominus Experimentorum." Peter has already been introduced to the reader in the chapter on Villard de Honnecourt—he was the scientist who devised two perpetual-motion devices: a magnetic perpetual-motion machine and "a globular lodestone which if it were mounted without friction, parallel to the celestial axis, would rotate once a day."

Unfortunately, we know very little of the life of this remarkable man, the greatest scientist of his time and the first man really to have undertaken planned experimental research. There are only two main documents to bring him to life: Bacon's description of him and his own epoch-making work on magnetism. Bacon wrote:

One man I knew, and only one, who can be praised for his achievements in this science [experimental science]. Of discourses and battles of words he takes no heed: he follows the work of wisdom, and in there finds rest. What others strive to see dimly and blindly, like bats in twilight, he gazes at in the full light of day, because he is a master of experiment. Through experiment he gains knowledge of natural things, medical, chemical and indeed of everything in the heavens or earth. He is ashamed that things should be known to laymen, old women, soldiers, ploughmen, of which he is ignorant. Therefore he has looked closely into the doings of those who work in metals and in minerals of all kinds; he knows everything relating to the acts of war, the making of weapons, and the chase; he has looked closely into agriculture, mensuration, and farming work; he has even taken notes of the remedies, lot-casting and charms used by old women and by wizards and magicians, and of the deceptions and devices of conjurors, so that nothing which deserves inquiry should escape him and that he may be able to expose the falsehood of magicians. If philosophy is to be carried to its perfection and is to be handled with utility and certainty, his aid is indispensable. As for reward, he neither receives nor seeks it. If he frequented kings and princes he would easily find those who would bestow on him honours and wealth. Or, if in Paris, he would display the result of his researches the whole world would follow him. But since either of these courses would hinder him from pursuing the great experiments in which he delights, he puts wealth and honour aside, knowing well that his wisdom would secure him wealth whenever he chose.[29]

Roger Bacon's praise of Peter of Maricourt was justified. In August 1269 Peter wrote *Epistolae de Magnete* (*Letters on the Magnet*), addressed to a Picard countryman, Suggerius of Foncaucourt. These letters, written while Peter was at the siege of Lucera in southern Italy with the Duke of Anjou's army, were so remarkable that no further experimental study of magnetism on a comparable scale is known to have been made before 1600, when William Gilbert, one of Queen Elizabeth's doctors, published in London his own *De Magnete*. Gilbert acknowledged his debt to his thirteenth-century predecessor and incorporated Peter of Maricourt's experiments into his own book.

One of the surprising things stressed in this thirteenth-century work was the importance of manual skill in the profession of the scientist. Peter of Maricourt opened his observations on magnets by writing:

You must realize, dearest friend, that while the investigator in this subject must understand nature and not be ignorant of the celestial motions, he must also be very diligent in the use of his own hands, so that through the operation of this stone he may show wonderful effects. For by his industry he will then in a short time be able to correct an error which he would never do in eternity by his knowledge of natural philosophy and mathematics alone if he lacked carefulness with his hands. For in investigating the unknown we greatly need manual industry without which we can usually accomplish nothing perfectly. Yet there are many things subject to the rule of reason which we cannot completely investigate by the hand.[30]

Peter's *Epistolae de Magnete* explains how to identify the poles of the compasses and states the laws of magnetic attraction and repulsion. It contains a remarkable description of an experiment with a repaired magnet, and it describes a number of compasses, with one of which "you will be able to direct your steps to cities and islands and to any place whatever in the world."

Compasses had already been used by navigators in Europe, occasionally in the twelfth century, and fairly widely in the thirteenth. Thanks to Peter of Maricourt, magnetic compasses now reached a higher degree of perfection than even those used in China, where the properties of the magnetic needle had originally been discovered, or other earlier compasses in Islam. It was the Europeans of the thirteenth century who, with the perfection of such instruments, led the way to the conquest of the seas, the circumnavigation of the African continent, and the discovery of America. During this century navigators began to use maritime charts, attempts were made to apply simple trigonometrical tables to sea travel, and the stern paddle of antiquity gave way to the modern rudder fixed to the stern port, an innovation that allowed much greater accuracy of steering.

European self-confidence was such that in 1291 two

Genoese navigators, the Vivaldi brothers, equipped two ships in Genoa and set out with two Franciscan monks—from the order to which Roger Bacon belonged—to reach India by way of the ocean (*ad partes Indiae per mare oceanum*). It has been suggested that they wanted to reach India by sailing west into the Atlantic Ocean, but it seems more likely that they hoped to reach India by sailing around Africa, for after sailing out of the Strait of Gibraltar they followed the African coast down beyond Cape Non (28 degrees, 46 minutes north), after which all trace of them was lost. More than two centuries elapsed before the Vivaldis' ambitions were realized. Not until May 20, 1498, was India at last reached, by Vasco da Gama.

The suggestion that the navigators with their two Franciscans were aiming to cross the Atlantic to reach India may in fact have some justification in that the Franciscans could have read the *Opus Majus*, or learned directly from their brethren the view expressed by Roger Bacon that the distance separating Spain from India was not great. Bacon's theories, as well as the statements of writers of antiquity, seem to have convinced Christopher Columbus that he should undertake his voyage westward.

Columbus was always searching in the past for confirmaton of his intuition that the world was covered by more land than sea. He believed he had found such confirmation in the Apocrypha, where it is written: "thou didst command that the waters should be gathered in the seventh part of the earth: six parts hast thou dried up. . . ." From this, Columbus drew the conclusion that the oceans only cover one-seventh of the world. He also read certain passages on the matter by Bacon, reproduced in Cardinal d'Ailly's *Imago Mundi*, which was written in the early fifteenth century and printed at Louvain in 1480. In a letter to Ferdinand and Isabella, written from Hispaniola in October 1498, Columbus quoted these passages as having influenced his great voyage.

Columbus must certainly have taken a great delight in

reading Bacon, what with the thirteenth-century author always producing proofs of the error of Ptolemy's belief that
land covered only one-sixth of the world.

> Aristotle says that the sea is small between the end of
> Spain on the west and the beginning of India on the east.
> Seneca, in the fifth book on Natural History, says that this
> sea is navigable in a very few days if the wind is favour-
> able . . . this fact is proved by the weight of another
> consideration. For Esdras states in the fourth book that
> six parts of the earth are habitable and the seventh is
> covered by waters. That no one may lessen this authority
> by saying that that book is apocryphal and of unknown
> authority, we must state that the sacred writers have used
> that book and confirm sacred truths by its means. . . . And
> Aristotle was able to know more [than Ptolemy] because
> on the authority of Alexander he sent two thousand men
> to investigate the things of this world. . . . And Seneca
> likewise; because Emperor Nero, his pupil, in similar
> fashion sent him to explore the doubtful things in this
> world. . . .

And further, Bacon writes again, "the water . . . extends for no
great width between the end of Spain and the beginning of
India. . . ."[31]

The curious fact about these passages on India is that
while they were known to Christopher Columbus, living more
than two hundred years later, they had probably been unknown up to then, even to the two Franciscans who sailed
from Genoa in Bacon's lifetime. The reason for this anomaly
is that in 1278 Jerome d'Ascoli, general of the Franciscans
(who was to become Pope Nicholas IV), had measures of
restraint placed upon the writings of Bacon.

All Bacon's numerous biographers have voiced opinions
on the reasons behind these measures of restraint, which were
accompanied by some sort of house arrest. Some have believed

that his scientific experiments led him to be accused of magic, others that he was accused of taking too great an interest in astrology, others again that he granted too much importance to the teaching of pagan authors such as Averroës. He may have earned disfavor for his outspoken criticism of the moral corruption of the Church, from the Court of Rome downward; or for criticizing respectable members of the rival Benedictine Order; or for his sympathies with the condemned prophetic movement of Joachim of Flora; or for his sympathies with the "left-wing" group of Franciscans known as the Spirituals.

It may have been a combination of all these. The important fact is that he was condemned in the year following the famous and dramatic condemnation of 219 doctrines by the Bishop of Paris, an act that effectively brought to an end the effort of the Church to marry faith and reason—and that opened the way to the mysticism of the fourteenth and fifteenth centuries.

9

The End of an Era

In the period following the condemnation of 1277 the medieval machine—the progress of technology—was checked, the thirteenth-century movement of enlightenment suffered a setback, and there followed a dark and increasingly decadent age.

In the years 1315–17 Europe was devastated by a hideous famine; in 1337 the Hundred Years' War began, and in the same year occurred the first bankruptcy that shook the European economy. Some ten years later, in 1347–50, Europe was decimated by the worst catastrophe Western civilization has suffered, the Black Death, and before the end of the century, in the years 1378–82, conditions led to a series of revolutionary uprisings throughout the continent.

The list of the 219 "execrable errors" (some of which were propositions held by Thomas Aquinas) condemned in 1277 shows the extent to which the University of Paris had become dominated by Greek and Arab ideas, many of them incompatible with Christianity. The creation of the world, personal immortality, and the freedom of the will were called into question. In certain intellectual disputations God no longer seemed to be the center of the universe. In place of the glorification of theology one had the glorification of philosophy. Scripture was suspected of inaccuracies.

As an immediate result of this action by the Church many Averroists, who had been leading the onslaught on Christianity, were forced to leave Paris. Many of them moved to Padua, where they continued to profess their beliefs, and it was in this milieu, in the next century, that Jacopo and Giovanni di Dondi built their astronomical clocks.

Siger of Brabant, the Averroist leader, was among those who left for Italy. He was later immortalized by Dante, who placed him in Paradise in the company of a brilliant circle of twelve souls, including Thomas Aquinas, whose doctrines had also come under attack in 1277. Introducing Siger to Dante, Aquinas says,

> *Lastly this, from whom*
> *Thy look on me reverteth, was the beam*
> *of one, whose spirit, on high musings bent,*
> *Rebuked the lingering tardiness of death.*
> *It is the eternal light of Sigebert*
> *Who 'scaped not envy, when of truth he argued,*
> *Reading in the straw-litter'd street.*[1]

The condemnation of 1277 had two long-term results. On the one hand, by separating philosophy from theology it served to establish the intellectual climate in which science developed almost independent of liberal humanism; and on the other, it caused Christianity to revert to mysticism.

Mysticism is the attempt to penetrate the riddle of the universe not by logic, but by sympathetic intuition. The mystic rejects reason. The mystic starts where conscious, coherent thought ends. God again becomes the center of all devotion. Saint Bonaventure wrote that mysticism "is the reaching out of the soul to God through the yearning of love" and, later, Goethe defined mysticism as the "scholastic of the heart, the dialectic of the feelings."

The fourteenth and fifteenth centuries were to see an increasing devotion to ascetic exercises, to meditation, to retreats, and to ecstasies. More and more men and women tried to renounce the world, to dedicate themselves to holy lives and do penance for their sins. Their deep mystical vocation made them choose the strictest religious orders of the time, orders such as the Carthusians. In the Low Countries, for example, where 37 Carthusian monasteries had been founded in the twelfth century and 34 in the thirteenth century, 110 were founded in the fourteenth century and 45 in the fifteenth century.

The grip of mysticism was more powerful in the Low Countries and the Rhineland than anywhere else in Europe. Outbursts of mass mania became common, the most famous, ensuing from the Black Death, being the processions of flagellants, men who took it upon themselves to do penance for the sins of the community that they believed had caused the plague. In 1349, flagellant brethren were encouraged to start public flagellations. This is how a contemporary witness described the scenes of flagellation in London:

About Michaelmas 1349, over six hundred men came to London from Flanders, mostly of Zeeland and Holland origin. Sometimes at St Paul's and sometimes at other points in the city they made two daily public appearances wearing cloths from the thighs to the ankles, but otherwise stripped bare. Each wore a cap marked with a red cross in front and behind. Each had in his right hand a scourge with three tails. Each tail had a knot and through the middle of it were sometimes sharp nails fixed. They marched naked in a file one behind the other and whipped themselves with these scourges on their naked and bleeding bodies. Four of them would chant in their native tongue and another four in response like a litany.[2]

With the spread of mysticism, Europe began to show an interest, which soon grew into a fervid passion, for all the superstitious arts and occult sciences; for geomancy, hydromancy, aeromancy, pyromancy, chiromancy, augury, and necromancy; for alchemy, for astrology, and for witchcraft. As all these occult sciences spread, an irrational repression of frightening proportions followed in their wake. The first astrologer to be condemned by the Inquisition was Cecco d'Ascoli, burned at the stake in Florence in 1327 as a relapsed heretic. But the number of astrologers to meet this fate was small compared with the thousands of witches or those accused of being witches, who were hunted down, tortured, and burned.

A witch is one who has made a pact with the devil to effect his purposes on earth. The worshiper of the devil is a heretic, although "it was not until the fourteenth century that the existence of a definite sect of witches was finally accepted by the Church as an imminent danger."[3] "All witchcraft comes from carnal lust which is in women insatiable,"[4] wrote two fifteenth-century inquisitors, J. Sprenger and H. Kraemer, one of whom had boasted that he had burned forty-eight sorcerers in five years. "There are three things that are never satisfied, yea, a fourth thing, which says not, 'It is enough'; that is, the mouth of the womb."[5] The frustrated love of unmarried girls often led them to be accused of witchcraft by their lovers or the wives their lovers had married.

For when girls have been corrupted, and have been scorned by their lovers after they have immodestly copulated with them in the hope and promise of marriage with them, and have found themselves disappointed in all their hopes and everywhere despised, they turn to the help and protection of devils; either for the sake of vengeance by bewitching those lovers or the wives they have married, or for the sake of giving themselves up to every sort of lechery. Alas! experience tells us that there is no number to such girls and consequently the witches that spring from this class are innumerable.[6]

Many men who had for one reason or another become impotent accused the women with whom they had copulated of having bewitched them. Our two inquisitors devoted several chapters of their book *Malleus Maleficorum* (*The Hammer of Witchcraft*) to these problems and suggested remedies. In chapter II remedies are prescribed for those who are bewitched by the limitation of the generative power, and chapter IV contains remedies for those who by prestidigitatory art have lost their virile members or have been seemingly transformed into the shapes of beasts. But what do witches do with the virile members they have by prestidigitatory art made disappear? They

sometimes collect male organs in great numbers, as many as twenty or thirty members together, and put them in a bird's nest, or shut them up in a box, where they move themselves like living members and eat oats and corn, as has been seen by many and is a matter of common report . . . a certain man . . . when he had lost his member, approached a known witch to ask her to restore it to him. She told the afflicted man to climb a certain tree, and that he might take which he liked out of a nest in which there were several members. And when he tried to take a big one, the witch said: You must not take that one; adding, because it belonged to a parish priest.[7]

Even this passage cannot lead us to believe that these two inquisitors had a sense of humor, for their book on witchcraft was the most important and terrible ever written and contains, too, a detailed chapter on the different types of torture to be applied to the accused.

The spirit of enthusiasm which had inspired the Crusades to the Holy Land was, by the thirteenth century, much weakened. The higher standard of living at home was keeping men from searching for a better way of life abroad. The bloody failures of several previous expeditions were in the minds of many, who knew there was a high risk of being killed or taken prisoner, while the teaching of men like Saint Francis had begun to propagate the idea that it was better to convert infidels than kill them, and some men even began to be aware that infidels were human beings like themselves. When the King of France, Saint Louis, a man passionately religious when most others were less so, launched his first Crusade in 1248, he already had great trouble convincing his subjects of the necessity for another Crusade. The catastrophic disaster that followed—thousands killed and the army and the King made prisoner—led to the conviction that no more armed forces should be sent to the Middle East. When the King did decide in 1270 to lead another expeditionary force overseas, he was faced by nationwide opposition. The King, an idealist, had to promise material advantages to those who would follow him, and even had to go to such lengths as subsidizing his own vassals. His faithful companion and chronicler Joinville had to find excuses for not going. It was more important for him to stay at home and look after his subjects.

I was much pressed by the King of France and the King of Navarre to take the cross. To them I made answer, that while I had been in the service of God and the King across the seas, and since I came back thence, the officers of the King of France and the King of Navarre had ruined and impoverished my people for me; so there was never a time but that I and they would be worse for it. And I told them this, that if I meant to labour according to the will of God in this matter, that I would remain there to help and defend my people.[8]

For the next two centuries or so, European imperialism was held in check. It was not only because Europe's psychological drive was declining, but also because Islam was on the offensive again. The last stronghold in Syria, Saint John of Acre, fell in 1291, and the remaining Christians had to abandon the mainland they had occupied since the end of the eleventh century. The Ottoman Turks reduced what was still left of the Byzantine Empire and, crossing into eastern Europe, occupied vast regions of the Balkans, threatening Hungary and Poland. Europe was once more on the defensive.

Another "external" menace to Europe was the changing climate. Whereas favorable climatic conditions had assisted Europe's era of growth, now unfavorable conditions were to have an adverse effect on the continent's economy. The average temperature fell and rainfall increased. The trend, which had begun in the thirteenth century, became dramatically apparent at the beginning of the fourteenth century, notably in the years 1315–17. During this brief period, from Scotland to Italy, from the Pyrenees to the plains of Russia, Europe suffered weather conditions so appalling as to trigger the medieval economic depression, with effects that were to last about 150 years, right into the Renaissance.

The preceding period had seen famines virtually disappear from Europe. Two are recorded in the twelfth century, in 1125 and in 1197, but they did not affect all of Europe, and in thirteenth-century France only Aquitaine, in 1235, suffered a famine. There were years when crops were not bountiful, and the gap between harvests was often difficult to bridge, but both climate and economics remained relatively stable. The famines of 1315–17, however, were on a scale that stunned Europe. In the summer of 1314, northwest Europe was hit by heavy rains. Harvests were ruined, which in turn provoked a general rise in the price of corn and other foodstuffs. Confronted by this inflation, the King of France was requested on January 21, 1315, to draw up a schedule of prices for all domestic animals and fowls. The sheriffs were instructed to establish the maximum prices and see to it that these were not exceeded. Inevitably, these measures failed, and prices continued to rise.

The torrential rains that fell in France from the middle of April 1315, and in England from May 11, were more destructive still. It rained all through the summer and autumn of 1315, drowning the crops. The one consolation of this disaster was that it stopped a war. The rains checked the French army invading Flanders, as the soldiers became bogged down in a sea of mud in the low-lying lands. Unfortunately, many who were saved from dying on the battlefield died the following year of hunger or of diseases accompanying the famine. From May 1 to September 1, 1316, some 2,800 people died in Ypres, 190 a week, as against 15 to 16 in normal times. The toll amounted to 10 percent of the population. The Abbot of Saint Martin of Tournai, one of the chroniclers of the famine in Flanders, describes the miseries of the time:

> on account of the torrential rains and because the fruits of the earth were harvested in difficult conditions and destroyed in many places, there was a dearth of wheat and of salt . . . the human bodies started growing weaker and disabilities developed. . . . So many people died every day . . . that the air seemed to be putrefied . . . miserable

beggars died . . . in great numbers in the streets, on dung-hills. . . .[9]

One misery of the time he particularly deplored was the scarcity of French wine. In 1316 he was compelled to drink the local wine of Saint Jean des Clairfours.

Economic historians who have made an accurate measurement of the gross yield of wheat per annum for nearly 150 years, 1209–1350, on the fifty manors of the Bishopric of Winchester have found the average rate of seed germination for the whole period to be 3.83. It is interesting to observe that for 1315 the rate is as low as 2.47, a deviation of −35.77%. For 1316, the rate is even lower at 2.11, a deviation of −44.91%. In 1317, the rate is still below average at 3.33, a rate deviation of −13.05%. But in 1318, the rate at last picks up and reaches the figure of 5.07 a +32.38% deviation. The famine had passed, but the moral and material repercussions of this European disaster were still apparent.

The bailiffs, when there were extremes of weather in spring, summer, autumn, or winter, wrote down climatic observations in their manorial accounts. For the famine years, Table 6 shows that there were eight successive extremes of wet weather.

The documentation is shockingly vivid:

In Ireland, the agony dragged on into 1318 and proved especially severe, for the people dug up the bodies in the

TABLE 6. *Climate in the Bishopric of Winchester, 1315–16*[10]

Year	Yield deviation	Previous summer	Previous autumn	Winter	Summer
1315	−35.77%	Flooding	Very wet and long	Flooding	Very wet
1316	−44.91%	Very wet	Very wet and long	Flooding	Flooding

churchyards and used them for food and parents even ate their children. . . . In Slavic parts such as Poland and Siberia it appears that the famine and mortality were still common as late as 1319 and cannibalism is said to have been rife. . . . Parents killed their children and children killed their parents, and the bodies of executed criminals were eagerly snatched from the gallows.[11]

But the horrors of those famine years were surpassed by those of the Black Death. Perhaps there was even a direct relationship, for it has been suggested that the malnutrition suffered by Europeans in the aftermath of the famine lowered their physical resistance to the plague bacillus.

Plague is the most complicated as well as the most deadly of human epidemic diseases. There have been three recorded outbreaks, and the third one is still with us in the world today. The first ravaged the Byzantine Empire in the sixth century and western Europe in the seventh and eighth centuries. The second began with the Black Death in the fourteenth century and ended only in the seventeenth century, in 1665, with the Great Plague of London. Since the eighteenth century, Europe has been spared the horrors of this second outbreak, possibly because across the continent the black rat, which is host to the *Xenopsylla cheopsis*, the flea that harbors the plague bacilli, was driven out by the brown rat. While the brown rat can also be host to the flea, it lives more out of doors and is less likely to come in contact with human beings. In any case, the third outbreak started in Yunnan in 1892 and reached Bombay by 1896. "In India alone it is believed to have killed some six million people. It made a brief and mercifully unsuccessful foray into Suffolk in 1910, finding only a handful of victims. Quite recently it has made itself felt in the Azores and parts of South America. In many parts of the world it still has to run its course."[12] It seems to be endemic today in Uganda, western Arabia, Kurdistan, northern India, and the Gobi Desert.

One of the routes by which the epidemic reached Europe was through Genoese merchants who had been besieged by the Tartars in 1347, in the city of Tana, now Feodosia, on the Crimean coast. The besieging army had been riddled by the disease and, before withdrawing, thought that the Christians should also suffer their agony. So, using their giant catapults, they lobbed their plague victims high over the walls, hoping to contaminate the Genoese. Their plan was brilliantly successful. Infected with the germs, the Genoese fled the city and embarked on their ships. They sailed into the Mediterranean, and with them came the plague.

Boccaccio's detailed description of the Black Death in the introduction to his famous *Decameron* is still the most vivid and dramatic account of how medieval society reacted to this exceptional calamity:

> Tedious were it to recount how citizen avoided citizen . . . brother was forsaken by brother, nephew by uncle, brother by sister and often times husband by wife . . . fathers and mothers were found to abandon their own children . . . many died daily or nightly in the public streets; of many others, who died at home, the departure was hardly observed by their neighbours, until the stench of their putrefying bodies carried the tidings . . . one and the same bier carried two or three corpses at once . . . one bier sufficing for husband and wife, two or three brothers, father and son . . . nor, for all their number, were there obsequies honoured by either tears, or lights, or crowds of mourners; rather it was to come to this, that a dead man was then of no more account than a dead goat would be today. . . .[13]

By the end of 1348 the Black Death was decimating the Mediterranean islands, Italy, Spain, France, the south of England; by the end of 1349 Germany, central Europe, Flanders, and the north of England; and by the end of 1350 the Baltic countries, Scandinavia, and Scotland. The plague left no country untouched, although certain areas escaped lightly, especially Bohemia, large areas of Poland, an ill-explained pocket between France, Germany, and the Netherlands, and tracts of the Pyrenees.

The impact of this mighty catastrophe was extensive in nearly every area of medieval life, though one should not lose sight of the fact that the Black Death often only accelerated trends established prior to the outbreak. A demographic decline, for example, existed prior to the spectacular decline provoked by the epidemic. There was also a point in the Middle Ages at which the birthrate began to fall. In the aristocracy, which is the only social group for which there are sufficient documents for historians to amass statistics, we can observe the decreasing average number of children per couple. This trend is shown clearly by the index of population increase: 122 for the period 1150–1200, 113.1 for 1200–1250, but only 105.8 for 1250–1300.

The statistics offered by San Gimignano, a town in Tuscany now famous for its high-rise towers built for social status by its wealthy citizens, reveal clearly the medieval demographic decline before and after the Black Death. There is a table (Table 7) showing the number of hearths recorded in different years from the thirteenth to the sixteenth centuries, for both the city of San Gimignano itself and its *contado* (surrounding countryside), with the number of inhabitants per hearth at those dates. Though the number of hearths increased in the city from 1277 to 1332, from 1,331 hearths to 1,687, the population only increased by a bare 500 inhabitants, from 8,000 to 8,500, and in the *contado* the population, in fact, decreased between 1290 and 1332 by 20 percent (the hearths by 4 percent).

With the Black Death, the decrease in the hearths and population is dramatic. Between 1332 and 1350 the city of San Gimignano lost 59 percent of its hearths and 70 percent of its

TABLE 7. *Number of Hearths in San Gimignano*[14]
(approximate number of inhabitants per hearth in parentheses)

Year	1277	1290	1332	1350	1427	1551
City	1,331(×6)		1,687(×5)	695(×3½)	314(×4)	401
Contado		891(×6)	852	468(×4)	250(×7)	461

citizens, and in the *contado* respectively 45 percent and 55 percent. These figures are exceptionally high, possibly because there were two calamities—an epidemic in 1340 and a famine in 1347—over and above the Black Death. It is generally agreed among historians that there was in Europe an overall demographic loss of 33 percent to 40 percent (higher in the cities than in the countryside, as one might expect).

What is often not realized about this demographic catastrophe is that Europe only recovered its pre–Black Death level of population around 1600. In 1427 San Gimignano had 314 hearths and only 14 percent of the population of 1332, while in 1551 the city had still only 25 percent of the hearths it had in 1332. Figure 5 is a graph for ten European cities showing that Venice alone had recovered its population level of the first half of the fourteenth century by the early sixteenth century (1509). Florence in 1526 still had only 80 percent to 85 percent of its 1328 population, and Albi in 1601 still had less than 55 percent of the citizens it had in 1343.

Tens of thousands of European villages literally disappeared from the face of the earth. One of the most spectacular ways of rediscovering these lost villages is by aerial reconnaissance. The patterns of village houses and streets, which are absolutely invisible from the ground, show up remarkably in air photographs. In England the number of deserted medieval villages recorded up to 1968 was 2,263, a figure bound to increase considerably when all the counties have been systematically surveyed. Approximately 20 percent of English

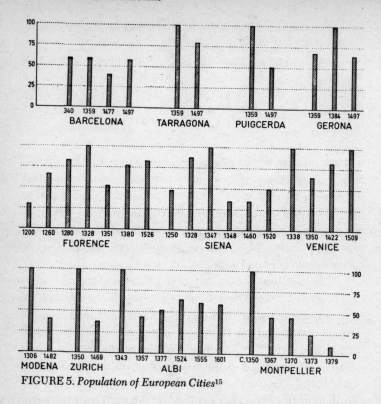

FIGURE 5. *Population of European Cities*[15]

villages disappeared in the late Middle Ages, and in some counties like Oxfordshire the proportion was as high as 25 percent. The map of the deserted villages of England is covered with black dots, especially in the Midlands and the northeast.

In Germany and certain Mediterranean islands, the number of lost villages is even higher than in England. Out of the 170,000 German villages recorded from 1300 (within the frontiers of 1933), 40,000 disappeared in the next two centuries, approximately 23 percent. In some regions, like Hesse, the proportion was as high as 44 percent. But most spectacularly hit were Sardinia and Sicily, where 50 percent of the villages disappeared.

The Black Death and its demographic and economic consequences were not entirely responsible for all these deserted villages. Another crucial factor was the falling productivity of the land. Land clearing no longer produced the rich soils it had originally opened up to the plow. Very soon the fertility of these new marginal lands was exhausted, and they had to be abandoned. Villages that had been established to farm them were forsaken, and the Black Death accelerated the flight of their people.

The effects of the Black Death were not always disastrous. For a great many of the surviving peasants and industrial workers, the plague actually brought about a higher standard of living. With the sudden shortage of manpower, the rural and urban proletariat was able to receive considerably higher wages. It was, of course, true that after the 1315–17 famine and depopulation, salaries had already been marginally raised. But now the landlords could not refuse the demands for higher wages, otherwise the peasants and their families would move to the next demesnes. In the city, the skilled as well as the unskilled workmen offered their work to the highest bidder. The shortage of labor was of greatest benefit to the unskilled, for it led to a substantial narrowing of wage differentials.

Though the price of wheat soared at the time of the Black Death, as it did in later epidemics and times of famine, the average price of grain decreased for the next 150 years or so, due to the decline in population. Demand no longer outran supply. The events of 1315–17 had already produced a 20 percent fall in the price of wheat in the second quarter of the fourteenth century. In Caen, in 1428, wheat was worth only half of its 1270 value.

The price of other agricultural products, such as wine and livestock, did not fall in the same proportion. In England the price of cattle fell on the average by only 11 percent between 1350 and 1450, and, exceptionally, the price of some semiluxury items like butter actually rose.

The price of industrial products also generally fell, with perhaps one important exception, iron—a result of the increasing demand for iron in guns, cannons, and every kind of weaponry in an age of almost permanent warfare.

This general decline in prices in the fourteenth and fifteenth centuries is a reversal of the trend of the twelfth and thirteenth centuries. Figure 6 shows fluctuations in the purchase price of oxen and in the prices of wheat and cheese for the period 1245–1325 in England. The price of oxen rose some 250 percent and the price of wheat over 200 percent. The sharp rise in the selling price of wheat for the 1315–17 famine is also clearly shown in the graph.

Figure 7's two graphs show the relative fluctuations in Paris of the price of wheat for the period 1340–60 and the daily salaries for workmen in the building trade. The wheat graph naturally shows a high point for 1350, the great plague year, but what is interesting is to compare the two graphs and observe that once the workmen got their wage increases, due largely to the high price of grain prevailing in the city, they were never relinquished. Over the years 1349–51 the authorities in France, England, and Spain issued statutes to compel the workmen to return to their preplague salaries, but to no avail.

A country gentleman, John Gower, writing in England in about 1375, deplored the revolutionary situation that had arisen:

> The world goeth fast from bad to worse, when shepherd and cowherd for their part demand more for their labour than the master-bailiff was wont to take in days gone by. Labour is now at so high a price that he who will order his business aright, must pay five or six shillings now for

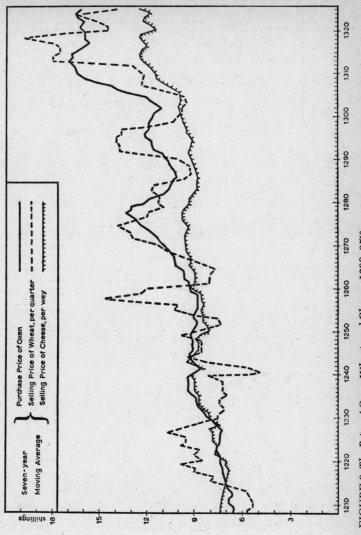

FIGURE 6. *The Price of Oxen, Wheat, and Cheese, 1208–35*[16]

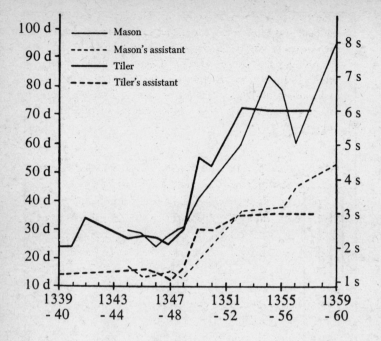

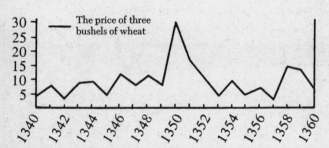

FIGURE 7. *Daily Wages in the Building Trade and* (below) *the Price of Wheat in Paris, 1339/40–1360*[17]

what cost two in former times. . . . Ha! age of ours . . .
the poor and small folk . . . demand to be better fed than
their masters. Moreover they bedeck themselves in fine
colours and fine attire, whereas (were it not for their
pride and their privy conspiracies) they would be clad in
sack cloth as of old. . . . Ha! age of ours . . . I see the poor
folk more haughty than their lords; each draweth whither
he pleaseth.[18]

The upstart spirit denounced by Gower was perhaps new
to England, but on the Continent it had for a century or so
fomented many bloody uprisings. In the chapter on the textile
industry we mentioned a number of revolts in Flanders in the
second half of the thirteenth century. In the fourteenth century there was a considerable increase, and in the years following John Gower's lamentation, Europe witnessed, between
1378 and 1382, a whole series of revolutionary uprisings, the
most famous being that of the Ciompis in Florence and the
Peasants' Revolt in England.

For the first time in European history, socialist and communist ideals, aspirations unknown to the classical world, were
being professed by revolutionaries. Even though these revolutionaries failed to put these ideals into practice for more than
a few days or weeks, they stand nevertheless as forerunners
of the socialist revolutionaries of later centuries.

For nearly twenty years, from 1366 on, the man behind
the Peasants' Revolt of 1381 had been going from village to
town, from Yorkshire to Essex, preaching the subversive doctrine that all men were equal, and that the lands of the Church
should be confiscated and distributed to the landless peasants.
His name was John Ball. Like many modern revolutionaries
he spoke, preached, and propagandized, and may have published and circulated seditious pamphlets. His famous "letters"
may be a few of these, written in cipher. He spent part of his
life in and out of prison, and he was interned for the last time

in Maidstone jail on April 21, 1381, but released six weeks later by an army of insurgents on their way to take London. Before entering the city they camped on the night of June 12 at Blackheath, and it was probably on the following day that John Ball preached his famous sermon on the text:

> *When Adam delved and Eve span,*
> *Who was then a gentleman?*[19]

His contemporaries recognized Ball as being largely instrumental in exciting the rebellious ideas that led to the Peasants' Revolt. He would say:

> My good friends, matters cannot go on well in England until all things shall be in common; when there shall be neither vassals nor lords; when the lords shall be no more masters than ourselves. How ill they behave to us! for what reason do they hold us in bondage? Are we not all descended from the same parents, Adam and Eve? And what can they show, or what reason can they give, why they should be more masters than ourselves? They are clothed in velvet and rich stuffs, ornamented with ermine and other furs, while we are forced to wear poor clothing. They have wines, spices and fine bread, while we only have rye and the refuse of the straw and when we drink it must be water. They have handsome seats and manors, while we must brave the wind and rain in our labours in the field; and it is by our labour they have wherewith to support their pomp.[20]

Led by Wat Tyler, the majority of the insurgents occupied London from June 13 to 15, 1381, freeing the prisoners from every prison in London, burning the houses of some of the wealthier citizens, beheading the Archbishop of Canterbury and playing football at a crossroads with his head, and getting the King to agree to their reforms. While this was going on, another group of insurgents from Saint Albans marched back to the abbey "to achieve ancient underground aspirations, like new town boundaries, free pastures and fisheries, revival of lost sporting rights, freedom to establish hand mills, the exclusion of the liberty's bailiffs from the town limits, and the return of bonds made by their sires to the late Abbot Richard of Wallingford."[21]

Here for the third time we come across Richard of Wallingford. We heard of him first seizing the millstones in 1326 and paving the cloisters with them to "the humiliation of the common people." Next he appeared as a famous inventor answering the King, who had rebuked him concerning his clock, that "there would be no successor, after his death, who could finish the work that had been begun." And now at last we find the townspeople of Saint Albans in a position to avenge the humiliation inflicted on them half a century earlier. They "went into the cloister . . . and ripped up millstones set in the parlour floor . . . smashing these, they distributed fragments like holy bread in a parish church."[22]

But the tide was turning against the revolutionaries. Wat Tyler was killed in London on Saturday, June 15. The insurgents of Saint Albans "now dismayed . . . hired an expensive lawyer to compromise with the Abbot, repairing damage, replacing as many millstones as were removed."[23] John Ball was arrested and brought to Saint Albans, where he was tried on July 13 and executed on July 15. The Peasants' Revolt was over.

Many of the uprisings during the Middle Ages' period of decline were prompted by the raising of taxes. The immediate cause of the Peasants' Revolt had been a further levy of the poll tax and continuing grievance against the devaluing or debasing of the currency.

We have seen how silver monometallism was introduced into Europe in the eighth century by the Carolingians. For five hundred years, until the middle of the thirteenth century,

Europe lived and worked with silver monometallism. Then bimetallism was reintroduced for the first time since the Romans: Genoa and Flórence minted gold coins in 1252, and France in 1266.

After returning in 1254 from the Middle East following nearly six years overseas, the King of France, Saint Louis, devoted much of his time to reforming his country's financial situation, which had deteriorated in his absence. A strong currency being essential for the welfare of France, he decided to mint a gold coin, the *écu d'or*, and a silver coin, the *gros tournois*, and took strong measures to protect their value. Nobody but the King had the authority to mint them. Not only were the feudal lords denied this privilege, but the currency of their own coinage was now confined strictly to their lands. Unfortunately, the *écu d'or* and the *gros tournois*, symbols of France's power and wealth in thirteenth-century, began to lose their prestige, and at the end of the thirteenth century the *gros tournois* suffered a series of devaluations. (In the Middle Ages, currency was devalued either by reminting a coin of lesser weight, or by changing the alloy and reminting the coin with less silver.)

As France entered its era of maturity in the mid-thirteenth century, it aspired to assume a leading political role and act as arbiter of the nations within its zone of influence, and for a while it succeeded. Its administration, however, was not sufficiently staffed or competent to deal with this new role, so it had to create and support a vast new bureaucracy of civil servants. At the same time an effort was made to concentrate greater power in Paris. A standing army in time of peace became necessary, and military expenditure began to weigh heavily on the economy.

The French King who first devalued the currency was Philip the Fair (1285–1314). In fact, he has remained famous for this; all French schoolbooks describe his financial operations. His first debasement in the years 1294–95 apparently did not attract much attention, but in 1306 he confidently announced in advance that he was now going to devalue by 39 percent. The result was a sensational rise in prices while creditors still demanded to be paid in predevaluation currency. Tenants protested violently against the rise in rents and started defacing their houses. The landlords called on the king's officers, who then tried to intervene and were badly beaten up by the tenants. In the following January, the situation deteriorated further, and there was concerted action by a number of citizens. Their anger was directed not against the King's officers, who were after all not responsible, but against Etienne Barbette, a bourgeois, formerly *Prévot des marchands* and now *Maître de la Monnaie*, who was held to be the instigator of the devaluation. Barbette's country house just outside Paris was ransacked, and after that his house in the city. His wine cellar was emptied and his furniture thrown out of the windows into the street. The demonstrators then moved on to besiege the King, who had taken refuge in the Temple. After a day of parlaying, the King moved in his troops and had the demonstrators thrown back. Philip took exception to their open defiance of his financial decisions, and arrested one leading representative from each of twenty-eight trades and had them hanged.

Philip the Fair devalued again in 1313, and to commemorate the event a charming song was written by a Parisian, possibly Geoffrey de Paris:

> *It seems that the King enchants us,*
> *For at first sixty made twenty for us*
> *Then twenty made four and thirty made ten*
>
> . . .
>
> *Gold and silver all is lost*
> *none of it ever to be returned.*[24]

The devaluations continued, were opposed, and more blood flowed.

The historian Carlo Cipolla has compiled a list of the causes that singly or in various combinations were, in his view, responsible for these devaluations in the Middle Ages.

a. The long term increase in the demand for money, resulting from the long term growth of populations and/ or of income and/or of the "monetization" of the economy.
b. The growth of government expenditure and deficits.
c. The pressure of social groups in the direction of profit-inflation.
d. Disequilibrium in the balance of payments.
e. The mismanagement of the mints.
f. The wear of the existing stocks of coins in circulation, occasionally aggravated by the practice of clipping.
g. Fluctuations in the market rate of exchange between gold and silver.[25]

A serious deficit in the balance of payments is generally a main contributory cause to devaluation. Although we do not have any documents to prove that France at the time of Philip the Fair had a balance of payments deficit, we do know that the English pound was devalued only marginally in the fourteenth and fifteenth centuries in comparison to French currency, possibly because her balance of payments was exceptionally favorable, due to her high exports of raw wool and finished cloth.

From A.D. 1000 to A.D. 1500, fluctuations in the market rate of exchange between gold and silver plagued the monetary history of Europe and the Moslem world. Gold and silver tended to shift from areas where they were undervalued to areas where they were more highly valued. When the ratio of gold to silver was 14 to 1 in the Islamic Empire, and 12 or even

10 to 1 in Europe, gold moved eastward and silver westward. To use a widely accepted expression, there was a famine of gold in the east and a famine of silver in the west. Merchant-financiers made fortunes on the fluctuating rates of exchange between the two monetary zones. But then, in the thirteenth century, there was a reversal of the trend. The Islamic world began to remint silver coins and Europe reminted gold coins, so silver now started to flow eastward and gold westward.

> By the early fourteenth century signs appeared of what was to become a spectacular boom in the price of gold. The South of Europe was hit first: in Venice the success of the ducat seems to have caused such a demand for gold that the ratio rose to over 13 by 1297 and over 14 by 1308, while in France the coining of large quantities of gold under Philip the Fair brought the ratio up to nearly 14 in 1299, 16 in 1309 and apparently over 19 in 1311 . . . the ratio in Germany . . . hit a peak of 21.6 in 1339.[26] . . . Rulers in all parts of Europe were ready to procure the metal needed to maintain a strong gold currency by sacrificing silver. They were prepared to let the common people who received their incomes in silver bear the burden of keeping intact a prestige coinage for the use of princes and merchants.[27]

By the middle of the fourteenth century, this outflow of silver produced a new monetary crisis, dramatically reported by the chronicler Giovanni Villani:

> This same year, 1345, there was a great scarcity of silver . . . because silver had been melted down and conveyed overseas. . . . It caused great difficulties to the textile merchants and other entrepreneurs who feared that the florin would fall too heavily in relation to silver. So it was prohibited to export silver from the city. . . .[28]

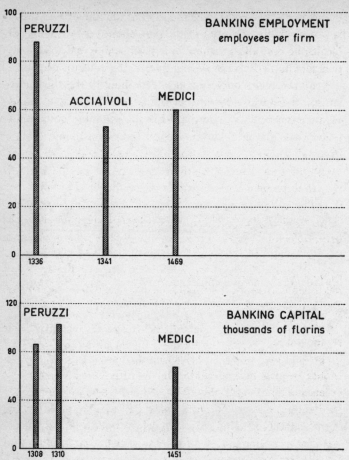

FIGURE 8. *The Principal Banking Houses of Florence*[29]

That same year Giovanni Villani wrote of another frightening disaster, "the greatest Florence had ever known": the bankruptcy of the famous banking company the Bardi. Two years previously the Peruzzi bank had failed, and now the most powerful financial city, not only of Europe but of the world, was thrown into financial chaos. Villani, who only a few years before had proudly recorded statistics showing the wealth of his city, was stunned. Bankruptcy followed bankruptcy, and there were repercussions all over Europe.

Florence was never again the formidable financial power she had been in the thirteenth century and in the first decade of the fourteenth. The Medici bank, with capital considerably lower than that of the Peruzzi, and fewer personnel, was the one and only great Florentine bank by the middle of the fifteenth century. And by the time Lorenzo the Magnificent took over its leadership in 1469, it, too, was in decline.

The aura of humanism that has always surrounded Lorenzo has long concealed the fact that he was unable to apply his intellectual gifts to his banking activities. The accusation leveled at him by Florentine chroniclers that he salvaged the Medici bank from bankruptcy by appropriating public funds has been proved by a recently discovered document, which states explicity that the payments were made "without the sanction of any law and without authority to the damage and prejudice of the Commune."[30] Lorenzo in his panic found other dubious ways of refloating his company, though it should be said in his defense that he was living in a time of great monetary instability. Florence had again been shaken by bankruptcies in the years 1464–65, and in the following decades the Florentine economic depression deepened.

The traditional view of historians that the depression of the Middle Ages was arrested by the Renaissance was questioned in an important article entitled "The Economic Depression of the Renaissance," written by R. S. Lopez and H. A. Miskimin (1962). They asked:

> Whether at the end of the fifteenth century the balance sheet . . . showed an overall retreat, advance, or stability as compared to the balance sheet of the early fourteenth century, or in absolute figures . . . whether the total mass of production and consumption increased or diminished

in size, or whether the rate of growth was high enough
in the fifteenth century to equal earlier achievements.[31]

The authors illustrated their article with a graph (Figure 9),
showing levels of international trade for which statistics are
available for Marseilles, Genoa, England, and Dieppe over
the period 1270–1550. In all four cases it is apparent that the
years between 1420 and 1465 were years of economic decline. Genoa's best trade figures occurred in 1293; the peak
reached in the second decade of the sixteenth century is still
lower than that of 1293.

We have seen that the aging era of the Middle Ages was
characterized by a cult of mysticism, witchcraft, and torture;
a decline in agricultural yields and the loss of vast acreages of
land; an increase in the number of famines and epidemics; a
dramatic fall in population with a dramatic rise in the number
of popular uprisings; and an economic depression leading to
devaluations and bankruptcies. But there was one calamity
that surpassed all the others: war.

For the greater part of the declining era of the Middle
Ages, wars raged all over Europe—in Spain, Italy, Germany,
Scandinavia, England. But nowhere was war more terrible
than in France, where for over a hundred years it was endemic.
It has been said that in our time a Vietnamese child could have
been born whose father and even grandfather had never witnessed real peace. But in the fifteenth century a child in
France could have been born whose great-great-grandfather
had never known what peace really was. A medieval chronicler tells us that even the livestock were conditioned to war.
As soon as the animals—horses, oxen, pigs, and sheep—
heard the signal of the watchman on his tower warning of approaching men-of-arms, they would rush back to the safety
of the city walls.

When the revolutionary fourteenth-century European
weapon, the bombard or cannon, appeared, it "made such a

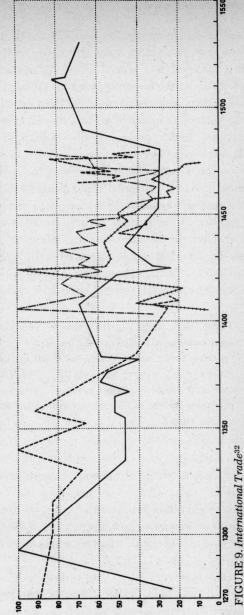

INTERNATIONAL TRADE
expressed as a percentage of the area maximum during
the time span for which statistics were available

------- MARSEILLE, 1304-41 = 100% = 60 LIVRES – Price of tax farm
——— GENOA, 1293 = 100% = 3,822,000 lb
——— ENGLAND, 1405-8 = 100% = 187,439 £.
+++++ DIEPPE, 1424-5 = 100% = 390 SHIPS granted permission to enter or depart

FIGURE 9. *International Trade*[32]

noyse in the goying as though all the dyvels of hell had been in the way."[33] Cannons went into action in the very decades when medieval decline took a turn for the worse, in the second decade of the fourteenth century (though some historians dispute the references) and in the third decade. The first official reference is found in a Florentine document dated February 11, 1326, concerning the acquisition of "pilas seu palloctas ferreas et canones de metallo"[34] and indicating that at that date bronze guns were used to fire iron balls. The following year a cannon is represented in the English Milemete manuscript, and in 1338 there is a reference at Rouen to "pot de fer à traire garros de feu," as cannons were then sometimes called. In the same year a Genoese battleship had firearms on board when it appeared with a French fleet in Southampton Water. From then onward, references are so numerous as to justify Petrarch's remarks on cannons in 1350:

> These instruments which discharge balls of metal with most tremendous noise and flashes of fire . . . were a few years ago very rare and were viewed with greatest astonishment and admiration, but now they are become as common and familiar as any kind of arms. So quick and ingenious are the minds of men in learning the most pernicious arts.[35]

Though gunpowder was mentioned by Roger Bacon and a formula was offered at the end of the thirteenth century by a certain Marcus Graecus, it was, of course, a Chinese invention of the ninth or tenth century. But the cannon itself was a European invention, and its spread very likely traveled from West to East. The first extant examples of cannons in China are dated as late as 1356, 1357, and 1377.

One of the great tragedies in history is that a declining society, hoping to live more peacefully than in the past, tends to regret its technology. What in fact usually happens is that civil engineering slows down and military engineering continues to progress. This branching off of technology into two different directions is one of the most important lessons to be learned from the history of technology. The factors that convince a society to accept technological change and those that turn a society against technology have rarely been studied, although such a study could be of the greatest benefit not only to developing countries but also to highly industrialized nations.

One of the few attempts to discover the social conditions necessary for the successful generation of or reception to technological innovation was made by Dr. R. A. Buchanan in his classic *Industrial Archaeology in Britain.* It is fascinating to see that the social prerequisites for the modern British Industrial Revolution were virtually the same as those for the medieval industrial revolution.

> For an invention to become a commercial success, three conditions are necessary, and these are all factors, in part or in whole, of the social environment. The first of these conditions is the existence within society of key groups who are prepared to consider innovations seriously and sympathetically.[36]

In the medieval era of growth, there were at least three such key groups: the landlords, who, among other achievements, built the 5,634 water mills of the Domesday Book; the Cistercians, who built the model farms and factories; and the bourgeois or self-made men, on whose ingenuity depended the financing of the expanding textile and other industries.

In the declining era, these key groups tended to innovate less and less. The landlords often became absentee landlords, and when their rents began to fall in value, they had less and less capital for investment. By the fourteenth century, the Cistercians were also on the decline, and the bourgeois had become *embourgeoisé* and, like all social groups who have reached a certain station, devoted their efforts to preserving the status quo.

Dr. Buchanan continues:

> However important this first factor, it can only operate effectively when technological innovation is being encouraged to match social needs. Such needs must be explicit—that is, they must be *felt* to be needs ... so that people are prepared to devote resources to their fulfilment. It may be that the pressure of increasing population is creating social need in the form of an enlarged market, or, paradoxically, that shortage of labour in specific areas of the economy is creating a need for labour-saving machines. Or it may be that some obdurate technical problem sets up a pressure for new solutions, like the shortage of timber. . . .[37]

In chapter 3 stress was put on the considerable population increase up to about 1300, which paved the way for an enlarged market. In the declining era, the fall in population narrowed the market. The Cistercians introduced labor-saving devices because of their labor shortage, since the lay brothers as well as the monks had to spend many hours praying. The rise in the price of timber in the thirteenth century put pressure on the society to find a new fuel. Coal was found.

> The third factor—social resources—is similarly indispensable. Many inventions have foundered because the social resources vital for their realization—capital, materials and skilled personnel were not available . . . the resource of capital involves the existence of surplus productivity and the organisation of a "capital market" capable of diverting the available wealth into channels where the inventor can use it. It presupposes, in other words, an adequate economic system.[38]

The Middle Ages produced a substantial surplus productivity, and this enabled the estate administration of Glastonbury, for example, to invest capital in a new post-mill. Again, Richard of Wallingford could not otherwise have invented his two astronomical instruments, the Rectangulus and the Albion, nor his famous clock, and Giovanni di Dondi could not have built his marvelous clock over a sixteen-year period.

In the declining era, the progress of technology was hindered by less readily available capital. The havoc wrought by the wars that raged across Europe for so many decades considerably diminished what we now call the Gross National Product (G.N.P.). What capital was still available was more often invested in war efforts: "The resource of materials involves the availability of appropriate metallurgical, ceramic, plastic substances, which in turn presupposes an adequate industrial system."[39] The medieval machine was, of course, dependent upon the available metallurgy. The exceptional advantages enjoyed by medieval miners demonstrate the crucial importance of mining in those centuries. When the great depression hit Europe, the majority of mines suffered a great fall in production, some because there was now a dearth of miners and others because the seams were running out. Some mines had been destroyed by military action and others were now too deep to exploit without new methods of raising water from the pits, methods that were far off in the future.

The last social prerequisite of technological innovations is the availability of skilled personnel. "The resource of skilled personnel implies the presence of expertise and technical 'know how' capable of constructing artifacts and devising processes, and this presupposes an adequate educational system."[40] The industrial revolution of the Middle Ages created its own skilled personnel. This phenomenon continued in the later Middle Ages, with a further refinement of skills in military engineering. The number of technological treatises published at the time is proof that the social conditions necessary

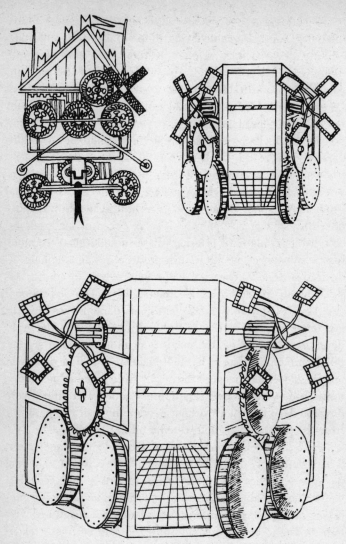

Wind-driven chariots by Guido da Vigevano (*above left*), by Valturio (*above right*), and by Taccola (*below*). Courtesy B. Gille: *Les Ingénieurs de la Renaissance*, Hermann, Paris.

for the successful generation of military innovations existed and corresponded to the needs of a society living in constant warfare. We have, for example, a military treatise written by a doctor, Guido da Vigevano, for the King of France, Philip VI of Valois, who in 1328 considered embarking on a Crusade. The treatise contains drawings of some extremely revolutionary machines, such as a war chariot driven by wind power—windmill wings were to drive the chariot to battle. Vigevano also sketched a boat in which oars have been superseded by propellers, and bridges in which pillars or similar supports have been replaced by floating drums. Another sketch shows an assault tower on the principle of the elevator, with mobile platforms.

Vigevano's project of a wind-driven chariot, although never realized, excited the imagination of engineers of later generations such as Taccola and Valturio, who drew their own similar chariots. Taccola, a Sienese military engineer born in 1381, was the first man to represent a chain transmission system, a pair of hydraulic bellows and a suction and pressure pump. He also offered the "solution of the perpetual movement that was already to be found in Villard de Honnecourt." Valturio in his treatise depicted a fantastic dragonlike machine, spouting death through a cannon lodged in the dragon's mouth.

Still other engineers such as Konrad Kyeser and the authors of the manuscript of the Hussite Wars managed to perfect some of this technology. Kyeser was born on August 25, 1366, at Eichstätt, a city halfway between Munich and Nuremberg. A workshop seems to have produced numerous copies of his military treatise, which for a century was considered to be the authoritative work on the science of machines. Kyeser drew floating and folding bridges, assault towers, and armored vehicles equipped with cannons. He offers us the first known representation of portable firearms, a long-barreled cannon, the culverin. He also drew multiple-tube

Diving helmet and deep-sea diver, as sketched in the manuscript of the Hussite Wars. Courtesy B. Gille: *Les Ingénieurs de la Renaissance*, Hermann, Paris.

cannons rotating like a revolver. (So, Leonardo was not the first to invent this type of artillery.)

The manuscript of the Hussite Wars, written in the following generation (*c.* 1430), contains the first drawing of a cannon, mounted on a carriage with two wheels. In a further drawing, reinforced gun screens were introduced, also a machine for boring cannons. The manuscript has the first known representation of a cannon on board a warship. The most remarkable of all the drawings is a hand mill with a rod and crank system, and perhaps equally noteworthy, if this time in the realm of science fiction, is the drawing of a diver and his diving suit (although this was not the first—for Kyeser had himself drawn two divers fighting underwater). "We have here a true piece of apparatus which strikes us by its modern appearance. We can make out the waterproof—or supposedly waterproof—tunic, the lead soled shoes and the helmet, details of which are given separately." Leonardo again was not the first to draw a deep-sea diver and it has even been observed that "Leonardo's drawing is much less precise."[41]

By 1453 artillery had become so powerful as to be decisive in a siege or battle. In the east, the Turks, who for centuries had tried to conquer Byzantium but had never been able to break the huge ramparts that protected Constantinople itself, now, with artillery, had the means to capture the city, and in 1453 Turkish guns battered down the walls. It was to be the end of an empire that had lasted eleven hundred years.

In the West, the French army, who a century earlier had been defeated by an English army with superior military equipment, including the first cannons, now defeated the English with artillery superior to any in the world. English citadels in France collapsed, and the English army was twice defeated on the battlefields with the help of cannons, at Formigny in 1450 and at Castillon in 1453. The Hundred Years' War was over. The year 1453 brings the medieval period to its close.

France's continuing progress in military technology had no parallel in nonmilitary fields, where toward the end of the thirteenth century stagnation set in that was to last for about 150 years. Nevertheless, during these years the rest of Europe benefited from the supremacy France had gained in the twelfth and thirteenth centuries, in particular in building techniques.

This is a perfect example of the way in which technical knowledge is transferred from the most advanced country to those less advanced, a phenomenon fundamental to the understanding of history. The country with the technological lead gradually slows down and the less developed countries with which it is in contact begin to catch up; in some industries they may even overtake it. For certain periods of time, which can last half a century or more, the world seems to reach a technological plateau. During the Middle Ages, this plateau lasted for approximately 150 years, from the last third of the thirteenth century to the first third of the fifteenth century. The few remarkable exceptions were to have no immediate or decisive influence—the mechanical clock, cast iron, the free-turning forecarriage, and the suction pump driven by a rod and crank. Basic areas of the economy such as agriculture, energy resources, and the textile industry remained at very much the same technological level until the Industrial Revolution of the eighteenth century. The building industry really only resumed progress with the introduction of iron structures in the nineteenth century.

Nevertheless, it was from a twofold medieval legacy—the innovations relating to navigational techniques and printing, both recognized landmarks in the history of mankind—that the Renaissance blossomed forth.

Epilogue

The picture of the Middle Ages as a dynamic and progressive period when inventions were at a premium differs
markedly from the generally accepted view of this era, a view
based on an overly neat contrast between the religion of the
Middle Ages and the rationalism of the Renaissance. The
truth is that medieval man was often less religious than is
widely believed, and the later humanists' faith in Christianity
was often deep and sincere.

The reputation of the Middle Ages has never really recovered from the attack launched by the Renaissance upon
the centuries that preceded humanism. Being passionately
interested in the literature and poetry of classical civilization,
people in the Renaissance were convinced that their fore-
bears in the Middle Ages—later to be termed the Dark Ages—
were altogether ignorant of or indifferent to ancient Greek and
Roman authors, whereas in actual fact the medieval men were
passionately interested—not so much in the literature and
the poetry of the classical world, as in its philosophical, scientific, and technological works.

While the Renaissance viewed medieval society as scholastic and static, the Reformation saw it as hierarchical and

corrupt, and the Age of Enlightenment considered it to have been irrational and superstitious. For many people in our contemporary Western world, these views of the Middle Ages are still very real. With the advent of Romanticism in the nineteenth century, enthusiastic efforts were made to lift the Middle Ages out of the Dark Ages, but this rescue operation led to some misrepresentation of social realities. Liberal Catholic reformers began to look back on those centuries as a time when there existed an ideal Christian society, a model for contemporary Christianity. For the French, the ideal Christian century was the thirteenth, the century of Saint Louis. A beautiful legend took root that faith was so great in those days that the population of the cities volunteered to help build the cathedrals without financial remuneration, and that the sculptors and architects chose to remain anonymous. The conservative elements in nineteenth-century Europe, faced with class warfare and industrial strife, believed that they had found in the Middle Ages an ideal social organization, the guild system, which brought together masters, apprentices, and workmen in one harmonious society. A study of the powerful capitalist textile industry of Flanders or Florence shows this belief to have been an illusion. But conservatives were not the only ones so deluded. The ever-increasing importance of industrial technology in the nineteenth century and its accompanying misery led social reformers also to turn to medieval times, believing that laborers then were all craftsmen or artisans, working with their hands in an age without machinery—that the medieval era was in fact blessed as being a *non*technological age.

Although twentieth-century medievalists have gradually reappraised the majority of nineteenth-century romantic fallacies about their period, they have generally left untouched this legend of a nontechnological medieval society.

The history of medieval technology is still very much in its infancy, and contributors to this vast field are rare. In 1953, when I submitted an article to *Techniques et Civilisations*, the magazine's editor, Bertrand Gille, was writing the majority of its contents under various noms de plume to give the impression that there was a substantial group of scholars interested in the history of technology. Louis Delville, the publisher of the review, had to be convinced that mine was not just another of Gille's nom de plume articles. With few authors and very nearly as few subscribers, the review published its last number in 1956.

Two years later, in 1958, Lynn White, then professor of history at U.C.L.A. and author of the only book at that time on medieval innovations, *Medieval Technology and Social Change*, took up the cause of Bertrand Gille's defunct review when he helped to found *Technology and Culture*. Almost the only other periodical devoted to the history of technology is the *Transactions of the Newcomen Society*, published in England, but it is mainly concerned with the English Industrial Revolution.

Lynn White remarks that while there has been since the middle of the fourteenth century

> a trickle of interest in the history of technology, there has been no professional academic discipline of the history of technology. The histories of law, politics, art, philosophy, religion and the like, all have long been developed by bodies of highly trained scholars, occupying university chairs, providing recognized curricula towards advanced degrees, organized in learned societies and research institutes, equipped with journals as clearing houses of new findings and interpretation. Within the past twenty-five years even the history of science, so curiously neglected, has achieved this status. In contrast what little has been done in the history of technology has been produced, with rare exceptions, with the left hand by men whose right hands were busy with practical technical problems.[1]

Our ignorance of the history of technology prohibits us from understanding fully the economic and political evolution of our time. It also distorts our picture of the past. We are convinced that we are living in the first truly technological society in history, and looking around we can see only continuous progress in technology and science. The historian of technology must correct this belief. Our Western civilization has reached a technological plateau that will extend well into the third millennium.

Technological progress is cyclical, as is most of history. The West has been privileged to live through two major cycles —the Middle Ages and the Renaissance—within a civilization that has lasted now for a thousand years. The majority of civilizations, like those of Byzantium or Islam, seem to have lived through only one cycle. Moreover, within the overall cycles of the West, each major nation has had its own dominant cycle. Italy in the fifteenth century, Spain in the sixteenth, France in the seventeenth, England in the nineteenth, the United States in the twentieth—these nations have provided an impetus to keep up the momentum of Western civilization. But today the West has no new young nation in reserve, and the momentum cannot be maintained.

The cycles are dependent on the close relationship between the psychological drive of a society and its technological evolution. Figure 10 represents this relationship graphically through three model eras. In the era of growth the curves of psychological drive and technological evolution are parallel— or the society would cease to progress. But as soon as the society reaches its maturity the curves stop rising and begin to converge. The psychological drive diminishes in intensity and begins a downward movement. In the declining era the technological evolution curve falls, though not as rapidly as that of the psychological drive, because aging societies continue to invest quite heavily in military technology.

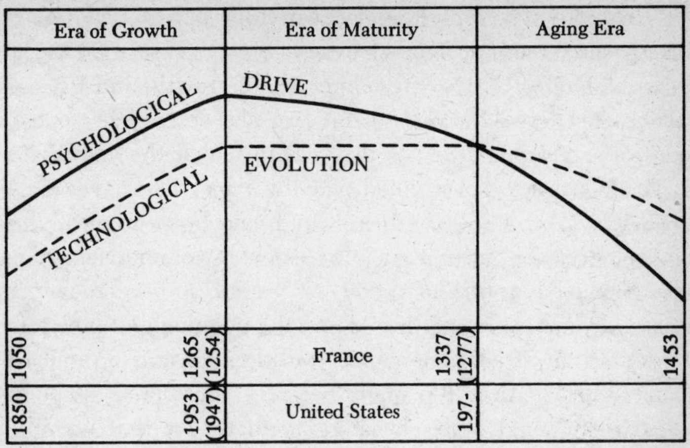

Era of Growth	Era of Maturity	Aging Era

FIGURE 10. *Cycles of Psychological Drive and Technological Evolution*

Shortly after World War II, I began a joint study of the Middle Ages and the United States and was continually impressed by the historical parallels suggested. The great Belgian medievalist Henri Pirenne had already noted a parallel between events of the eleventh and twelfth centuries in Europe and those of the American West in the nineteenth century. Similarities between new towns of the eleventh and twelfth centuries and towns preplanned by American businessmen to follow the development of the railroads are striking. In both cases one finds the emigrant, the pioneer, and the self-made man, and both economies arose from freedom of work and free enterprise.

Taking the graph of Figure 10 as my model, I decided to work out in detail the parallel developments in the two societies. At first I established that the era of growth of medieval France had lasted from 1050 to 1265 and her era of maturity from 1265 to 1337, but eventually I placed the beginning of France's mature age not in 1265 but in 1254, when Saint Louis returned from the Crusades and stamped the age with his own decisive maturity, and its end not in 1337 but in 1277, when mysticism gained ascendancy over reason. I chose 1850 as the year the United States entered her era of growth, and I tentatively considered 1953 to be the year she entered her era of maturity, because that was the year in which the celebrated Lever House was constructed on New York's Park Avenue. A glass structure only thirty stories high and built primarily for aesthetic reasons rather than with a view to commercial profit, it symbolized a turning point in American psychology: a greater awareness of aesthetics and the beginning of a certain contempt for strictly monetary considerations. Eventually I came to believe that 1947 might better be considered the point when the United States became "mature," for that was the year of the Truman Doctrine, when the United States took upon herself the responsibility for all the "free world."

When would the United States move out of her era of maturity into her aging era? I forecast that this could happen as early as the 1970s, since the absolute preeminence of a nation often lasts only some twenty-five years. Originally I tried to be even more precise and saw the change occurring in 1975, but later erased the date as being too conjectural.

In 1956 I crossed the Atlantic and gave a talk at Yale on the very subject of this parallel between the Middle Ages and the United States. The American psychological drive was well past its peak, but almost no one in the country seemed conscious of the fact. The United States citizen at that time was deeply, even fanatically, convinced that he was living in a nation that was still young. To imply the contrary was blasphemy, an insult—though an insult that was not to be taken seriously since it was made by someone who came from a decaying continent, and from the most decadent country of that continent—France. In 1956, the United States had a superiority complex, as do all nations when they are dominating the world. It must have been the case with the Romans, as it was with the British in the nineteenth century. This superiority complex made almost futile any attempt on my part to attract the attention of Americans to the historical trends I was observing. The Americans of 1956 were only interested in their own history and could not imagine that there could be a period in world history that was in any way relevant to the period they were living in.

Yet America's leveling off to maturity could be observed in many ways. No longer was the United States obsessed by a world-record-breaking spirit so often characteristic of young nations. The aesthetic of the Lever House was in sharp contrast to the 1,472 feet of the Empire State Building. The Americans were no longer ceaselessly proclaiming that they had the largest and fastest planes in the world, the greatest dams in the world, the most miles of highways in the world, the most powerful hydraulic presses. Their general attitude to life was changing. There was no longer a fascination with gadgets. In the years immediately after World War II, many Americans would proudly offer their newest gadgets to their friends in Europe as evidence of their inventiveness. This custom was dying out, and the number of new gadgets produced each year was itself falling.

The idea that Europe had of America, and that America had of itself in 1956, was of a country where there was a powerful psychological drive, where everyone in the street was in a hurry, working hard, where new millionaires rose by the thousand every month, where initiative was the motto.

Yet I noticed that the men and women in the streets were in no way running to and from their work—they walked as leisurely as in Europe, and many top executives were taking two hours or more over their lunches, just like their counterparts in Paris. And as for self-made men reaching the top of the ladder, they were fewer and farther between. Sons, instead of going into the world to make their own way in life, were increasingly content to go into their fathers' businesses. The American ideal of free enterprise and of an absence of governmental intervention was being seriously undermined by numerous groups—veterans, farmers, laborers, among others—who turned more and more to the federal government for help. The budget of the Department of Health, Education, and Welfare was to be increased in 1957 by half a billion dollars, from $2½ billion to $3 billion. The number of civil servants in federal, state, and local governments had topped the seven million mark.

At the end of my stay in the United States in 1956, I believed I had acquired enough documentation on America's psychological drive and technological evolution to discover many points of correspondence with the Middle Ages. I chose forty-eight factors from the broad spectrum of human activity —including economics, ideology, education, inventiveness, and industrialization—common to medieval France and twentieth-century America.

For each of these factors I found corresponding examples in both societies in the era of growth. Here are a few significant parallels.

la Beauce (medieval wheat country)	*with*	the prairies
the heavy plow	*with*	mechanization of agriculture
faith	*with*	the ideal of democracy
the cathedral	*with*	the automobile
Beauvais	*with*	the Empire State Building
Cistercians	*with*	Henry Ford
Chartres	*with*	Times Square
the gold louis	*with*	the dollar
the water mill	*with*	the steam engine
the horse	*with*	the combustion engine

Other factors—some already evident in 1956, others predicted —proved to be clear indicators of the evolutionary stage of the society.

In the left-hand column below are some of the main factors in the era of growth in both societies, and on the right the corresponding factors in the era of maturity, both medieval and American. If there are conclusions to be drawn, they are even more apparent now than they were in 1956.

rising Gross National Product (G.N.P.)	Gross National Product levels off
growth of population	growth of population levels off
free enterprise	free enterprise limited
free labor market	labor market restricted
economic independence	interdependency of economy
specialization of labor	higher specialization of labor
external crusade	diminishing crusading spirit
surplus of wealth	tendency toward self-interest
cult of the new	resistance to change
record-breaking spirit	loss of interest in record-breaking
aestheticism undeveloped	greater awareness of aesthetics
community spirit	private living
strong currency	monetary reform (devaluation)
beginning of inflation	inflation increases
plentiful natural resources	limited natural resources
education	higher education over-extended
new visual arts	entertainment more private
decentralization of power	centralization of power

functional technology	technical sclerosis (e.g., automobile industry)
exploitation of inventions	resistance to inventions begins
industrialization	survival of obsolete techniques

At the peak of its self-confidence, American society could not imagine that her enterprising and crusading spirit would decline, that she would have to face devaluation, increasing inflation, and a critical crisis of power. But what was perhaps even more unimaginable to the Americans, and for that reason to the Europeans, of 1956, was that nonmilitary American technological progress might be substantially arrested.

To forecast what could happen to the United States in her declining era, I brought in another parallel, that of France from the later nineteenth century into the twentieth, a period of decline that began with a long phase of antitechnology and arrested industrial expansion. The leaders of France's nineteenth-century "counterculture," like those in the modern United States, denounced the materialistic spirit of the ruling class and the dangers of mechanization and industrialization. They rejected reason and turned to mysticism, to dreams of the past—and some to drugs. They longed to return to nature. The anti-American feeling in France goes back in part to this period of the nineteenth century, a time when America represented the most materialistic country in the world, more mechanized and industrialized than any other nation. It was the "gaslight of America," according to Baudelaire, that had asphyxiated the genius of Edgar Allan Poe. What the American counterculture has discovered about America and the corporate state has been the common view of most Europeans for many decades.

I chose 1885 as the year in which modern France moved into her declining or decadent era. This is, in fact, an arbitrary date, and earlier dates could be suggested and substantiated, but it was in 1885 that the French intelligentsia lost their inhibitions about decadence. The following year a new French literary journal was launched entitled *Le Decadent*.

I extended my parallels into the declining era with examples from French history since 1885, situations or possibilities that one now sees clearly are or could be applicable to the United States. However, I noticed an interesting phenomenon, namely that under exceptional conditions, an aging society, like France, can for a time arrest the course of history. The defeat of 1940, the German occupation, the liberation, and the Marshall Plan are some of the events that helped reverse the trend.

The economic revival of France was not generally appreciated by the outside world until 1973 when Herman Kahn published his report on the country's remarkable industrial expansion. At one period only Japan had a higher Gross National Product growth rate.

I do not think the Frenchman of the present day has yet grasped that, in order to succeed economically, he has reverted to a more dynamic outlook and has become more American than the Americans—in other words, he is actually closer to the American of twenty years ago or so than is the United States citizen of the 1970s. He is more go-ahead and efficient. The reverse of the coin is that the Americans are now more "civilized" than the French. Fewer books are read in France than in most other countries of the Western world. The Americans are now against technology and the French for technology.

The renewed French psychological drive has had other very unexpected results. It has made the French regard the English as the English regarded the French before 1940, with condescension; as an ailing, even decadent nation. The Englishman before the last war was hesitant to send his son to Paris, and today the Frenchman hesitates to send his daughter to permissive London.

But this does not mean that France will not decline. It is part of the declining Western world, of which the United States was the last ascending nation, and it cannot escape the larger trend. Though it has reverted to a certain extent to its mature era, it is nevertheless being influenced by America's aging era, for example in the concern France has shown to protect its environment—recently it even established a Ministry of the Quality of Life.

In the United States the emergence of the counterculture about 1965 undermined the confidence Americans had in the excellence of their society, and those who chose to look deeper discovered that their country was evolving as others had in previous centuries. When in 1972 I was invited to give a seminar at the School of Architecture at the University of Southern California in Los Angeles, the students accepted spontaneously the historical parallel themes I proposed they should study:

cathedrals and Los Angeles freeways
cathedrals and dams (e.g., T.V.A.)
world-record-breaking spirit in the Middle Ages and in the United States
Gothic and twentieth-century international style
Villard de Honnecourt and Frank Lloyd Wright, Le Corbusier, Wachsmann, Gropius, Nervi
restrictive practices in the building profession in the Middle Ages and the United States

The student who chose the first of these themes ended his paper by stating that, like the cathedrals, the Los Angeles freeways would never be finished, and the student who chose the last theme discovered an amazing parallel between the restrictive practices of the Paris plasterers at the end of the thirteenth century and those of the American plasterers of the 1970s.

On the occasion of this trip to California I rediscovered my graph, which had lain neglected in a file for sixteen years, and found that the evolution I had forecast was happening: decline of civic virtues and of the crusading spirit, increased interest in aesthetic values, limited growth of the G.N.P., interdependence of the economy, decline in energy resources, devaluation, increasing inflation, resistance to new technology. I was now able to date the entry of the United States into her aging or declining era: 1971. In 1971 the United States Congress refused to allocate funds for the supersonic transport project, and this antitechnological vote represented a complete reversal of the traditional attitude of the United States toward technology. If we accept 1947 as the beginning of the previous era, the United States had an era of maturity of almost twenty-five years. The Golden Age of Pericles, which was sometimes recalled during John Kennedy's time in the White House, lasted about the same number of years.

Both American society and medieval society had reacted violently against the establishment, which had disappointed them. Both wanted to reform themselves by returning to a past which they believed was a Golden Age. The counterculture wanted to throw aside Consciousness II to reintroduce the age of the pioneers of Consciousness I, while medieval society wanted to reform the Church of Rome with its hierarchy and return to the primitive Christian Church. In so doing, the Americans and the men of the Middle Ages broke down their traditional ways of life. Neither society was ever to be the same again.

The psychological drive that impelled both societies to a high peak of civilization began to decline rapidly. One of the main consequences of this—and the one I am most concerned with in this book—was to slow down their technological evolution. Investment in science in the United States has been slashed in many areas, and the scientist has been thrown from the pedestal that he mounted with such pride in the 1941–45 war and again after *Sputnik*. Advanced technology has also had to retreat, including the space programs, and old technology is being reintroduced; hand crafts and bicycles are flourishing. This is just the sort of slowing down of technological progress that occurred in the later Middle Ages.

In the medieval industrial world, the psychological drive was progressively curbed also by the introduction of legislation that favored those already in positions of power, and aimed to preserve the status quo. These same restrictive practices exist in the United States today.

The age of maturity of any civilization will coincide with a waning economy, or in the words of a historian of comparative civilizations: "The peak of civilization in any culture would be expected at the time when economic decline begins."[2] He comments further that when a disproportionate amount of the energy of a society is directed to cultural achievements and appreciation, the economic well-being of that society is in jeopardy, and is unlikely to be prolonged.

As the United States moved into her aging era in 1971, she was suddenly made aware that she was losing her monetary stability, her technological leadership, and her entrepreneurial daring. In March of that year *Fortune* magazine published an article denouncing the "irrational campaign" against science and technology, and predicting that if it did not end soon the United States could "become a second-rate power and a third-rate place to live in."[3] Equally "irrational" was the 1277 campaign against Thomism and Averroism, which silenced Roger Bacon's faith in reason, mathematics, and experimental science. The geneticist and Nobel Prize winner Dr. Joshua Lederberg has remarked most judiciously that today technology is often thought of as evil. "If we think of technology as the devil," he has said, "we will waste our strength in vain theological controversies over the best ritual formula for exorcising it."[4]

In 1971 the all-powerful dollar was twice devalued by 17 percent. Wage and price controls were imposed, and free enterprise was limited. *Newsweek* magazine on April 24, 1972, published an article "Can the U.S. Compete?" The writer had his doubts. "Almost 100 percent of all tape recorders and 35 mm. cameras, 70 percent of the radios, 49 percent of the sewing machines, 40 percent of the glassware and more than 15 percent of all automobiles sold in the United States come from abroad." The percentage of imported automobiles has since increased considerably, and the United States has lost its technological superiority in other industries such as textiles, steel, and electronics.

The decline of the American psychological drive was also discussed in the same issue of *Newsweek* in an article entitled, "Too many U.S. Workers No Longer Give a Damn." It quoted absenteeism rates as high as 20 percent on Fridays and Mondays in some automobile plants. It reproduced a cartoon showing a company executive comfortably watching TV at twenty to ten in the morning. He is told by his wife, who is holding the telephone, "Your office won't take 'The General Malaise' as an excuse."

When a society moves out of its era of ascendancy—into its era of maturity and subsequently into its aging era—the birthrate tends to fall. The Romans were faced with this problem and so was France prior to 1940. The United States is inevitably moving in the same direction. The census bureau study of the United States population in 1970 reveals that Americans are marrying later and women are bearing fewer children. The average American family in 1970 consisted of 3.6 people, slightly down from 1960. Half of the Americans were over 28.1 years of age, with a median age of 29.5 in 1960, and this trend will be continued in the succeeding decades due to women bearing fewer children. The decline in fecundity results from a rise in the standard of living, and a greater desire to profit from the increasing material comforts of society. It is evidence of a decline in social responsibility and of increased individualism. The eventual increase of the median age in the aging era is another major factor in precipitating the decline of the psychological drive.

Though American prowess has been overtaken in some industrial areas by other Western powers, in which I include Japan, these limited advances do not conceal the fact that the whole of Western civilization is approaching the end of its historical cycle.

Can such a momentous trend ever be reversed and a once-great civilization begin a new historical cycle without a fundamental change in ideology? The only example one can look to is China, which suffered an inevitable decline lasting for many centuries. The revolutionary ideology adopted by China in 1947 may indicate that it has the possibility of attaining for the second time in its long history an era of growth in which psychological drive and technological evolution will rise in parallel curves. China might be at the beginning of a cycle that could last for more than a millennium, while Western civilization stands at the end of a cycle that is already a thousand years old.

Notes

Preface

1. Oswald Spengler, *Man and Technics* (New York: Alfred A. Knopf, Borzoi Books, 1932), p. 103.
2. Ibid., p. 102.
3. Plato, *Gorgias*, 512, tr. W. D. Woodhead, from *The Complete Dialogues of Plato*, E. Hamilton and H. Cairns, eds., Bollingen Series, LXXI (New York: Pantheon Books, 1961), p. 294.

Chapter 1

1. Quoted in David Luckhurst "Monastic Watermills," Society for the Protection of Ancient Buildings, no. 8 (London), n.d.: 6.
2. Quoted in L. Sprague de Camp, *The Ancient Engineers* (Cambridge, Mass.: M.I.T. Press, 1963), p. 229.
3. Suetonius, *Vespasian*, XVIII, tr. J. C. Rolfe, Loeb Classical Library, vol. II (London: Heinemann; Cambridge, Mass.: Harvard University Press, 1970), pp. 311, 313.
4. G. Sicard, *Aux Origines des sociétés anonymes. Les moulins de Toulouse au moyen age* (Paris: Armand Colin, 1953).
5. E. M. Carus-Wilson, "An Industrial Revolution of the Thirteenth Century," *The Economic History Review* (London), 1941: 38.
6. E. M. Carus-Wilson, "The Woollen Industry," in *The Cambridge Economic History*, vol. II (Cambridge: Cambridge University Press, 1952), p. 409.

7. Quoted in Lynn White, Jr., *Medieval Technology and Social Change* (London: Oxford University Press, 1965), p. 87.

8. H. E. Butler, trans., *The Chronicle of Jocelin of Brakelond, Concerning the Acts of Samson, Abbot of the Monastery of St. Edmund* (London: Thomas Nelson, 1949), pp. 59–60.

9. Chaucer, "The Reeve's Tale," *The Canterbury Tales*, tr. N. Coghill (Harmondsworth, Eng., and Baltimore, Md.: Penguin Books, 1951), pp. 131–33.

Chapter 2

1. R. J. Forbes, *Studies in Ancient Technology*, vol. II (Leiden: Brill, 1965), p. 85.

2. G. Duby, *Rural Economy and Country Life in the Medieval West* (London: Edward Arnold, 1968), p. 110.

3. Dorothea Oschinsky, ed., *Walter of Henley and Other Treatises on Estate Management and Accounting* (Oxford: Clarendon Press, 1971), chap. 36, p. 319.

4. Ibid., chap. 37, p. 319.

5. Ibid., chap. 41, p. 319.

6. Ibid., p. 148.

7. Ibid., p. 148.

8. Ibid., chap. 46, p. 321.

9. Ibid., chap. 44, p. 321.

10. Ibid., chap. 62, p. 325.

11. Ibid., chap. 23, p. 271.

12. Ibid., chap. 41, p. 279.

13. Chancellor's Roll 8, Richard I (Roll of Escheats).

14. Duby, *Rural Economy*, p. 140.

15. *The Rule of St. Benedict*, XL, tr. by a monk of St. Benedict's Abbey, Fort Augustus (London and New York: Burns and Oates, 1886), p. 123.

16. J. S. Donnelly, *The Decline of the Medieval Cistercian Lay-brotherhood* (New York: Fordham University Press, 1949), p. 32.

17. Ibid., p. 27.

18. Quoted in G. C. Coulton, *Social Life in Britain from the Conquest to the Reformation* (Cambridge: Cambridge University Press, 1918), pp. 29–30.

19. Lynn White, Jr., *Medieval Technology and Social Change* (London: Oxford University Press, 1965), p. 76.

20. Jean Gimpel, "Population and Environment in the Middle Ages," *Environment and Change*, vol. II, no. 4 (London), December 1973: 235.
21. L. Stouff, *Ravitaillement et alimentation en Provence aux XIVe et XVe siècles* (Paris and The Hague: Mouton, 1970), p. 220.
22. Gimpel, "Population and Environment," p. 236.
23. Stouff, *Ravitaillement,* pp. 245–46.
24. Ibid., p. 246.
25. J. M. Thoday, "The Problem," *Population and Food Supply*, Sir Joseph Hutchinson, ed. (Cambridge: Cambridge University Press, 1969), p. 1.

Chapter 3

1. Quoted in Jean Gimpel, *The Cathedral Builders* (New York: Grove Press, 1961), p. 149.
2. Quoted in H. M. Colvin, *Building Accounts of King Henry III* (Oxford: Clarendon Press, 1971), p. 151.
3. Gimpel, *Cathedral Builders,* p. 63.
4. Quoted in T. A. Rickard, *Man and Metals,* vol. II (London: McGraw-Hill, 1932), p. 879.
5. L. F. Salzman, *Building in England down to 1540* (Oxford: Clarendon Press, 1952), p. 304.
6. Ibid., p. 288.
7. Ibid., p. 288.
8. R. J. Forbes, "Metallurgy" in *A History of Technology*, C. S. Singer, E. J. Holmyard, A. R. Hall, T. I. Williams, eds. (Oxford: Clarendon Press, 1956), p. 75.
9. Tacitus, *Germania*, V, tr. M. Hutton, Loeb Classical Library (London: Heinemann; New York: The Macmillan Co., 1914), p. 271.
10. John U. Nef, "Mining and Metallurgy in Medieval Civilisation," in *The Cambridge Economic History of Europe*, vol. II (Cambridge, 1952), 437.
11. Rickard, *Man and Metals,* p. 522.
12. L. F. Salzman, *English Industries of the Middle Ages* (Oxford: Clarendon Press, 1923), p. 65.

Chapter 4

1. E. Panofsky, ed. and trans., *Abbot Suger, on the Abbey Church of St. Denis* (Princeton, N.J.: Princeton University Press, 1946), p. 31

Notes

2. Ibid., pp. 95–97.

3. D. M. Stenton, *English Society in the Early Middle Ages* (Harmondsworth, Eng., and Baltimore, Md.: Penguin Books, 1951), pp. 104–5.

4. T. Bowie, ed., *Sketchbook of Villard de Honnecourt* (Bloomington, Ind.: Indiana University Press, 1959), p. 120.

5. Ibid., p. 130.

6. Stenton, *English Society*, p. 109.

7. Quoted in F. R. S. Smith, *Sea-Coal for London* (London: Longmans, 1961), p. 3.

8. Quoted in R. L. Galloway, *A History of Coal Mining in Great Britain* (Newton Abbot: David and Charles Reprints, 1969), p. 10.

9. Ibid., p. 20.

10. L. F. Salzman, *English Industries of the Middle Ages* (Oxford: Clarendon Press, 1923), p. 20.

11. Galloway, *History of Coal Mining*, p. 24.

12. Salzman, *English Industries*, p. 20.

13. Quoted in G. C. Coulton, *Life in the Middle Ages,* vol. III (Cambridge: Cambridge University Press, 1929), p. 99.

14. G. Fagniez, *Etudes sur l'industrie et la classe industrielle à Paris aux XIIIe et XIVe siècles* (Paris: 1877), p. 22.

15. W. Page and J. H. Round, eds., *The Victoria History of the County of Essex,* vol. II (London: 1907), p. 459.

16. G. C. Coulton, *Social Life in Britain from the Conquest to the Reformation* (Cambridge: Cambridge University Press, 1918), p. 330.

17. Quoted in R. de Lespinasse and F. de Bonnardot, eds., *Le Livre des métiers d'Etienne Boileau* (Paris, 1879), pp. 156–57.

Chapter 5

1. Registers of the Black Prince, II, 178.

2. Quoted in A. Zycha, *Das Böhmische Bergrecht des Mittelalters auf Grundlage des Bergrechts von Iglau,* vol. II (Berlin: 1900), p. 39.

3. B. Gille, "Les problèmes de la technique minière au moyen age," *Revue historique des mines,* vol. I, no. 2 (Paris), 1969: 282.

4. G. R. Lewis, *The Stannaries. A Study of the English Tin Miner* (Cambridge, Mass.: Harvard University Press, 1924), p. 36.

5. Ibid., p. 36.

6. Ibid., p. 94.

7. G. A. J. Hodgett, *A Social and Economic History of Europe* (London: Methuen, 1972), p. 144.

8. Quoted in E. M. Carus-Wilson, "The Woollen Industry," in *The Cambridge Economic History*, vol. II (Cambridge: Cambridge University Press, 1952), p. 415.

9. Ibid., p. 412.

10. Arnold Hauser, *The Social History of Art*, vol. I (London: Routledge and Kegan Paul, 1951), p. 285.

11. L. F. Salzman, *Building in England down to 1540* (Oxford: Clarendon Press, 1952), p. 74.

12. Ibid., pp. 54–55.

13. H. M. Colvin, *Building Accounts of King Henry III* (Oxford: Clarendon Press, 1971), p. 301.

14. Ibid., p. 401.

15. D. Knoop and G. P. Jones, *The Medieval Mason* (Manchester, Eng.: Manchester University Press, 1949), p. 206.

Chapter 6

1. John Fitchen, *The Construction of Gothic Cathedrals: A Study of Medieval Vault Erection* (Oxford: Clarendon Press, 1961), pp. xi–xii.

2. John Harvey, *English Mediaeval Architects, A Biographical Dictionary down to 1550* (London: Batsford, 1954), pp. 114–15.

3. L. F. Salzman, *Building in England down to 1540* (Oxford: Clarendon Press, 1952), p. 47.

4. Quoted in Teresa G. Frisch, ed., *Gothic Art—1140–1450, Sources and Documents* (Englewood Cliffs, N.J.: Prentice-Hall, 1971), p. 55.

5. T. Bowie, ed., *The Sketchbook of Villard de Honnecourt* (Bloomington, Ind.: Indiana University Press, 1959), p. 92, plate 41.

6. Ibid.

7. Ibid., p. 96, plate 43.

8. Fitchen, *The Construction of Gothic Cathedrals*, p. 23.

9. Bowie, *Sketchbook*, p. 100, plate 45.

10. Ibid., p. 94, plate 42.

11. Frisch, *Gothic Art*, pp. 56–57.

12. Bowie, *Sketchbook*, p. 108, plate 49.

13. Ibid., p. 14, plate 2.

14. Lynn White, Jr., *Medieval Technology and Social Change* (London: Oxford University Press, 1965), p. 134.

15. Bowie, *Sketchbook*, p. 134, plate 62.

16. White, *Medieval Technology*, p. 133.

17. G. C. Coulton, *Social Life in Britain from the Conquest to the Reformation* (Cambridge: Cambridge University Press, 1918), p. 476.

18. White, *Medieval Technology*, p. 133.

19. Bowie, *Sketchbook*, p. 129, plate 58.

20. Ibid., p. 129, plate 58.

21. White, *Medieval Technology*, p. 118.

22. Bowie, *Sketchbook*, p. 129, plate 58.

23. *The Sketch-Book of Villard de Honnecourt*, ed. and tr. R. Willis (London: 1859), p. 161.

24. Bowie, *Sketchbook*, p. 129, plate 58.

25. Ibid., p. 130, plate 28.

26. A. Martindale, *The Rise of the Artist* (London: Thames and Hudson, 1972), p. 51.

27. Bowie, *Sketchbook*, p. 132, plate 61.

28. Ibid., p. 130, plate 59.

29. Ibid., p. 64, plate 27.

30. Vitruvius, *The Ten Books on Architecture*, I, 1, tr. Morris Hicky Morgan (New York: Dover, 1960), pp. 5–6.

31. Bowie, *Sketchbook*, p. 72, plate 31.

32. Willis, *Sketchbook*, p. 238.

33. Vitruvius, *Ten Books*, III, 1, p. 72.

34. Paul Frankl, *The Gothic. Literary Sources of Interpretations Through Eight Centuries* (Princeton N.J.: Princeton University Press, 1960), p. 44.

35. Quoted in F. Bucher, "Medieval Architectural Design Methods, 800–1560," *Gesta*, vol. XI, no. 2, 1973: 40.

36. Ibid.

37. Ibid., p. 120, plate 55.

38. Ibid., p. 120, plate 55.

39. Jean Gimpel, *The Cathedral Builders* (New York: Grove Press, 1961), p. 125.

40. Vitruvius, *Ten Books*, IX, intro., p. 252.

41. Leonardo da Vinci, *Treatise on Painting*, Codex Atlanticus 119, in J. P. Richter, ed., *The Literary Works of Leonardo da Vinci*, vol. I, 2nd ed. (1939), p. 116.

42. Ibid., Codex Atlanticus 117a.

43. C. P. Snow, *The Two Cultures* (Cambridge: Cambridge University Press, 1964).

44. Quoted in S. Lilley, *Man, Machines and History* (London: Cobbett Press, 1948), p. 49.

Chapter 7

1. Quoted in Jean Gimpel, *The Cathedral Builders* (New York: Grove Press, 1961), p. 165.
2. Ibid.
3. Quoted in Lynn White, Jr., "The Expansion of Technology 500–1500," in *The Fontana Economic History of Europe*, vol. I (London: Fontana, 1969), chap. 4, p. 24.
4. Quoted in Lynn White, Jr., "Cultural Climates and Technological Advance in the Middle Ages," *Viator*, vol. II, 1971: 174.
5. Lewis Mumford, *Technics and Civilization* (New York: Harcourt Brace, 1939), pp. 14–15.
6. J. Needham, W. Ling, and D. J. de Solla Price, *Heavenly Clockwork* (Cambridge: Cambridge University Press, 1960), p. 6, n. 3.
7. Ibid., p. 141.
8. H. Alan Lloyd, *Some Outstanding Clocks over Seven Hundred Years 1250–1950* (London: Leonard Hill, 1958), p. 5.
9. Ibid., p. 11.
10. Dante Alighieri, *Il Paradiso*, canto X, verses 139–419, tr. H. F. Cary, introd. by E. G. Gardner, Everyman's Library, vol. I (London: J. M. Dent; New York: E. P. Dutton, 1937), p. 339.
11. R. T. Gunther, *Early Science in Oxford*, vol. II (Oxford: Clarendon Press, 1923), p. 32.
12. Ibid.
13. S. A. Bedini and F. R. Maddison, "Mechanical Universe. The Astrarium of Giovanni di Dondi," *Transactions of the American Philosophical Society*, vol. 56, part 5, October 1966: 6–7.
14. Ibid., p. 7.
15. Ibid., p. 8.
16. Ibid., pp. 15–16.
17. Lynn Thorndike, *A History of Magic and Experimental Science*, vol. III (New York: Columbia University Press, 1934), pp. 392–93.
18. Bedini and Maddison, "Mechanical Universe," p. 19.
19. Ibid., p. 18.
20. Ibid., p. 20.
21. Lloyd, *Some Outstanding Clocks*, p. 11.

Notes

22. H. Alan Lloyd, *Old Clocks* (New York: Dover Publications, 1970), pp. 198–99.
23. Quoted in Carlo M. Cipolla, *Clocks and Culture, 1300–1700* (London: Collins, 1967), pp. 40–41.
24. Ibid., p. 41.
25. Mumford, *Technics and Civilization*, p. 14.

Chapter 8

1. Anselm, *Cur Deus Homo*, plates 158, 362.
2. Quoted by Robert S. Lopez, *The Birth of Europe* (London: Dent, 1971), p. 180.
3. J. Le Goff, *Les Intellectuels au moyen age* (Paris: Ed. du Seuil, 1957), p. 51.
4. A. C. Crombie, *Robert Grosseteste and the Origins of Experimental Science 1100–1700* (Oxford: Clarendon Press, 1953), pp. 29–30.
5. Charles H. Haskins, *The Renaissance of the Twelfth Century* (Cambridge, Mass.: Harvard University Press, 1971), p. 258.
6. A. C. Crombie, *Augustine to Galileo, The History of Science A.D. 400–1650*, vol. I (Harmondsworth, Eng., and Baltimore, Md.: Penguin Books, 1969), pp. 55–63.
7. Le Goff, *Intellectuels*, p. 23.
8. Ibid., p. 24.
9. Ibid., p. 14.
10. C. G. Crump and E. F. Jacob, *The Legacy of the Middle Ages* (Oxford: Clarendon Press, 1951), p. 238.
11. Crombie, *Augustine to Galileo*, p. 46.
12. Quoted in L. Thorndike, *A History of Magic and Experimental Science*, vol. II (London: Macmillan, 1923), p. 59.
13. Ibid., p. 58.
14. Ibid.
15. Lynn White, Jr., "Cultural Climates and Technological Advance in the Middle Ages," *Viator*, vol. II, 1971: 187–88.
16. A. Katzenellenbogen, *The Sculptural Programs of Chartres Cathedral* (New York: W. W. Norton, 1959), pp. 20–21.
17. Le Goff, *Intellectuels*, p. 28.
18. Lopez, *Birth of Europe*, p. 324.
19. Thorndike, *History of Magic*, p. 441.
20. Ibid., p. 442.
21. Ibid.

22. Roger Bacon, *The Opus Majus*, tr. R. B. Burke, vol. II (Philadelphia, 1928), p. 574.

23. Ibid., p. 582.

24. Ibid.

25. Crombie, *Robert Grosseteste*, p. 153.

26. Bacon, *Opus Majus*, vol. I, p. 306.

27. Ibid., pp. 290–96.

28. Bacon, *Opus Majus*, vol. II, p. 583.

29. Crombie, *Robert Grosseteste*, p. 205.

30. Ibid., pp. 207–8.

31. Bacon, *Opus Majus*, vol. I, pp. 311–12.

Chapter 9

1. Dante Alighieri, *Il Paradiso*, canto X, verses 133–38, tr. H. F. Cary, introd. by E. G. Gardner, Everyman's Library, vol. I (London: J. M. Dent; New York: E. P. Dutton, 1937), p. 339.

2. W. O. Hassal, *They Saw It Happen, 55 B.C.–A.D. 1485* (Oxford: Basil Blackwell, 1973), p. 156.

3. J. Sprenger and H. Kramer, *Malleus Maleficorum, The Hammer of Witchcraft*, ed. P. Hughes, tr. M. Summers (London: The Folio Society, 1968), p. 15.

4. Ibid., p. 29.

5. Ibid.

6. Ibid., p. 51.

7. Ibid., p. 93.

8. Sire de Joinville, *The History of St. Louis*, Natalis de Wailly and Joan Evans, eds., (London: Oxford University Press, 1938), p. 222.

9. J. Glenisson and J. Day, eds., *Textes et documents d'histoire du moyen age XIVe–XVe siècles* (Paris: S.E.D.E.S., 1970), pp. 8–9.

10. J. Titow, "Evidence of Weather in the Account Rolls of the Bishopric of Winchester 1209–1350," in *The Economic History Review*, 2nd ser., vol. XII (London), 1959–60: 403.

11. Henry S. Lucas, "The Great European Famine of 1315, 1316 and 1317," *Speculum*, vol. V (Cambridge, Mass.), 1930: 376.

12. P. Ziegler, *The Black Death* (London: Collins, 1969), p. 25.

13. Boccaccio, *Il Decameron*, 1st day, introd., tr. J. M. Rigg, Everyman's Library, vol. I (London: J. M. Dent; New York: E. P. Dutton, 1930), pp. 8–10.

14. C. M. De la Roncière, P. Contamine, R. Delort, Armand Colin,

eds., *L'Europe au moyen age, fin XIIIe siècle–fin XVe siècle,* vol. III (Paris: Armand Colin, 1971), p. 109.

15. R. S. Lopez and H. A. Miskimin, "The Economic Depression of the Renaissance," *The Economic History Review,* 2nd ser., vol. XIV (London), 1962: 418.

16. M. M. Postan, *The Medieval Economy and Society* (London: Weidenfeld and Nicolson, 1972), p. 242.

17. Glenisson and Day, eds., *Textes et documents,* p. 37.

18. G. C. Coulton, *Social Life in Britain from the Conquest to the Reformation* (Cambridge: Cambridge University Press, 1918), p. 353.

19. Hassal, *They Saw It Happen,* p. 166.

20. Ibid., p. 167.

21. Ibid., p. 172.

22. Ibid., p. 174.

23. Ibid., p. 177.

24. Quoted in Regine Pernoud, *Histoire de la bourgeoisie en France,* vol. I (Paris: Ed. du Seuil, 1960), p. 201.

25. C. M. Cipolla, "Currency Depreciation in Medieval Europe," *The Economic History Review,* 2nd ser., vol. XV (London), 1962–63: 414.

26. A. M. Watson, "Back to Gold and Silver," in *The Economic History Review,* 2nd ser., vol. XX (London), 1967: 25–26.

27. Ibid., p. 33.

28. Glenisson and Day, eds., *Textes et documents,* p. 15.

29. Lopez and Miskimin, "Economic Depression," p. 624.

30. R. de Roover, *The Rise and Decline of the Medici Bank 1397–1494* (Cambridge, Mass.: Harvard University Press, 1963), p. 367.

31. Lopez and Miskimin, "Economic Depression," p. 410.

32. Ibid., p. 421.

33. Quoted in C. M. Cipolla, *Guns and Sails in the Early Phase of European Expansion 1400–1700* (London: Collins, 1965), p. 22.

34. Ibid., p. 21.

35. Ibid., p. 22.

36. R. A. Buchanan, *Industrial Archaeology in Britain* (Harmondsworth, Eng., and Baltimore, Md.: Penguin Books, 1972), p. 38.

37. Ibid., pp. 38–39.

38. Ibid., p. 39.

39. Ibid., pp. 39–40.

40. Ibid., p. 40.

41. B. Gille, *The Engineers of the Renaissance* (London: Lund Humphries, 1966), p. 125.

Epilogue

1. Lynn White, Jr., "The Discipline of the History of Technology," *Journal of Engineering Education*, vol. LIV, no. 10, June 1964: 349.
2. J. B. Clough, *The Rise and Fall of Civilization* (New York: Columbia University Press, 1961), p. 7.
3. L. Lessing, "The Senseless War on Science," *Fortune*, March 1971: 88.
4. Ibid., p. 89.

Index

Index

Index

Palazzo Capitano, Padua, 160
paper mills, 1, 14
Paradiso, Il (Dante), 154–55
Paris, Matthew, 97
Paris, Bishop of, 198
Paris, France, 181–82; baths in, 91; dams, 17–20; horsepower used near, 13th century, 36; peace in, 56–57; stone quarrying in, 60; water mills in, 16–17
Peasants' Revolt, 16, 217–19
perpetual motion devices, 127–30, 193, 233
Perruzzi bank, 102, 224
Peter of Blois, 178
Peter of Maricourt, 129–30, 144; Roger Bacon on, 193–94; *Epistolae de Magnete*, 194–95
Petrarch, Francesco, 159, 228
Petrus Peregrinus, *see* Peter of Maricourt
Philip VI of Valois, King of France, 233
Philippe de Maisières, 160
Philip the Fair, King of France, 99, 220–22, 223
philosophy and theology, *see* reason and faith
phylloxera epidemic, 48
Physics (Aristotle), 184
Pico della Mirandola, 143
Pierre de Montreuil, 119, 120
Pirenne, Henri, 241
Pius II, Pope, 83
plagues, *see also* Black Death, 56, 208, 226
Plato and Platonists, x, 141, 175, 179, 189
plow, 32, 213; heavy-wheeled, 40–43; iron plowshare of, 64
plowing: horse vs. ox for, 35–38; methods of, 41
Pneumatics (Hero of Alexandria), 132
Poland, 205, 208
Polizano, 143
pollution, *see* environment and pollution
Poppaea, 34

population: decline after 1300, 210–11, 226, 230; increase to 1300, 56–58, 230
"post-mill," 24
printing, 13, 236
Prosdocimo de Baldomandi, 160
prostitutes, 3, 91
Ptolemy, 177, 197

quadrivium, 178, 179, 181
Quaestiones Naturales (Seneca), 175
quarrymen, 60–61

reason and faith, 171–98, 200, 250
Rectangulus (astronomical instrument), 155–58, 231
raw materials, 105; common purchases of, 22; factories and, 5; timber as, 75–76; wool as, 46, 99, 100
Raymond (master of the works of Lugo Cathedral), 115
Reginald, Abbot, 50
Renaissance, viii, 134, 142–43, 224–26, 236, 237
"renaissance of the twelfth century," 174–75
Rhineland, mysticism and, 201
Ricci, Matteo, 152
Richard de Melton, 108
Richard I, King of England, 64, 80, 97–98
Richard of Wallingford, Abbot, 16, 219; inventions of, 155–58, 231
Robert, Abbot of Molesmes, 46
Robert de Courcy, 118–19
Robert of Chester, 176
Robert the Englishman, 152–53, 154
Roger, Abbot, 15
Romance of the Rose, The, 185
Roman era, 64, 242, 251; agricultural methods, 32, 39, 51–52; bronze and, 63; medieval knowl-